Manteo's World

Manteo's World

Native American Life in
Carolina's Sound Country
before and after the Lost Colony

Helen C. Rountree
with Wesley D. Taukchiray

Original paintings by Karen Harvey

The University of North Carolina Press CHAPEL HILL

Publication of this book was supported in part by
a generous gift from Kim and Phil Phillips.

© 2021 The University of North Carolina Press
All rights reserved
Paintings by Karen Harvey © 2021 Karen Harvey
Set in Merope Basic by Westchester Publishing Services
Manufactured in the United States of America

The University of North Carolina Press has been a member of the
Green Press Initiative since 2003.

Library of Congress Cataloging-in-Publication Data
Names: Rountree, Helen C., 1944– author. | Taukchiray, Wes, 1948– author. |
    Harvey, Ren (Karen), illustrator.
Title: Manteo's world : Native American life in Carolina's Sound Country
    before and after the Lost Colony / Helen C. Rountree with
    Wesley D. Taukchiray ; original paintings by Karen Harvey.
Description: Chapel Hill : The University of North Carolina Press, 2021. |
    Includes bibliographical references and index.
Identifiers: LCCN 2021009993 | ISBN 9781469662923 (cloth ; alk. paper) |
    ISBN 9781469662930 (pbk. ; alk. paper) | ISBN 9781469662947 (ebook)
Subjects: LCSH: Algonquian Indians—North Carolina—Outer Banks—
    Civilization. | Algonquian Indians—North Carolina—Outer Banks—
    History—16th century. | Algonquian Indians—First contact with
    Europeans—North Carolina—Outer Banks—History—16th century. |
    Cultural fusion—North Carolina—Outer Banks—History—16th century. |
    Outer Banks (N.C.)—History—16th century.
Classification: LCC E99.A35 R68 2021 | DDC 974.004/9755—dc23
LC record available at https://lccn.loc.gov/2021009993

Cover illustration by Karen Harvey. Used by permission of the artist.

To Paulette Rae Taukchiray
(1981–2020)

Contents

Figures, Maps, and Tables

TABLES

Preface

I have been researching southern Algonquian speakers for half a century, beginning with Virginia in 1969 (first visit to modern people in 1967) and emphasizing culture as well as history, and then expanding my data gathering geographically to include Maryland and North Carolina. When the Smithsonian Institution's *Handbook of North American Indians*, vol. 15, *Northeast* came out, the chapters on the Algonquian-speaking Indians of the Mid-Atlantic region (written in 1972–73) were done by the only published scholar on Virginia Indians available as of 1970, when the contract was drawn up: Christian F. Feest, an Austrian. No other American anthropologists were interested. Several students of Frank G. Speck who had done Virginia fieldwork in the 1930s and 1940s were still actively working, but they were doing it elsewhere. I met several of them in 1970–71 and found none to be willing to supervise my Ph.D. dissertation. Christian, who contacted me in 1972 and with whom I have been friends since, was and still is primarily a museum scholar, concentrating on artifacts rather than on people. We agreed at the outset that his chapters in the *Handbook* (Feest 1978a, 1978b, 1978c) were pitifully small, given the riches of the documents that were "out there," but he had to work within the constraints of a handbook. He also had to do all his research in the one calendar year he could spend in the United States, so the quality of the history part of his chapters is remarkably good. He did not plan to go on and do in-depth books on the culture and history, as I hoped to do, so I decided then that my life's work as a cultural anthropologist—then training to be a historian as well—would be to see that book-length treatments of all the southern Algonquian speakers reached publication. This volume is the last piece of that project.

In doing my project, I have worked with several other scholars who researched Native American history in depth in areas adjacent to eastern Virginia: Thomas Davidson for the Maryland Eastern Shore (Rountree and Davidson 1997), the late Rebecca Seib for Southern Maryland (Seib and Rountree 2014), and, with this volume, Wesley D. Taukchiray for the Carolina Sounds region. All three found themselves, when they completed their research, in jobs that did not allow writing time. My university professorship and, beginning in 2000, my retirement did allow me time, so I have been glad to become their scribe while making additions of my own. I also made or acquired the needed illustrations and then fought the manuscripts into publication for us.

Wes Taukchiray has worked as a contract historian in the Carolinas and Virginia for over forty-five years. During most of that time, he generously sent me photocopies of anything he found related to the Algonquian speakers in North Carolina and Virginia, so I regard him as my history researcher for this volume and as, deservedly, the senior author on the history chapter. Several other historians have tackled one or another of the Carolina Algonquians, but as of 2014, no one was working toward a book-length treatment of all of them together, nor of the culture of the 1580s. I had waited nearly forty years to see someone fill the gap, not wanting to invade someone else's "territory," but now, with Wes's help, I am wading in.

I am indebted to several other people for their invaluable help in getting this book completed. The editorial staff at the University of North Carolina Press acted as a sounding board as soon as I contacted them, something I badly needed because I was too close to the manuscript (seeing the trees) to have a proper "feel" for continuity and proportion (seeing the forest). The people who served as readers for the Press were likewise helpful. Wes and I received excellent assistance at the North Carolina State Archives; in particular, Edward Vann did some serious hunting for us when our time in Raleigh ran out. Karen Kupperman read an early draft of the "merging-in" chapter and recommended further readings to strengthen it. Last but not least, I profited greatly, when writing the first chapter, from having worked with "hard scientists" in Maryland during my time as senior author on *John Smith's Chesapeake Voyages, 1607–1609*. I had been doing pleasure reading about the Sounds region's hydrology and geology for many years, but these colleagues—especially marine biologist and historical biologist Kent Mountford, ichthyologist Bob Lippson, geologist Jeff Halka, and plant biologist/paleontologist Grace Brush—gave me the grounding I needed to do a better job with other aspects of the region's natural history.

A WORD ABOUT THE ARTIST

Karen Harvey ("Ren") is a part-time artist in Nashville. She grew up in Ontario, Canada, near the Grand River Reserve, and seeing so many Indian faces in her youth, she easily draws them more accurately than poor John White could when seeing Indians for the first time. She has been doing Native American portraits with people from many times and tribes, in a variety of mediums and for a long time now, always backed up by careful research.

In September 2018, Ren embarked upon a new, longer-term project: redoing the portraits that John White painted in the Carolina Sounds in the mid-1580s, so that in face and body build they were more Indians than freakish anatomy lessons (especially needed for the de Bry engravings, made from White's paintings). The portraits in the originals, at the British Museum, are small (less than letter-size), and some of the paints have oxidized, so Ren sought the assistance of various scholars, including Kim Sloan of that museum. Since some of the questions involved items of dress and ornamentation, Sloan recommend that Ren contact me for what I could tell her from the historical documents in my database. Ren did so in mid-November 2018. That began an eight-month collaboration that I had been hoping (and failing) to find with an artist for several decades. When I suggested that Ren not only redo the portraits she planned but also incorporate the Indian subjects into multiperson village and foraging scenes that I could imagine, she agreed. The result of both of her efforts is displayed in this book. Her portfolio from the project is larger: she painted the portraits not only in color (the hunter on the book's cover is one example) but also in the same black-and-white watercolor she used for the multiperson scenes, so several *accurate* portraits could also be used in this book while keeping its price down.

Helen C. Rountree
April 2020

Manteo's World

Introduction

The Algonquian-speaking Indians of North Carolina have been touched upon in many books because of their association (unwilling, as it was) with the famous "Lost Colony." Yet up to now, there has been only one book-length treatment that even attempts to include the Indians' world: *The Head in Edward Nugent's Hand: Roanoke's Forgotten Indians*, by historian Michael Leroy Oberg. That book tells the Roanoke colonies' history in detail, with small chunks of Indian culture added, the better to explain why the Native people, being rational human beings, behaved as they did toward the English. Some new light was shed on the interactions between the two peoples, but not enough, and Oberg's story stopped with the 1587 departure of John White to fetch more supplies from England, which also halted the written records about the people he left behind. The Native people of the Carolina Sounds remain little more than stick figures compared to the fleshed-out English, and readers are left to assume that they conveniently disappeared soon thereafter. In this book we hope to change those views significantly. The Indians and their world were a long-established entity in the region, and it was one that the "Lost Colonists" eventually had to merge into. Then, far from disappearing, Indian people met the later English onslaught with their lifeways intact for a surprisingly long time, and their descendants are among us to this day.

This book goes about viewing the Native people in a manner different from simply recounting "history" with cultural additions. It is written by a cultural anthropologist specializing in North American Indians, with over a half-century's background in researching the Algonquian speakers of the Mid-Atlantic coast: not just in Early Contact times but also through the middle centuries and right down to the present, including fieldwork with modern Indian people in Virginia. (Taukchiray, the historian who is senior author in chapter 8, has done the same long-term work in the Carolinas.) The book therefore does what my own first two books did for the better-recorded Powhatans of Virginia: it describes the people's culture in detail (part 1) and brings the story forward (part 2), mainly but not entirely through historical records. Chapter 7 (in part 2) goes farther and does something that anthropologists are accustomed to doing but that usually makes traditional historians' blood run cold: it compares the Algonquian speakers' culture with the culture of Tudor England, whence the would-be colonists came. The goal is to reconstruct in detail what it would have been like for the abandoned colonists to have to merge with the Native people in order to survive—for that is what we believe actually happened after 1587. Speculation beyond the fringe for historians; business as usual for cultural anthropologists.

Each of the two parts of the book therefore has a distinct "feel." Part 2, being mostly history, moves in a linear way, like walking along a road. Part 1, being an ethnography, is more like standing in a huge, elaborately decorated room and looking all around. The many things to see all contribute to the overall ambience of the room, and it is hard to know what to stare at first. But we ethnographers have evolved a useful order for helping readers to take in the whole. We begin by describing the environment in which the people lived, then go on to how they fed and sheltered themselves within it, then to the social bonds that drew them together, and finally to the belief systems that made it all meaningful to them. Because every part of a culture is related to and affected by the other parts, there have to be "see belows" and "described in chapter X" in places. That is the norm in writing an ethnography; otherwise the ethnographer, not to mention the reader, would go mad.

Part 2, the history, departs from the norm in another way besides that of including chapter 7: it focuses very heavily upon the Indians, not the English. Anyone wanting more background on the English at various points in the history can use the endnotes to find books and articles about it. The English have been getting and are still getting most of the attention because scholars have many, many more records about them to work from. But in addition, the readership (namely, you) is English speaking and, aside from any prejudices picked up from history taught you in childhood, you are more at ease with characters who have English names rather than yards-long Algonquian ones. Our aim in this book is to right that imbalance. The text of part 2 is mostly about Algonquian-speaking Indian doings; for instance, there is no lengthy disquisition on the Tuscarora War because few Algonquians suffered reprisals over it. In addition, we use Indian people's personal names whenever possible (no one expects you to pronounce them—we can't either) and omit nearly all the English personal names. That adds to the humanization of a people too often written off as "aliens."

Some of the Englishmen who left us records from the 1580s were military men, with interests usually limited to that area: Arthur Barlowe, who described the first, actually a reconnaissance, visit in 1584, and Ralph Lane, who went on the exploring missions of 1585–86. Others had wider interests, including recording what the Native people were like and how they lived: Thomas Hariot, who lived in the colony in 1585–86, and John White, who made those invaluable paintings from life and who also left us a record of the 1587 colony he had to leave behind (along with his daughter and granddaughter).

However, there were two other people who contributed immensely to our knowledge of the Carolina Sounds people, and neither one left any writings at all: the Indian interpreters, Manteo and Wanchese. Both were young men who came from the Roanoke chief's territory: we know specifically that Manteo was from Croatoan, at Cape Hatteras. They went voluntarily to England with the reconnaissance voyagers in 1584 and returned to their homeland the next summer, having learned English and come to understand something of English ways. The English did not stay very long in the Carolina Sounds, for their colonizing attempts failed. They did not actually live there long enough to learn very much by themselves. Without the translating and explaining that Manteo and Wanchese did for them, it would be immeasurably harder for an anthropologist to reconstruct what their people's world was like and thus why they acted as they did toward those bearded foreigners.

PART I | The Indian World, 1583

CHAPTER ONE

The Land and the Waters

The people native to the Carolina Sounds region inhabited a natural world of interlaced land and waters, much of the land being wetlands that did not seem like land at all. In this world they lived by hunting, fishing, foraging for plants, and farming, all of which required them to know exactly what they were doing in order to survive. Over many millennia they had learned to cope expertly. But any Europeans who became stranded there were in danger of starving, unless they could tap the locals' knowledge.

The territory of the North Carolina Algonquian speakers stretched between approximately 35 degrees and 36 degrees 35 minutes north latitude and 75 degrees 27 minutes and 77 degrees west longitude. That is the area from the Atlantic Ocean over to the Suffolk Scarp that runs past the west end of Albemarle Sound and then up the Chowan River, with Indian lands being on both sides; and from roughly the North Carolina–Virginia line southward to the Pamlico River, again with Indian lands being on both sides. It is a region of broad sounds and wide estuaries, with generally low-lying lands around them.

The climate is one of cool, humid winters and hot, humid summers. The Appalachian Mountain barrier to the west, as well as the area's latitude, means that winter cold fronts often bypass it, hitting New York and New England instead with heavy snowfall. The Gulf Stream that passes by North America's east coast makes its nearest approach off Cape Hatteras, contributing further warmth. Thus northeastern North Carolina sees snow only infrequently, and then it does not last long on the ground.

Those winter storms usually approach from the northwest, though some genuine northeasters do occur in the wintertime. But in summer it is different. Storm tracks usually come from the southwest, after deluging the Gulf Coast, while less frequent ones take the form of hurricanes making their way northward from the Caribbean or swinging in from the Atlantic. North Carolina, with its coastline protruding so far eastward, is a major target for hurricanes, exceeded only by Florida, Texas, and Louisiana in the number of "hits" in the past century. That would have held true for the late 1500s, too, as the English would-be colonists found out.

The climate in general, however, was somewhat colder back then, in terms of average annual temperature, because the Little Ice Age (ca. 1550–1800) was in progress. It affected mainly the northern hemisphere, and what lowered the annual *average* temperature by one and a half to two degrees Celsius (up to three and a half degrees Fahrenheit) was the tendency toward considerably colder winters.[1] Written records in the Carolina Sounds region are lacking, but literate eyewitnesses at Jamestown two decades later wrote of obstructing ice in the James and York Rivers, something that is rare nowadays.

Longer, colder winters shrank the growing season for crops, though at the territory's southerly latitude and low altitude it would have made little difference to Native American farmers. Another factor, however, did affect their crop year: droughts. The Mid-Atlantic region suffers a drought roughly one in every three or four summers. Multiple-year droughts are not common, but tree-ring studies have shown that a major drought occurred in 1587–89.[2] It would not have affected people during the first two English visits (1584, 1585–86), but it must have made real difficulties for Indians and English alike, beginning in that winter of 1587–88.

The Algonquian speakers' lands lay mainly on the outer coastal plain, though the Chowanokes' foraging territory extended some distance into the inner coastal plain. In that westerly area the land rolls gently, cut through by small streams and transected by old beachfronts like the three-million-year-old Suffolk (or Pamlico-Chowan) Scarp. East of it, the terrain is flat and often poorly drained. The soil is sandy, and the land consists of low-lying, often marshy peninsulas cut by sluggish rivers (or more properly, estuaries), with broad, open sounds to the east (map 1.1).[3] Wetlands can be good foraging territory, but they are not amenable to farming.

The Carolina Sounds are extensive, shallow estuaries mostly closed off from the Atlantic Ocean by narrow barrier islands that are punctuated by inlets, some relatively permanent (e.g., Hatteras Inlet), some fairly long-term (e.g., Oregon Inlet, formed by a hurricane in 1846), and some quite temporary (e.g., the inlet that keeps trying to form just north of Cape Hatteras).[4] Therefore the waters in the Sounds range from salty-brackish near inlets to oligohaline (slightly salty) farther away, to fresh still farther away in Albemarle Sound, northern Currituck Sound, and up the tributary rivers (map 1.2). Variations in the waterways' salinity make for considerable variations in plants and animals living in them, including those species useful to people.

A map of the salinities in the 1580s would differ, however, from the map of today's, especially in the Albemarle Sound. And understanding the resources available to Indian people of that time requires us to try to reconstruct what things were like in their day, not ours. In a nutshell, in the

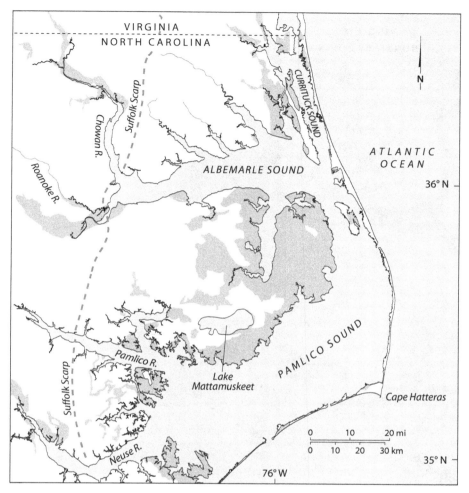

MAP 1.1 Wetlands (tidal flats, marsh, swamp) in the
Carolina Sounds region, shown in gray.

Albemarle Sound, the salty-brackish waters extended somewhat farther
westward from the barrier islands than they do today, in spite of the modern rise in sea level. There are at least two good reasons for this situation.

First of all, the layout of inlets was somewhat different from today's, when
the sandbank barrier stretches continuously from Virginia Beach, Virginia,
to Cape Hatteras with only one breach: Oregon Inlet. In the 1580s, that barrier across the east end of Albemarle Sound had four breaches: Old Currituck Inlet (pre-1585 to 1731), near the present-day North Carolina–Virginia

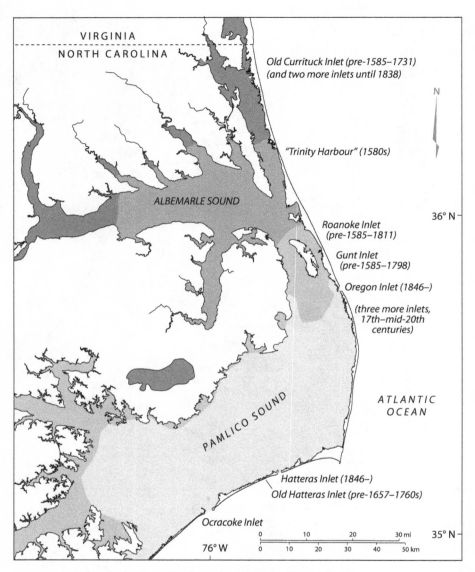

VIRGINIA
NORTH CAROLINA

Old Currituck Inlet (pre-1585–1731)
(and two more inlets until 1838)

"Trinity Harbour" (1580s)

ALBEMARLE SOUND

N

36° N

Roanoke Inlet
(pre-1585–1811)

Gunt Inlet
(pre-1585–1798)

Oregon Inlet (1846–)

(three more inlets,
17th–mid-20th
centuries)

ATLANTIC
OCEAN

PAMLICO SOUND

Hatteras Inlet (1846–)
Old Hatteras Inlet (pre-1657–1760s)

Ocracoke Inlet

0   10   20   30 mi
0   10   20   30   40   50 km

35° N

76° W

MAP 1.2 Inlets in the Outer Banks and resulting modern salinities
in the Carolina Sounds and their tributaries. Salinities run from
ocean saltiness (white) through salty-brackish (light gray) and
fresh-brackish (darker gray) to fresh (black).

line; Trinity Harbour Inlet (pre-1585 to mid-1600s), several miles north of the modern Currituck–Dare County line; Roanoke Inlet (pre-1585 to 1811), near the eastern end of the U.S. 64/264 connector between the Outer Banks and central Roanoke Island; and Gunt Inlet (pre-1585 to 1798), just north of modern Oregon Inlet. These four openings made southern Currituck Sound, eastern Albemarle Sound, and Roanoke and Croatan Sounds saltier than they are today, and they would have contributed more seawater yet at high tides and during storms to the central and western Albemarle Sound than Oregon Inlet can do today by itself.[5] Thus the progression of salty to freshwater salinities would have lain farther west in the sound, and higher up the tributaries, than it does today. That in turn would have affected which shellfish (oysters, clams, and the like) were available in which locations to people wanting to eat them.

Secondly, the amount of rain runoff into the waterways differed four centuries ago, though to a lesser extent than in the Chesapeake Bay, where there are fewer huge wetland areas and more large cities and vacation houses along the waterfront. Modern building by humans covers land with hard, impenetrable surfaces: roofs, paving, and so on. Not only that, but the human population of the Sounds region today is much, much larger than it was in the 1580s. Back then, most of the rain that fell over land was absorbed by the forest-covered land itself and did not run off into the waterways. Therefore, as in the Chesapeake Bay region, less rainwater was reaching the waterways, resulting in higher salinities reaching farther upstream than today's. The upshot, for people living partly by fishing and shellfishing, was that oyster grounds were found farther west in Albemarle Sound, farther north in Currituck Sound, and farther up all of the sounds' tributary rivers than they are today. And people had to go farther still upstream to find big cypress trees for canoes (or else trade for them).

Even though the region's land does not vary all that much by altitude, and the rivers and sounds are all relatively shallow, there is a wealth of different habitats for plants and animals to live in. Waterways vary not only in salinity and depth but also in the types of bottom they have: mud, sand, or a combination thereof in the coastal plain. Even low-lying lands vary in the composition of their soils and thus in the plants their soils will support, aside from the matter of drainage. The animals feeding on the plants vary in turn.

Northeastern North Carolina has several types of tree cover. Most of the forest on the dryer lands, with their sandy soils, used to be a Southern mixed pine forest, the dominant species being longleaf pine (*Pinus palustris*), which needs forest fires at intervals in order to reproduce. Since deer like to feed on the grasses that grow after a fire, the Native people were known to start forest fires in order to attract deer to those localities later. The trees grow tall and straight, and they were logged almost out of existence after the arrival of the English; only a few small pockets of that kind of original forest remain. The dominant pines today, given modern fire-prevention techniques, are loblolly and shortleaf pine (*P. taeda* and *P. echinata*), which grow and reproduce without any need of fires. Therefore, growing in the 1500s in much more restricted places than now was the kind of forest we see most often today: loblolly and shortleaf pines as colonizers in clearings, being gradually replaced in part by hardwoods consisting of several kinds of oak, resulting in a mature mixed deciduous forest.

As for the higher grounds on the Outer Banks, aside from the mixed hardwoods at Nags Head Woods, there are two other kinds of forest to be found—all of which botanist Jim Senter says have been there since pre-European contact times.[6] One is a tall pine forest, which can be seen at Buxton Woods. The other is more widespread along the barrier islands and near sandy beaches on the mainland. Its canopy consists predominantly of live oak (*Quercus virginiana*), mixed with southern magnolia, sweet bay, red bay, and myrtle oak. Spanish moss often hangs from the boughs, and under that canopy is wax myrtle and yaupon holly (*Ilex vomitoria*). Close to the beaches there may also be prickly pear cactus and yucca. The forests are not continuous along the Outer Banks, and Senter makes a compelling case for that being true long before Old World grazing animals were ever introduced there. Geologic and climatic processes are the main culprits, although the narrowing of the barrier islands in the last century, thanks to human building projects on the sound-side preventing westward growth of the islands, has also had an effect. The islands themselves are not stable, for with the rise in sea level since the last ice age, they are rolling over on themselves and moving westward, a process that has been going on for a very long time now.[7] The forests move along with them: storms wash away plants on the eastern, ocean side and also push sand and other materials westward into the sound, and then new plant cover begins growing on the materials deposited on the sound side; eventually there is more forest.

Wetlands in the Carolina Sounds region are of several kinds, and all of them produced things that humans needed, either for eating or for building. Wetlands without trees, commonly called marshes, may be salty, brackish, or fresh and have sandy or muddy bottoms. We will return to them later, to discuss the plants they contain that were useful to people. Forested wetlands include bottomland hardwood forest, whose trees include the bald cypress (*Taxodium distichum*; Carolina Algonquian word for it: *rakíock*). When those are the main trees, the place is called a cypress swamp. There is also a mixed hardwood swamp forest, in which the water tupelo (*Nyssa aquatica*) is dominant, but oaks and swamp and water hickories (*Carya glabra* and *aquatica*) also grow there, as do pawpaws (*Asimina triloba*, aka "custard apple") in the understory. There are pocosins, flat and damp, sandy, or peaty areas cut off from waterways and receiving their water entirely from rainfall. They contain pond pines (*Pinus serotina*) scattered among luxuriantly growing evergreens like gallberry (*Ilex glabra*). And lastly, along the "blackwater" (high in leached-out tannin from the surrounding forest floor) rivers, there is another kind of forest that is dominated by the swamp white cedar (*Chamaecyparis thyoides*).

All these kinds of forest have understory trees and also a large variety of smaller plants adapted to each habitat. And within them are a goodly variety of animals, each species living where they find appropriate food in enough quantities to allow them to grow and reproduce. There are so many of these—mammals, marsupials, reptiles, amphibians, and birds—that we will not attempt to list them here. Instead we will pay attention only to the ones the Native people took an interest in as they went about their business of living in the region.

The Algonquian speakers of the Carolina Sounds region were part-time farmers whose world lacked the large domesticated animals that Europeans were accustomed to. Therefore any meat in the people's diet came from fishing and hunting. To feed a family with regularity, these animals needed to be either big or else smaller but catchable in large quantities. Adult men went after the big animals, while boys got their target practice by hunting the small ones; trapping and snaring also went on constantly. Wild plants were in the purview of women, and being "working mothers" (i.e., caring for children, doing the farming, and making the family's clothes and utensils), women preferred plant species that produced large amounts of human food with the minimum amount of processing needed to make it edible. These considerations narrow the list of "available" plant and animal species rather drastically.[8]

On land, any forest with oaks, at least, if not also chestnut, chinquapin, various hickories and walnuts, provides nuts in the fall that attract deer and wild turkeys in the fall, not to mention bears and squirrels—and people. Other attractions in those woods included persimmon trees for their fruit. Dry forest edges with fruit-producing trees (pawpaw, wild cherry, wild plum) and open, weedy ground with summertime berry-producing bushes (blackberry, blueberry, elderberry, huckleberry, raspberry, wild raisins) and vines (wild grapes) also attracted bears as well as people. Opossums and raccoons, being omnivores, live in all environments except sandy ocean beaches. The Native people were thus in competition with these animals at times, so it made sense to eat the animals and then eat the food that had attracted them. (Live oak acorns have so little tannin that they can be eaten raw by humans. The taste is woody, with a hint of vinyl floor-covering.[9])

On marshes and waterways, mammals, birds, and reptiles do not care about salinity, but the prime game animals (deer and wild turkey) are rarely found there. Instead, the adult hunters' prey consisted mainly of ducks, geese, swans, and even herons and egrets among the birds, and muskrats, opossums, otters, raccoons, and beavers.

Fish and shellfish do care about salinity, as well as depth and (for many fish) temperature of water. Many of the larger fish available in the warm months retreat out into the Atlantic during the cold months — croaker, rockfish, striped bass, trout, and white perch from the sounds' brackish water, for instance; and croaker and spot from all salinities. Anadromous fish — alewife, herring, shad, sturgeon — pass through the sounds in the spring,

TABLE 1.1 Year-round fish and shellfish, by salinity (parts per thousand)

Salty (25+ ppt)	Salty-brackish (15–25 ppt)	Fresh-brackish (5–15 ppt)	Fresh (<5 ppt)
Windowpane	Hogchoker	Hogchoker	Hogchoker
Hogchoker	Sturgeon (juv.)	Pickerels, redfin and chain	Long-nosed gar
Blue crab	American eel	Sturgeon (juv.)	Sturgeon (juv.)
Oyster	Long-nosed gar	Long-nosed gar	Shads, redfin and threadfin
Whelks, knobbed and channeled	Blue crab	Blue crab	Crappies, white and black
	Clams, hard and soft	Crayfish	Mussels

CAROLINA ALGONQUIAN WORDS FOR FISH

Croaker: *manehaemec*

Striped bass: *mesickek*

White trout: *ribuckon*

Alewife: *chaham* or *wundúñaham*

Long-nosed gar: *arasémec*

headed into the fresh waters upstream to spawn. Besides the season, another factor limited the availability of fish and shellfish: most of the Indians' fishing technology precluded going after marine animals in water deeper than about ten feet at high tide. Some of the very biggest fish in the sounds, considered the best game fish by modern sportsmen, prefer deep water and were thus out of the Native people's reach.

Other marine species, however, were within reach year-round (see table 1.1).

Year-round wild plant foods were also important to people who lived in a region where every few years the garden crops were poor or nonexistent. Therefore the Native women had to know about plants other than the nut and fruit trees and berry bushes and vines already mentioned. For very physically active people, the species with the most food value for the least labor in preparation were usually those with starchy rootstocks and tubers,

A CLOSER LOOK AT TUCKAHOE

"Tuckahoe" (*tockawhogh* in Powhatan) probably referred to several emergent plant species (plants growing in water with their leaves and flowers appearing above the water line), including golden club (in Secota/Pamlico, *coscushaw*) and duck-potato (*kaishúcpenauk*). Another species in the group would have been yellow cow lily (*Nuphar advena*), whose uncooked tubers, even the ones taken from clean water, taste like sewage (they grow in semi-stagnant swamp water). Filling their bellies was the Indians' goal, not a delicious taste.

Arrow arum (*Peltandra virginica*) is the variety of tuckahoe that John Smith saw being used by the Powhatans. It grows best in large marshes open to direct sunlight; such marshes are most likely to occur within the meanders of rivers—and the Carolina Sounds region has very few of these. We have found from our own experience in trying to grow it that it does not thrive in nonmoving water (we tried a bucket of mud and water on the back porch); the water has to be either tidal or riverine for the plant to grow enough to produce tubers. Nowadays, city park ponds with water being flushed slowly through them also harbor healthy arrow arum plants.

most of which were found in the waterways and wetlands of the region (table 1.2). The most famous kind is the tuckahoe that Captain John Smith described being gathered and prepared. Meanwhile, the drier forests provided hog peanuts (*Amphicarpa bracteata*) and groundnuts (*Apios americana*), the latter being especially easy to dig and edible either raw or cooked. Of the two, only the Indian word for groundnut was recorded: *openauk*.

Forested lands provided people at all seasons with firewood, which, until they adopted large, grazing, dung-producing animals later on, was their one and only fuel. The Algonquian speakers may also have preferred certain deciduous trees (e.g., "ironwood") to cut as saplings and use in building houses.[10] There is archaeological evidence from Woodland Indian sites in other states that the inner bark of red cedar (*Juniperus virginiana*) was collected and felted (pounded into a fabric) to make blankets. Fortunately, red cedar, like the fruit-bearing persimmon tree, grows in most land habitats in the Carolina Sounds. All the kinds of marshes provide reeds of some sort—

TABLE 1.2 Starchy food-producing root plants, by salinity

Salty (25+ ppt)	Salty-brackish (15–25 ppt)	Fresh-brackish (5–15 ppt)	Fresh (<5 ppt)
None	Phragmites	Phragmites	Phragmites
		Cattail	Cattail
		Arrow arum	Arrow arum
			Broad-leaved arrowhead
			Cow lily
			Skunk cabbage
			Jack-in-the-pulpit

from brackish-water phragmites through freshwater cattails — for making into mats and, if woven finely enough, blankets.

Even the people's clearing of garden plots provided useful things besides the crops grown in them. After a few years of farming, the plots were allowed to go fallow for at least several years before being cleared again. And during those fallow years, while the soil regenerated, the women would return to them with harvesting in mind. Some very important wild plants — weeds, to most of us — grew there. In the first year or two, there could be the fruits of passion flower and blackberries. More importantly, Indian hemp (*Apocynum cannabinum*) and common milkweed (*Asclepias syriaca*) were there, with stems lined with long, extractable fibers in them that could be cleaned beautifully (hence the nickname "silkgrass" for the plants), twined into cordage, and then, if desired, made into nets, carrying bags, and so on. Indian women used literally miles of cordage each year,[11] and those weedy former gardens were the main source of it. They called that kind of plant *wysauke*. In the third to seventh year, a thicket would spring up, with wild grape vines growing at its edges along with several kinds of berry bushes. After that, the thicket became forest, with pines being dominant. But if there were no forest fires for long enough, and if there was enough topsoil that was drained well enough, some of the pines would gradually be replaced by deciduous trees, making the rich mixed forest that fed deer and wild turkeys — and also people — in the fall.

In short, all of the region's places except oceanfront beaches and treeless sand dunes could produce food, or utilitarian plants, or both, for human beings. All areas of the people's territory were useful to them, even burnt-over pine barrens. Nothing was wasted.

CHAPTER TWO

First View of Indian Settlements

The Algonquian-speaking (Algic-speaking, to linguists) people of the Sounds region were linguistically related to peoples northward up the Atlantic coast as far as Nova Scotia, including the Powhatans in Virginia (map 2.1). The more northerly Sounds people and the James River Powhatans probably spoke mutually intelligible dialects; people farther apart would have had more difficulty understanding one another. As Thomas Hariot put it, "The farther they are distant [from one another] the greater is the difference [in speech]."[1] Records from the 1580s and the 1600s show that the people of Chowanoke and Weapemeoc both had regular communication with Nansemond people in Virginia (see chapters 3 and 8). The geographical link was the north-south-running Nansemond and Chowan Rivers, with a portage between them (possibly along modern State Route 32). The Roanoke and Chesapeake peoples were in regular contact, indicated archaeologically by a shared pottery style (Roanoke shell-tempered wares). It was the Roanoke chief who told visiting Englishmen in 1585 about the Chesapeakes' existence.

All the other neighbors of the Algonquian-speakers had languages that were as different from Roanoke/Powhatan as English is from Arabic. To the northwest, up the rivers that bore their names, were the Meherrins and the Nottoways; westward lived the Tuscaroras. All three peoples, called "Mangoags" by the Roanokes, spoke languages that belonged to the Iroquoian language family, whose best-recorded members were the Five Nations Iroquois far to the north and the Cherokees far to the southwest. The Neuse River people, whose name of Niwasiwac became Anglicized to Neuseock, may also have been Iroquoian speakers, though the evidence is slight. Farther south were people such as the Woccons (Waccamaws), whose languages came from yet another language family, the Siouan-Catawban, whose most famous member was Lakota, far to the northwest. Relations with all these neighbors shifted back and forth, from peace to war, independent of language affiliation. Because of the widespread practice of capturing and adopting enemy women and children, as well as the far-flung luxury goods trade (see chapter 5 for both), it was easy to find multilingual people in the Indian towns.

The first thing about the Native people that a visitor would notice was the location of their settlements. The people of the Sounds region considered

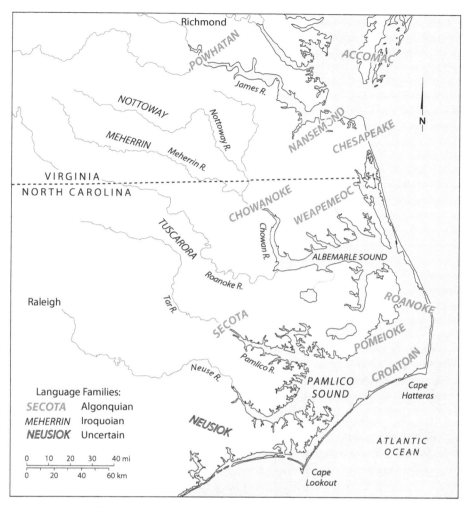

MAP 2.1 North Carolina borderlands and language families.

themselves to be town-dwellers—however scattered out their houses might be in the vicinity—and when given a choice, they looked for certain things in choosing town lands. First of all, the site had to be on or near the water-front, with easy access to fish and shellfish and easy loading of the dugout canoes that were their heavy-duty mode of transportation. The latter requirement meant that there should not be too wide a marsh between the land and the open water, though a big marsh fairly close by was desirable for its reeds in mat making. Second, there had to be good corn-growing land at the site, because maize was a major part not only of the people's diet but also of their diplomatic activities. Soils vary considerably, as the USDA's soil surveys show. Some land is good for farming, and other lands have soils better left forested; across the centuries, Indian women had learned where the former were located. Third, there had to be at least a minimal source of drinking water nearby. Washing could be done in salty water, but there had to be at least a spring or seep that yielded fresh water for drinking and cooking. Seeps could be created. Lacking the materials to make a hard-surfaced catchment area, the people took advantage of the high water table: they would dig a ditch down to the rain-fed water table and let its bottom fill naturally with groundwater, as at the town of Pomeioke.[2] (Interestingly, the sixteenth-century sources show no towns near the big freshwater lakes such as Mattamuskeet. The reason may have been their being landlocked, so that a long portage was needed to reach other Indian towns in the region.) Last but not least, an Indian town site had to have adequate foraging territory adjacent to it—either a tract of rich deciduous forest or a larger expanse of less rich forest to produce the same amount of nut-bearing trees and animals.

All the recorded Indian towns of the Carolina Sounds had these prerequisites in some degree. The spacing, as well as the locations of the towns (see figure 2.2), shows roughly how rich—for humans—the foraging territories were: the closer together, the richer the foraging. Thomas Hariot wrote in 1590 that "near the sea coast but few" towns were to be found.[3] And those towns, the ones best known to the would-be colonists, probably had smaller numbers of residents than towns farther west. When people live at least partly by foraging, there is a correlation between the richness of the land in foods for humans and the number of humans able to maintain a population on it. With or without intensifying food production by farming, the term "carrying capacity of the land" applies to human populations as well as animal ones.

The Algonquian-speakers' towns will now be listed according to their geographical location (map 2.2), rather than their political affiliation, since the English accounts are not clear about which chiefdoms some of the towns— located between two capitals—belonged to. Matters are further complicated by the fact that John White's map, painted in 1585–86, does not always agree with Theodor de Bry's map, based upon it and engraved in 1590—as though White were consulted and remembered things he had left out. Not only that, but various written accounts mention still other towns that do not appear on anybody's map. Very few of the towns have been located archaeologically, at this writing. There is also little indication in the historical record about how the yards'-long names were pronounced.

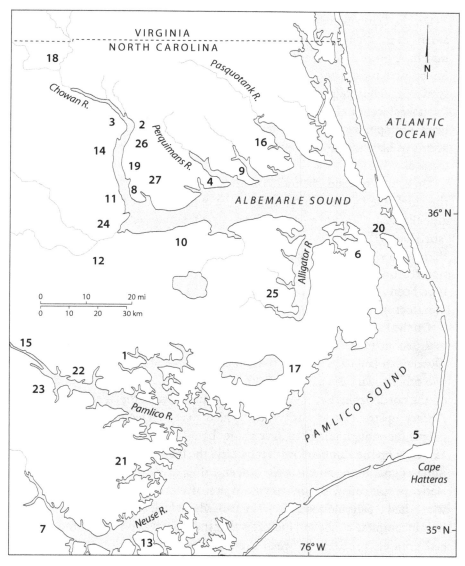

MAP 2.2 Village locations in 1585–86. 1. Aquascogoc 2. Cautaking 3. Chowanoke (White map only) 4. Chepanoc (de Bry map only) 5. Croatoan 6. Dasemenkapeuc 7. Marasanico (possibly not Algonquian speaking) 8. Mascomenge 9. Masquetuc (White map only) 10. Mequopen (de Bry map only) 11. Metaquem (de Bry map only) 12. Moratuc (possibly not Algonquian speaking) 13. Neiasiwac (possibly not Algonquian speaking) 14. Ohanoak (de Bry map only) 15. Panawaioc (de Bry map only) 16. Pasquenoke (de Bry map only) 17. Pomeioke 18. Ramushonnouk (de Bry map only) 19. Ricahokene (White map only) 20. Roanoke 21. Secotaóc 22. Seco 23. Secoton 24. Tandaquomuc (de Bry map only) 25. Tramaskecooc 26. Warawtani 27. Weapemeoc (White map only).

On the Outer Banks, there was only one town we can be sure of: Croatoan, in the vicinity of modern Buxton at Cape Hatteras. That settlement may have been a seasonal fishing camp, although there was enough dune forest, with topsoil lying under it, to enable a small amount of clearing and gardening.[4] But Ralph Lane wrote of it as a place where "the people [i.e., Roanokes] went to forage while their crops ripened."[5] There may also have been a temporary settlement on the island of Woccocon, since the name seems to have meant "fort"; the location of it would have been at modern Ocracoke village.[6]

On Roanoke Island, the Indian town of Roanoke was at the north end, and the chief ruled a subsidiary town on the opposite mainland named Daseamenkapeuc. "Roanoke" could have meant either "northern people" or "shell beads," while the latter name probably meant something like "where there is an extended land surface separated [by water]," which fits the location reasonably well.[7] (The river called "Roanoke" nowadays seems not to have been related to the tribe of the 1580s; back then, the river was called Moratock.)

On the Pamlico River were three towns, comprising what historians refer to as Secota. One, near the river's mouth, was Secataóc, which, according to Algonquian language plurals, could mean "people of Secota." Upriver were two other towns: Secoton (de Bry's "Secota") on the south bank and Seco on the north bank. "Secotan" may have meant "town at the bend of a river."[8] Farther upstream was Panawaioc, which may in fact have belonged to people far enough inland to have made them Iroquoian-speaking Tuscaroras. Over on the Pamlico River's tributary, the Pungo River, was the town of Aquascogoc. To the north, at the east end of Lake Mattamuskeet, which the Native people called Paquip, was the capital of another chiefdom, Pomeioke, which had a palisade around it. The palisade, which will be explained later (it is incomplete as shown) indicates that the town was on some kind of social frontier, probably between the on-and-off antagonists, the Secotas and the Roanokes.

On the Alligator River, somewhere around its westward turn, was the town of Tramaskecoke. Along the south shore of Albemarle Sound, there was one town: Mequopen, in modern Washington County. The name might mean "where there are red tubers," or dyeing roots.[9]

Along the Albemarle's north shore, starting in the east, the town of Pasquenoke (no connection to the name Pasquotank)[10] lay on one shore — archaeologists are not certain which — of the Pasquotank River a couple of miles up from its mouth. On Durants Neck, at the mouth of the Perquimans

River, was Masquetuc. On Yeopim River, on Harveys Neck, stood Chepanoc, a name that may have meant "cemetery."[11] And at modern Edenton, the chief's town of Weapemeoc stood. The name was probably pronounced "way-YAH-peh-meh-ock," since it later became Anglicized to "Yawpim" (modern Yeopim). It may have meant "where shelter from the wind is sought"—a good description of Edenton Bay.[12] Farther up Pembroke Creek, a tributary of Edenton Bay, was Mascomenge.

At the west end of Albemarle Sound were two towns, possibly belonging to Algonquian speakers or else to Iroquoian-speaking Tuscaroras. One was Moratuc, an Algonquian name that may mean "dangerous river," which the Roanoke River definitely is due to its strong current. The other was Tanda-quomuc, which, if Algonquian, could mean "where the road goes by the big evergreens."[13]

Lastly, there were towns along both sides of the Chowan River (pronounced "cho-WAHN"). On the right bank (west side) near the river's mouth was Metaquem, which may have meant "big trees."[14] Upstream near modern Colerain was Ohanoak, called "Blind Town" by the English, a site now destroyed by development.[15] The Chowanoke chief's town of the same name was a bit downstream from the mouth of Wiccacon River; the name may mean "people to the southward."[16] On the left bank (east side) near modern Rockyhock Creek was the town of Ricahokene. Upstream, near modern Arrowhead Beach, was Warawtani (Anglicized to Waritan; name could mean "village in a hollow"),[17] and above that, near the mouth of Bennetts Creek, lay Cautaking (a name that may mean "where the land bulges out [into the river]").[18] That area would later comprise the historic Chowanoke Indian Reservation. Finally, at Parkers Ferry, where the Meherrin River splits off from the Chowan, lay Ramushonnouk, probably a Chowanoke town but possibly a Meherrin one; no one is sure. The historic Meherrin Indian Reservation would be sited there later on. The name may mean "those who paddle back by the inside way."[19]

Down on the Neuse River, the people in the towns of Newasiwac and Marasanico may not have been Algonquian speakers. Accordingly, they do not figure often in this book.

It is not possible, from the early colonial records, to reconstruct where one town's or one chiefdom's territory ended and the next one's began. The reason is that the Algonquian speakers' concepts of landownership and boundaries differed so much from English ones that foreign observers did not comprehend them at all. In Native minds there *were* no concrete territorial boundaries as such, because people did not own the land; they were only the stewards of it. A family could clear and plant a field, and it was "theirs" for as long as they used it (a practice called *usufruct*); when they abandoned it and went on to other fields, the "old field" reverted to common use. Anyone could gather from it the useful wild plants that were taking over. Away from the towns, all of the land and marshes were in common use by foragers: men hunting, women and children collecting firewood and other plant materials for house building, mat making, and so on. Especially for the hunters, boundaries would not have been practical, anyway: a wounded deer was chased until it was brought down, wherever that was. Everyone agreed that a man's family really needed that deer (see chapter 3), and it did not matter if he killed it fairly close to someone else's town. The people of that town had the same privilege near the man's town. The arrangement ended only if the townspeople became enemies.

It is nearly impossible to estimate how many Algonquian speakers lived in northeastern North Carolina in the mid-1580s. No sixteenth-century English observer in the Sounds region left the equivalent even of Captain John Smith's "warrior counts" from the Powhatan area in Virginia. Ralph Lane wrote in 1585 that seven hundred people were once seen together, probably in a Chowanoke town in the far west, and he wrote the next year that the town's population was that size.[20] Thomas Hariot wrote in 1590, perhaps about the same meeting, that "the greatest wiroans [chief] that yet we had dealing with had but . . . above seven or eight hundred fighting men at the most."[21] But that one meeting was probably a special occasion, and the English were seeing people from numerous towns, come to gawk at the strangers.

Already by that time, the region's Native people may have suffered a reduction in population because of some fairly drastic events. For one, there may or may not have been epidemics of European diseases before the second English visit in 1585–86; there had been contacts with other Europeans before then (see chapter 6). Certainly, some diseases to which the local people had no immunity began making inroads on the population shortly after the English began exploring. Hariot wrote that "there was no town [in which] we had any [difficulty with the residents and left it unavenged] but that within a few days after our departure . . . the people began to die very fast, and many in short space; in some towns about twenty, in some forty, in some sixty, and in one six score [120], which in truth was very many in respect of their numbers."[22] The perception that only unfriendly towns were affected may be inaccurate. It is also probable that Hariot was reporting only on a very early contact situation, when large numbers of people would gather to meet the newcomers and get exposed to the foreigners' viruses (and vice versa).

However, for truly drastic epidemics to decimate a population, the people would need to be living year-round in densely settled cities[23]—something that was foreign to coastal Algonquian speakers. Secondly, Arthur Barlowe wrote in 1584 that continual warfare had already taken a toll: because of war and "civil dissentions which have happened of late years amongst them, the people are marvelously wasted, and in some places, the country left desolate."[24] That was probably another exaggeration, with a kernel of truth. Matters would get worse, though, in 1587, when the three-year drought mentioned in chapter 1 set in, killing all the growing crops. Therefore, a safe guess for the population of Algonquian speakers would be a few thousand men, women, and children at the most—less than the ten-thousand-plus Powhatans, living in their larger and ecologically richer country to the north.[25]

Like most Eastern Woodlands Indian people, the Carolina Sounds folk were town-dwellers for only two parts of the year: during the winter and in late summer's harvest time. In between, they moved around among widely scattered camps in order to live off the land—to survive in spring before the crops came in, and to stock up for winter in the fall. Therefore, some of the settlements in figure 2.2, other than the chiefs' towns, may have been more camps than towns; they were simply named places that people returned to annually. And many of the Indian artifacts found in the region are in fact hunting or fishing camp debris: arrowheads, animal bones and shells from meals, and perhaps some broken pottery that campers left behind. There are fewer but bigger concentrations of remains where real towns stood: posthole patterns from buildings, more variety of household and tool-making debris, often in large trash pits, and also human burials.

The "typical" Indian town in most modern people's minds is a palisaded one, like Pomeioke,[26] but in spite of the de Bry map using palisades to denote towns,[27] only two settlements are actually known to have been fortified that way: Pomeioke and Roanoke. Two different methods of town wall–making were used: either close-together stakes or, as at Pomeioke (figure 2.1), fewer stakes with bark or cedar boughs tied onto them. (White and de Bry use artistic license that omits the bark/boughs, the better to show the town inside.) Blocking enemy sharpshooters' line of sight was the goal in each case.[28] Roanoke town may have been fairly recently palisaded, as Europeans came calling more often in the second half of the sixteenth century. Among the Native people's relatives to the north, the Powhatans, palisaded towns were few, being found only where people felt threatened enough by somebody else that they took on the truly laborious task of cutting poles—with stone tools, not metal ones—and digging holes—with sticks, not metal

FIGURE 2.1 De Bry engraving of Pomeioke.

shovels—to insert them all the way around a town. Builders of palisades did not make gates in those walls. Instead the entry was a corridor, between overlapping ends of the walls, forcing enemies (most of whom were right-handed) to make a left turn once they came through and emerged into the town. (The John White painting shows this clearly, while the de Bry engraving omits it.) Such entryways have been found archaeologically in some Virginia and Maryland Algonquian speakers' sites.

The alternate, and much more common, settlement pattern in North Carolina, as elsewhere to the north, was houses scattered among gardens and

FIGURE 2.2 De Bry engraving of Secota.

groves of trees along the waterfront of the rivers. John White tried to paint one in his rendering of Secota,[29] but to get everything in, he had to use artistic license (shown more clearly in the de Bry engraving: figure 2.2). The town is too compact, the "streets" are too straight, and the crops are planted in neat rows (European) rather than in the nodes of a grid, in the Indian way. The real scatter of the houses looked much less organized; it was also spread so far and wide that it was impossible for enemies to attack a whole town successfully unless they staged a mass assault with several hundred warriors, something that almost never happened in the Indian world.

All towns among the North Carolina Algonquian speakers, even the more densely built palisaded ones, had relatively few houses in their centers. Roanoke with its fortifications had only nine houses; many towns had "but 10. or 12. houses"; and the largest town had only thirty of them. The houses that did exist inside the palisades belonged to "the king and his nobles," with the priests' temple safely nearby.[30] Thus many of the people belonging to palisaded Pomeioke, being commoners, would have been living scattered out among their fields, like everybody in Secota; they would come inside the walls mainly for political meetings, ceremonies, or in times of danger. The town names, "Roanoke" or "Secota," however, would have referred to the satellite homesteads as well as the town centers.

Town "services," such as we expect nowadays, were few, with every family looking after itself. Sanitation seems to have consisted of informal latrine areas (English observers are silent on the subject), the trash pits found by archaeologists (used to keep out night prowlers such as raccoons and opossums), and the waterways in which people frequently bathed.[31] There were also the local dogs—another of nature's scavengers—that engaged in cleanup when allowed. Indian dogs were fairly small, their shoulders only coming up to a man's knee.[32] They could not be used as beasts of burden, and they may not have been used in any hunting except (as among the Powhatans) for wild turkeys, but living on the fringes of town as they did (they were not pets), their ability as an alert system for prowlers was invaluable.[33] One more factor contributed heavily to the towns' sanitation: they were "aired out" twice a year. Once the crops were planted in the spring, except for commuting back for occasional weeding, the people broke up into camping groups and lived off the land and waterways until the crops came in. Then again, in the fall, all able-bodied people left the towns, formed into large camping parties, and went nutting and hunting in the forests. These in-and-out movements in the annual cycle made for cleaner towns and also less chance for epidemics to take hold.

Sanitation around Indian towns was therefore probably good enough, and the people washed themselves often enough, that the prevalent smell around the houses would have been not people or animals but wood smoke. If the North Carolina folk followed the same customs as the Powhatans did, they would have had fires both in a hearth inside the house and at least one in the yard, where the cooking was done. The former would have been kept going day and night, partly because people believed that letting it go out brought bad luck.[34] A practical reason, though, was the fact that making a new fire was very hard work, involving rubbing an up-right stick hard into the hole made in a stick (of a different wood) laid on the ground, generating enough friction and therefore heat to set alight the spunk (the corky inner bark of trees) surrounding the contact point. Once there was smoke, the spunk, being blown on gently to fan the flame, was applied to dry twigs, and from there to larger deadwood. It required very strong arms to rotate the stick fast enough, while bearing down very hard, to generate the needed heat.[35] Nobody wanted to take that much trouble making a new fire daily—especially the hardworking mothers in Indian society. It was far simpler to keep an old fire going, even though it meant continuous wood-gathering.[36] Fire, in the Indian world, had many uses besides cooking; as we shall see, it was used in hunting, in punishing mis-creants, and as a cutting tool in woodworking.

Houses, palisades, fishing weirs, and canoes had to be made very labori-ously, because the Native people lacked not only draft animals for hauling heavy building materials but also metal cutting tools for shaping those ma-terials. The copper they imported from the west was nearly pure "native" cop-per, too soft to be used for anything but jewelry. Using sharpened stone tools, which do not keep an edge as long as iron or steel, affected in turn how substantial Indian buildings were, and it made the people's dugout canoes more expensive in terms of human time and effort. Thus the English thought the Indian houses, even the largest ones, in the towns were rather "flimsy," although they were, in fact, more aerodynamically sound than English ones and also much less likely to catch on fire from the family's central hearth.

The Native people built their houses using locally available materials that had to be collected and prepared in advance by family members. The main components were saplings for the framework, reeds for mats or bark for shingles, and an immense amount of cordage for lashing mats together, saplings together, and finally mats or bark to the saplings.

House frameworks were bent-wood structures. The saplings, best cut in the spring when the sap was running and the bark looser for peeling, were four inches or less in diameter, preferably from hardwood trees so they lasted longer; they were peeled after cutting (to discourage insect pests), and one end would be sharpened and perhaps fire hardened.[37] They would have to be bent into a half-barrel-shaped vault (see figure 2.3), so they may have been bent right after peeling and then staked into place while drying. If they had already dried, they could be salvaged by heating them for a few minutes over a roaring fire and then bending them.[38] All of this could have been the work of men or women or both.

Reeds for mats are best gathered in the summer, when they are still green but have reached their full growth. Women would cut quantities of them and transport them home in canoes. Indian canoes were not "toys for overgrown boys" in that culture; women did very physical work away from town on their own. Once dried (and smoked) in the loft of an Indian house, the reeds were ready for the mat-making process (see chapter 3).

Cordage was an item that women needed to make constantly for many uses besides house building, and all of it had to be hand-twisted by rolling the fibers along one's thigh.[39] Building a small Indian house could literally use up a quarter-mile of cordage. Cordage was also used in the continual mat-making the women did, and mats had a multitude of uses around the town outside of house covering.

With the materials ready to be assembled, the house building could begin. No eyewitness tells us who did what; the women and children could have been the entire labor force involved, but the process was laborious enough that it is likely whole extended families and sets of neighbors were involved, like a barn raising among nineteenth-century European-Americans.[40] Shallow holes were dug at intervals around the area the house was to cover; in North Carolina the shape could be either rectangular, as shown in White and de Bry, or oval, as has been found so far in Virginia.[41] The Carolina Sounds people seem to have built larger houses than their Powhatan relatives, whose houses rarely extended beyond twenty feet in length. Thomas Hariot wrote that the houses he saw were "commonly double to the breadth, [though] in some places they are but 12 and 16 yards long, and in other some we have seen of four and twenty."[42]

Saplings were then placed in the holes and their tops bent and tied together (figure 2.3), making either a barrel-shaped vault (yielding the rectangular posthole shape) or a vault with two rounded ends (apsidal-shaped, very good for resisting gale-force winds end-on). The bending-in and tying sounds simple, but it required the lashing on of saplings placed horizontally around the house's circumference, by way of both bracing the structure and providing a sort of scaffolding to stand on as the builders worked higher on the vault. Vertical poles would then be tied into the interior at intervals, further bracing the overall framework. All along in the process (given the people's limited cutting tools), gaps would be left in the walls for doorways, and another gap (two, in a longer building) would be built into the roof saplings for a smoke hole placed directly over the hearth(s) inside. Next, the mats were lashed onto the house's framework, placed in such a way—length of mat horizontal, reeds vertical—that rain would roll down the length of

FIGURE 2.3 House framework with vaulted roof partially tied. A completed house is in the background (photo taken at Jamestown Settlement, © Helen C. Rountree).

the reeds before it penetrated between them. Low platform-beds made of saplings were then built adjacent to some of the walls; these would be covered with mats and deerskins as bedding, with privacy—visual, if not sonic—ensured by using the interior upright poles to hang more mats around the beds like bed curtains. Finally, mats were hung to close the doorways, and the smoke-hole cover was made: a square sapling framework covered by a small mat, which could be propped open, resting on a short stick.

Indian houses were dark inside, lit only by whatever light could get in at the doorways and smoke hole.[43] John White's painting and de Bry's engraving of Pomeioke, with walls cut away, are artistic license intended to show the houses' interiors. Doorways were low enough that people had to crawl through them; in Virginia, Henry Spelman wrote that the door in an Indian house was "a little hole to come in at."[44] In addition, the smoke hole did not let all the smoke from the hearth out, nor did the house's inhabitants consider that desirable. Smoke seasoned the reed mats of the roof so that they lasted longer,[45] and in the warmer months it drove mosquitoes out of the house. So the smoke hole may not have been kept wide open, even in sunny weather; this would have reduced the limited amount of light that could come through it.

Most everyday work that Indian people did was done outside in the yard, not only for better light but especially if that work produced food scraps and sharp stone and bone chips from toolmaking that nobody wanted to step on. As in many parts of the developing world even today, houses were mainly places for sleeping and, remembering the hearth and its smoke, for drying things. Meanwhile, people working outdoors, in sight and sound of everyone else in the family, lacked visual as well as sonic privacy. That fact had a strong impact upon interpersonal relations in the towns (see chapter 3).

Given the biodegradable materials and the method of putting them together, Indian houses left a far smaller "footprint" on the land than our houses, whatever their size and shape, do today; all of our dwellings require heavy foundations (or pilings) and trenching for sewers and water lines, not to mention the concrete, metal, gypsum, or glass above ground. Indian houses were different. A few postholes and perhaps the remnants of a central hearth are all that remains of such houses, because biodegradable houses rapidly do just that: they start to fall apart. Even making a house last four years or so—which was the norm among people practicing shifting cultivation—necessitated frequent repairs, especially to the mats, after the first year. If nothing else, lashings became loose and had to be retied.

There was another ordinary-looking house at a distance from the family dwellings in each town: the women's menstrual house. It was built for the women to live in during their monthly periods. There is only a passing reference to it for the Powhatans,[46] but most Native Americans traditionally believed that menstrual blood was physically and ritually dangerous to men; it is certainly a scary scent to animals like deer. Men, the providers of meat for their families, therefore had to be protected from contact with it. The answer was for the women to tie on a waist cord and pass a perpendicular cord between the legs to hold wads of moss to catch the menstrual blood, after which they retired to the menstrual house and its environs for the duration of their periods—and probably also for the forty days of seclusion from men after giving birth.[47] No man would come near where they were. The other women in their extended family would cover their work (except possibly caring for female children, who could "safely" stay with their mothers) and also bring them food and drink. It would be almost a vacation for them—a week every month.

There were other, less elaborate structures in the Indian towns as well. From the Virginia Algonquian speakers, who were better recorded, we know that people built their houses under large, shady trees, both for the shade and for partial protection from rain and wind. They also had wall-less shades ("arbors") to work under outdoors; the shades had lofts in which corn and other foods were dried.[48] Lastly, there were houses for camping out. When families left the towns for the intensive fall foraging, and to forage in the spring and early summer while the crops grew, the women took along rolled-up mats as well as cooking pots. Once at a camping place, either there was a small house framework left over from a previous year (John Smith called it a "hunting house"), or the women and girls would erect a new, rough-and-ready framework. Unrolling and fastening the mats to the framework, they had a reasonably waterproof sleeping place that was ready, according to William Strachey, "in two or three hours."[49]

One more thing that every family had in their yard was a grill, consisting of sticks ("hurdles") lashed to a wooden framework built over a fire. On it fish were cooked for eating or smoked for storing.[50]

A different kind of structure ran from the shoreline into the water in front of many Indian towns and also out from sandy beaches around the Sounds (a wide, gently descending bottom was necessary): one or more fish weirs. Each weir consisted of a hedge running out into deeper water, perpendicular to the shoreline, with a mazelike trap at the end. The materials used were sapling stakes laid out in a line, in the case of a broad waterway, or in a small creek, in a pair of zigzags, converging in a "V" that all but closed the creek's entrance.[51] There were either reed mats lashed between the lined-up stakes, or boughs (probably cedar ones) piled up within the zigzag: either one would create a barrier to sizable fish trying to get through. Fish, when they encounter a barrier like that, will turn and swim into deeper water along the obstruction until they get clear of it. But waiting for them at the end of the hedge or "V" was a trap.

Closing the zigzags, at the downstream end, was a movable net something like a purse seine, into which fish in the creek were driven by the noise of paddles slapped into the water. The other kind of trap was more permanent (figure 2.4). That sort, incorrectly placed along the hedge by sixteenth-century illustrators, was out at the end, with an entrance on either side of the hedge's end, and consisted of one or more pairs of "bays," heart-shaped affairs that let fish enter by a funnel-opening but not leave again. Fish and shellfish are not analytically minded: they will go through a funnel to get into a baited trap or crab/lobster pot, but it never occurs to them to escape by going back out the way they came. Once in, they only see the funnel's narrow end as an obstacle, and they keep going around and around it. There is no need to build hatches or doors in such traps. The first set of bays fed fish into the next set (if there were two), and so on until the final square compound

FIGURE 2.4 Approaching a fish weir (painting by Karen Harvey, based on an idea of the author's).

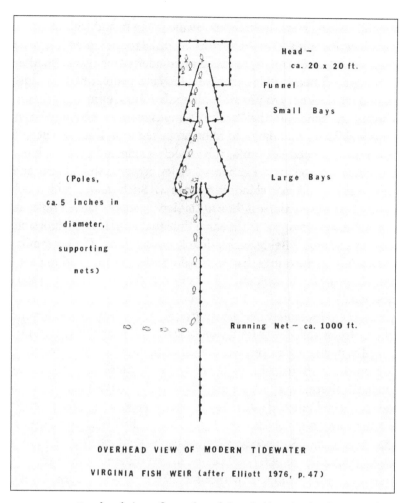

Head —
ca. 20 x 20 ft.

Funnel

Small Bays

(Poles,

ca. 5 inches in

diameter,

supporting

nets)

Large Bays

Running Net — ca. 1000 ft.

OVERHEAD VIEW OF MODERN TIDEWATER

VIRGINIA FISH WEIR (after Elliott 1976, p. 47)

FIGURE 2.5 Overhead view of a modern fish weir (drawing by the author).

was reached (figure 2.5). There the fish remained until they were dipped out by people intending to eat them (or fishing birds who got there first). Weirs of this kind caught fish 24/7/365, swimming in either direction along the shore, so they were well worth the effort required to build them. It takes an expert, however, to angle the bays correctly, so English colonists in both North Carolina and Virginia, being beginners at it, urged the Indians to build truly workable weirs for them.[52]

On the waterways around Indian towns observers would find people in canoes pursuing various errands: checking fish weirs, going after reeds and marsh tubers, visiting relatives in other towns, going to and from political meetings and ceremonies. Canoes were as essential to Indian people, who lacked draft animals and wagons, as cars are to modern Americans. But they were not the graceful bark affairs that New England peoples had, because white/paper birch does not grow in Mid-Atlantic latitudes, even in the mountains. Instead, the canoes in the Carolina Sounds were exceedingly heavy log dugouts—so heavy that they had to be propelled by at least two people standing on the flattened bottom of the canoe's inside and pushing long-handled paddles (i.e., poling the canoe) using leg power as well as back and arm power. (See how the man stands in figure 2.4.) Such canoes, which lack a keel, are hard to keep on course if the wind is blowing more than five miles an hour. They are also very tippy, at the same time that it is almost impossible actually to capsize one.[53] Being such valuable possessions of every family, and being made of cypress logs that eventually rotted, canoes had to be replaced. Making a new one took quite a bit of time; the process had to start well in advance.

A cypress tree—preferably one growing along a riverfront—was girdled repeatedly with controlled fires until stone axes could finish felling it. A line was fastened to it, and it was towed to the canoe makers' town's waterfront, hauled up onto the shore, and made stable there. More controlled fires were then used, alternating with scraping out the charcoal with shells, until the canoe had been hollowed out.[54] The danger was burning clear through the side or bottom, in which case the log had to be discarded and the process begun over again.[55] Somebody therefore had to tend the fires when they were burning; any adult or older child could do it if other jobs allowed.

No Indian town was complete without its gardens, where corn, beans, squash, and tobacco were raised. Their appearance differed somewhat from John White's and Theodor de Bry's renderings of the Secota ones, which are far too clean and neat. The time-capsule views that the short-lived English colony recorded also failed to note that the gardens were moved around from year to year (i.e., shifting cultivation). However, that moving was done within the town's areas of good farming land.

Tobacco, being a highly esteemed if not sacred plant, was grown in its own plot, and few details were recorded about its cultivation.[56] It was not the mild Orinoco tobacco that later became a cash crop shipped to Europe. It was *Nicotiana rustica*, a much stronger species that could cause hallucinations if smoked too freely. A puff or two, however, showed respect for the plant's power, and the reverent sharing of a pipe served to give the meetings between important men a slow, decorous beginning.

Corn, beans, and squash were originally Mesoamerican domesticates and were only partially adapted to the somewhat drier Mid-Atlantic climate. That meant both taking some extra care in cultivating them and also holding them in more esteem, when they became ripe, than was the case with wild plant foods. Englishmen visiting friendly towns at any season, including summertime when the last year's supplies of dried corn were low, were nonetheless presented by the chief with plenty of corncakes to eat.[57]

Clearing new fields occurred every year because older fields were becoming less productive; no Algonquian speakers in North Carolina (or Virginia) used fertilizer.[58] For each new field cleared, a three- to four-year-old field would be abandoned—and it would begin growing useful weeds like Indian hemp. As the main focus of gardening shifted around, up and down the waterfronts, so did those biodegradable houses that families lived in. As a result, for most Algonquian speakers, "towns" were in fact extensive areas along a river or creek, which were used and reused over and over again. From early eighteenth-century Virginia we have a vivid description of a town: it was "a row of cabins half a mile long."[59] That kind of settlement pattern drives archaeologists to distraction.

None of the fields was very big. We have to use Powhatan information here: "some [fields were] 100 some 200 feet square."[60] Clearing even that size of field out of the forest was quite an accomplishment for people who did not have steel axes or machetes. We have to turn to accounts of the Powhatans to find out how they did it. When dealing with small second-growth trees, they used stone axes and controlled fire to girdle them (chop or burn off the bark all the way around) down near the ground, after which a year or more was allowed for the trees to die and begin rotting, and then they could be mostly pushed down. Large, mature trees were chopped through, about "a yard above the ground" (the natural height of swing for the average man) and felled.[61] Such fields could be planted soon after these operations. Robert Beverley wrote in 1705 that "the ground was plantable, and would produce immediately upon the withering of the trees."[62] Sunlight reached the ground and any crops growing on it, but such fields were studded with jagged stumps and/or fallen logs. Planting was done around these obstacles with digging sticks, not plows. The Indians' attitude was one of getting by—as John Lawson put it, "taking care for no farther than what is absolutely necessary to support life."[63] Considering all the other jobs the people had to do (see chapter 3), that attitude made sense.

Preparing fields two years old or less (not yet growing low bushes) involved merely digging up the weeds and cornstalks to expose their roots, letting them dry for a day or two, then raking them into heaps and burning them. Nothing was then done with the ashes, which could have been used to enrich the soil. Men and women alike did this work.[64]

Actual planting among the Carolina Sounds people differed in a few ways from the method practiced by their Powhatan relatives to the north. Starting at one corner of a field, they used an imaginary grid, with intersections about three feet from one another. At each intersection, a shallow hole was made. Into it were dropped four kernels of corn, placed an inch from one another, and then the hole was filled in. Beans and sunflowers were then planted between the corn holes—a practice called "intercropping" that resulted soon afterward in a plant cover that prevented moisture from evaporating from bare soil. (It also made the fields look even messier.) The bean vines would eventually reach and climb the cornstalks; the Powhatans planted corn and beans together, so that it happened even sooner.[65] Planting in the Carolina Sounds region was done in late April, as opposed to May in Virginia. From April onward, there were staggered plantings in various fields, as in Virginia, to provide fresh produce well into the fall.[66]

Weeding would have been done by women and children. Adults also built a raised scaffold in each field, and someone sat on it to make noise to scare off any intruding animals. If the "scarecrow" was a boy, he may also have used the marauders for target practice, any resulting carcasses being donated to the family stewpot.[67] The harvest would have been gathered by all able-bodied people, for time would have been precious: they would have needed to get it in before the weather or vermin ruined it. (An amazing number of wild animals in the region love corn on the cob.) All the crops were divided, with some being eaten immediately and some being dried for future use.

Field crops had considerable variety and were prepared in multiple ways.[68] Any visitor to an Indian town on ordinary days, let alone special occasions, would have seen stewpots, at the very least, kept simmering continuously to feed the active, hardworking residents whenever they were hungry.

Corn (*pagatowr*) was multicolored and of two sorts: one grew to be six or seven feet high and ripened in eleven or twelve weeks, while the other grew ten feet high and ripened in fourteen weeks. The ears were dried, and later shelled, the kernels being treated in several ways. They might be boiled whole, until they were soft, or pounded into flour and the flour made into mush. Or the flour would be made into ash cakes, a sort of bread that was cooked in hot ashes in hand-fashioned patties. Corn kernels could also be ground to flour and then parched, to make a trail food carried in a buckskin pouch; in Virginia, at least, it was called *rockahominy*.[69]

Beans (large ones called *okindgier*, small ones called *wickonzówr*) ripened in ten weeks. They were either boiled until soft in a broth (perhaps a meat broth), or they were boiled with corn (in a dish ancestral to succotash). Or they were pounded in a mortar and the flour made into "lumps of doughy bread."[70]

Squash (*macócqwer*, or nowadays, "macaug," applied to only one kind) came in several kinds that nevertheless tasted alike, according to Hariot, who called them "pumpkins, melons, and gourds."[71] One of them ripened in a month, another in two months, but Hariot was not specific. The bottle gourds were dried, the loose seeds were removed, and the remaining shell was used for carrying water and the like.

Sunflower seeds were beaten into flour and used to make bread and thicken broth. The species shown in illustrations of Secota was *Helianthus giganteus*, the same species we raise commercially today.[72]

An orache-like plant was also encouraged, if not domesticated; its seeds were ground and the flour used as a broth thickener.[73] Today we consider it a weed.

Before the crops were planted and while waiting for them to become ripe, as well as after the harvest, the townspeople broke up into family camping groups and lived off the land, leaving the towns almost deserted except for the times that family members returned to do some weeding.[74] In both spring and fall, they were using the very extensive hunting and collecting territories that surrounded each town, lands that were left uncultivated (if they could be cultivated at all), giving the English the impression that most of the region was wilderness. In Indian minds, it would have been nothing of the sort.

People of both sexes went into the forests almost daily. House-building materials, the makings of pots and baskets and nets, and the makings of bows and arrows all came from the foraging territory, a territory that in the Algonquian speakers' minds had a river or large creek as its center, not its boundaries (figure 2.6). People grew up knowing, season by season, where the things that they would need could be found; this was true for many miles around, which required a major feat of memorization. Men, and women when they went along, had an even larger regional map in their heads, probably based upon rivers and their tributaries that they had both seen and heard about from others, including members of foreign tribes.[75] Not only that, but certain places along the network of trails through the woodlands were commemorated for events that had happened nearby, sometimes by cairns of stones,[76] but always in oral tradition. Altogether, what was "wilderness" to the English in the 1580s must have been alive with meaning, memories, and possibilities for the Native people.

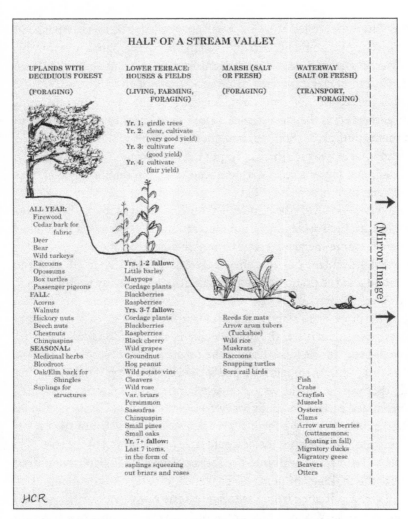

HALF OF A STREAM VALLEY

UPLANDS WITH DECIDUOUS FOREST	LOWER TERRACE: HOUSES & FIELDS	MARSH (SALT OR FRESH)	WATERWAY (SALT OR FRESH)
(FORAGING)	(LIVING, FARMING, FORAGING)	(FORAGING)	(TRANSPORT, FORAGING)

Yr. 1: girdle trees
Yr. 2: clear, cultivate
(very good yield)
Yr. 3: cultivate
(good yield)
Yr. 4: cultivate
(fair yield)

ALL YEAR:
Firewood
Cedar bark for
fabric
Deer
Bear
Wild turkeys
Raccoons
Opossums
Box turtles
Passenger pigeons
FALL:
Acorns
Walnuts
Hickory nuts
Beech nuts
Chestnuts
Chinquapins
SEASONAL:
Medicinal herbs
Bloodroot
Oak/Elm bark for
Shingles
Saplings for
structures

Yrs. 1-2 fallow:
Little barley
Maypops
Cordage plants
Blackberries
Raspberries
Yrs. 3-7 fallow:
Cordage plants
Blackberries
Raspberries
Black cherry
Wild grapes
Groundnut
Hog peanut
Wild potato vine
Cleavers
Wild rose
Var. briars
Persimmon
Sassafras
Chinquapin
Small pines
Small oaks
Yr. 7+ fallow:
Last 7 items,
in the form of
saplings squeezing
out briars and roses

Reeds for mats
Arrow arum tubers
(Tuckahoe)
Wild rice
Muskrats
Raccoons
Snapping turtles
Sora rail birds

Fish
Crabs
Crayfish
Mussels
Oysters
Clams
Arrow arum berries
(cuttanemons;
floating in fall)
Migratory ducks
Migratory geese
Beavers
Otters

(Mirror Image)

HCR

FIGURE 2.6 Half of a stream valley (drawing by the author).

A world such as that should not be owned by anyone, in Indian thinking. It belonged to everyone—everyone, that is, except hostile peoples whose incursions had to be guarded against. Likewise, the land where the soil was good for farming should not be owned absolutely; it should only be used temporarily by families and then returned to public use as foraging territory while the soil rested. After all, the wild plants that grew there in successive years were too valuable to hoard at the expense of fellow tribesmen who were also one's relatives. Good social relations, for women as well as men, depended upon knowledge of resources, bringing them in, and then sharing them.

CHAPTER THREE

The People and Their Everyday Work

The Roanokes and other Algonquian speakers were what they looked like: American Indians. They had pale yellowish skin if it was not suntanned or painted—but most men did paint their faces with red dye. That misled some Europeans into thinking Native people were born with dark skin.[1] The plant used for the dye, called "true" puccoon (*Lithospermum caroliniense*), had to be imported, and will be discussed in chapter 5. The people's hair and eyes were dark brown to black, although some children's hair was auburn or chestnut-colored before it darkened. That trait—parallel to blonde children growing up to be brunettes, among European-descended people—misled the producers of the colorized de Bry engravings into showing *everybody*, including adults, as redheaded (see, for instance, the 2007 edition of Hariot).[2] Hariot remarked that the people had "small eyes," but he may have meant eyes partially covered by epicanthic (above-the-eye) folds, a trait common among full-blooded American Indians. The men showed another American Indian (and Asiatic) trait: they had only scanty beards and never went bald.[3]

The people were taller, on average, than the English of their time. Precise figures are lacking at this writing, but the Carolina Sounds people may have been comparable to their linguistic relatives in Virginia and Maryland, in which case the male average was about five feet seven inches (170 cm) and the female average was about five feet three and a half inches (160 cm). By contrast, the average among early seventeenth-century Londoners was an inch shorter for men and two and a half inches shorter for women.[4]

To these basic physical traits were added numerous culturally determined ones. Both sexes tattooed their skins—the men with tribal, or perhaps kinship-determined, designs on their backs; the women with geometric figures on their arms and chests and sometimes their faces.[5] Body paint was worn by men on various occasions, especially those concerned with war.[6]

Men wore a short, greased, stand-up roach that extended along the crown from front to back. Side hair was treated variously: put into a knot at the nape of the neck among the Roanokes or plucked out (with bristles coming in) along the sides among other tribes.[7] This contrasted with the practice of their relatives to the north, who wore the roach but plucked the right-side hair and knotted the long left-side hair. The aim was to avoid getting one's long hair tangled in a bowstring. Men plucked their facial hair until they grew old, after which they allowed it to grow into a sparse goatee. Women favored various hairstyles. Some wore bangs, with shoulder-length hair elsewhere. Others had bangs in front but a knot of long hair done up in back.[8]

Clothing for both sexes was minimal by European standards, except in really cold weather, when people wrapped deerskin mantles around their bodies.[9] Wealthy people wore mantles with the fur dressed on, or with appliqués of iridescent green head-skins of male mallard ducks sewn on, or other feathers embroidered in patterns, the latter including "several pretty figures wrought in feathers, making them seem like a fine flower silk-shag."[10] In cold weather, though, the plain, workaday mantles were not very practical for doing hard physical work such as chasing a wounded deer, or prying tuckahoe roots out of the marshes. Therefore people strove to be both acclimatized before winter came and stoic about discomfort after it arrived. John Lawson wrote that they "are the patientest and most steady people under any burden, that I ever saw in my life."[11]

Everyday wear consisted of little more than a buckskin apron covering the private parts in front. Wealthier people, having more deerskins, could cover themselves fore and aft. Young children wore very little, at least when in town, which undoubtedly reduced the need for doing laundry. Unmarried girls wore a thong of silk grass around their waist, with another thong of it brought forward between their legs and tied to the waist thong; moss was then inserted in the groin area for modesty (figure 3.1). There was no underwear, although wads of moss tied between the legs were also used for cleanliness for babies and for menstruating women and girls.[12]

When working away from town, where they might encounter brambles, people wore deerskin moccasins on their feet. (The people in the White paintings and de Bry engravings are all barefooted because their portraits were made in town.) They may also have worn long leggings to protect their legs, as the Powhatans are known to have done.[13]

"Dressing up" meant adding not clothes but jewelry, consisting of necklaces, earrings, and bracelets of copper beads, freshwater pearls, "bones," and bird talons. Small copper beads might be strung between larger beads of pearl or bone.[14] Men sometimes wore feathers in their knots of long hair; if the rest of their heads had short hair, then it is likely that they left one lock long so they could attach such things (the feathers were not glued on somehow: figure 3.2). Chiefs who owned more luxury goods could dress up more elaborately with them: more jewelry, more furs, more earrings in each ear.[15]

FIGURE 3.1 A woman and her daughter (painting by Karen Harvey,
based on the John White portraits).

In fact, chiefs made a point of collecting trade copper; they used it not only for jewelry but also to give to allies when planning a war.[16]

The Women's World

For people staying in town, there was not a rigid division of labor between men and women, at least on special occasions such as feasts and in a season like harvest time, when all able-bodied people were expected to rally around and get the work done. For instance, Thomas Hariot saw the preparations for feeding him and other English guests, and he wrote that filling the big stewpots with water was done "by them [the men] or by their women."[17] He seems to have been unaware that every English visit automatically turned the day into an extraordinary one, so that he was not observing everyday behavior. Normally it was the women and older girls who carried the water, as well as going out into the woods to gather firewood for boiling it.

Women did, in fact, go in and out of town daily in the course of their work. Given the needs of their families, and the fact that they had to go and get the materials to meet those needs, no woman was confined by her work to the house and its vicinity (as were English housewives) unless she were physically disabled—or menstruating or in seclusion after giving birth. Women had business that took them into many of the same kinds of countryside as the men, albeit not so far afield, especially if they had small children with them. The many jobs they did, requiring a computerlike memory of what useful things were located where, gave them a good deal of autonomy from the men of the family, who in any case were totally absorbed in other matters.

Women's autonomy was indicated by two things. One was their use of canoes. Canoes in the Woodland Indian world were not for recreation. They were necessary modes of transport for hauling goods, including great quantities of reeds for mat making and marsh tubers for making bread when the corn had run out. That shoved canoes deep into the women's realm. The other indication of female autonomy is found in the Carolina Algonquian speakers' customs concerning sex and marriage. (The English in the Mid-Atlantic completely overlooked another possible indication: kinship groups such as clans. In *matrilineal* clans, the eldest woman, the "clan mother," wields real power over both sexes, sometimes including in the political realm when choosing leaders, which was documented among some Iroquoians to the north. But we have no record indicating such things among Algonquian speakers in either North Carolina or Virginia.)

Both sexes were free to engage in premarital sex. If a child resulted, it belonged to the mother's family just as children born within marriage did. That does not mean that the people were matrilineal: the practice of children going with their divorced mothers does not require matrilineality, as twentieth-century American divorce customs proved. Among the Secotas and others, a woman had the right to refuse to sleep with a man, who then had to withdraw his attentions. No forcing of women was allowed. That custom, still prevalent in the early 1700s, led John Lawson to think that "the Indian men were not so vigorous and impatient in their love as we are."[18] What he was seeing instead were cultures in which men (as well as women) were always supposed to be in complete control of their impulses. Indian men also knew better than to boast of their conquests when they succeeded. In those small towns, the word would rapidly get back to the women, who would thereafter snub them unmercifully. Lawson observed that forbearing to boast about conquests was not done to protect a young woman's reputation, which among the Indians had more to do with her economic performance than with her sexual behavior.[19] Instead, keeping quiet about liaisons was desirable because it prevented jealousy and quarrels in the town.

Men were allowed as many wives as they could support through their hunting and fishing. No English observer seems even to have asked if the converse were true: multiple husbands. But in a very real sense, wives supported husbands (with plant foods and making household goods) just as their husbands supported them (with meat and defense of the town against enemies). Lawson called the women "mercenary," because they valued a good provider over any other qualities a man might have. A truly expert hunter would have no trouble marrying more than one woman at a time. And older men who no longer hunted but who had income in foodstuffs or others' labor because of being politically important could attract much younger women—often "three or four" of them, as Lawson observed.[20] Marriage to a pair of sisters was allowed. In many societies with that custom, the reasoning is that sisters will get along better than unrelated cowives. Men, already married or not, were also allowed to marry a widowed sister-in-law (technically called the *sororate*). The rule made sense in a world with continual albeit guerilla-style warfare, and thus with constant attrition on the male population; the sororate provided unemployment insurance for widows. Other than the support issue, the only serious brake on men's acquiring wives was the prohibition against marrying relatives—first cousins or closer. Incest was punished with death. A century later, when the Indian populations had been severely reduced, the rule still stood, forcing people to marry outsiders or remain unmarried. Lastly, homosexuality seems to have been "never heard of" among the Carolina tribes, to the extent that there was no word for it in the tribes John Lawson met.[21] However, it is possible that the Indian people Lawson met were aware of the horror that most Englishmen felt about it and so may simply never have discussed the matter with their visitor. It is also possible that Lawson was speaking of the Tuscaroras, whom he knew better than the Secotas he had met.

Marriage in the Indian towns was a civil matter, not a religious one; however, it was very much a family and town matter, not just a relationship between two isolated individuals. After what was probably a quiet courtship and mutual agreement, the man made the first public move by going to the girl's parents or nearest relatives and sounding them out. If they said they would consider it, then the next step was to have a conclave of all the elderly relatives of both the man and the woman, and sometimes also the chief and his council. If they approved of the match and the girl was willing—apparently her people talked with her openly about it only at this late stage—then the groom paid bridewealth for her in valuable goods. Bridewealth is the opposite of a dowry, and paying it shows how valuable the woman, her reproductive powers, and her kinsmen as in-laws are to the groom and his family; it is not the selling of an individual like a piece of furniture. Marriages were not fully in force until the whole amount was paid. The couple could live and run a household together, but they could not have sexual relations, "all which is punctually observed."[22] That is more evidence for what we would consider extraordinary self-control.

Some adultery did occur after marriage, though it was not considered admirable. The woman was considered weak-willed, and the man, if caught, was publicly ridiculed. The husband demanded compensation in goods from the man, whose life was in danger until he had paid up. Nothing was recorded about what wives of adulterous husbands could get. Marriages broke up easily whenever a couple no longer got along and self-control might be stretched too far. Either party could be the one to leave. But the woman's new husband, if she remarried, had to pay the bridewealth to her ex-husband, not her family. She kept the children after a divorce. If the marriage endured and she was widowed, she usually remarried—fast. It was not due to a lack of sentiment toward the dead spouse; it was a matter of survival. Neither marriage partner could live for long on their own without the complementing work of the other one to keep the household going, especially if there were small children involved. A century later, when trade with Europeans had put many families in debt, another rule was in force: any new husband had to pay the deceased husband's debts. And as long as a widow stayed single, she was not responsible for those debts—debts were men's business.[23]

Women's business included work that was strenuous enough that some working mothers began developing arthritis in their thirties.[24] First, there was the daily hauling of water and firewood and the preparing of vegetables and animal carcasses to make stew for the family. Then there was the training of children, described below. There were hides, from the animal carcasses, to be tanned and made into garments. There were fields to be tended part-time, and until the crops came in the family's diet had to be supplemented with wild plant foods that might grow several miles away and some distance down in the mud of a marsh. And last but far from least, there were houses to repair and broken pots, mats, and baskets to be replaced—all with materials hauled in by women on foot or by canoe from the town's foraging territory and then processed by hand. Other than the priests, there were no specialists in the Indian towns, no one to make quantities of one or two things and sell them to neighbors. Every family's women had to know and practice all the skills it took to keep a household going.

House building and upkeep have already been described in chapter 2. Women made mats from various reeds, according to what grew in the local waterways; cattails were popular because of their length (Hariot wrote of "long rushes"). Reeds and rushes might be dyed red before being laid out and sewn together or sometimes woven into patterns. Mats were usually about five feet by twelve feet in size, and they were used not only as house coverings and partitions but also as makeshift umbrellas, bedding, and burial shrouds, as well as clean surfaces on which to dry things. And important visitors were given a double-thickness mat to sit on, rather than sitting on the bare ground.[25] With all those uses, mat making must have gone on nearly all the time. There would have been variation among the mats: some coarse and quick to make, others fine. William Strachey wrote in Virginia about "a delicate-wrought fine kind of mat the Indians make, with which [when the English could buy them or steal them during raids], our people do dress [hang on the walls of] their chambers and inward rooms, which make their houses so much the more handsome."[26] A piece of such a stolen mat has been found in an archaeological dig on Jamestown Island.[27]

There were also nets and bags to be made out of cordage: nets for carrying bags, nets for dipping fish out of weirs. The materials were various: soft inner bark of certain trees such as red cedar, deer sinew, and long fibers from some wild field plants. The finest were woven from silk grass (identified in chapter 2). The materials would be gathered and dried, after which, in the

ANOTHER CLOSE LOOK AT JOHN SMITH'S TUCKAHOE

Arrow arum is especially plentiful in coastal plain wetlands because it can grow in slightly salty water and also in odd places where other emergents do not. (We once spotted an isolated arrow arum plant growing at the margin of water flowing rapidly through Natural Bridge in Virginia.) For Indian women, that availability was offset by the fact that the tubers are horribly labor-intensive to dig: the bigger the tuber, the farther down in the mud it is (up to three feet for giant tubers). The starchy tubers want to float, so the plant anchors them in the mud by hundreds of small, thin rootlets, each with the tensile strength of a steel hawser. (A chef friend of ours once attempted it, using his best kitchen knives; each knife went dull in a matter of minutes, sawing away at those rootlets.) The roots that actually feed the plant are thick, soft, and easy to break. In our field experiments, the best way to excavate the tubers proved to be this: at least two muscular adults (women, of course, in the Indian world) sit around the plant, gouging into the mud with their feet and using a wooden pry bar with both hands, to find and loosen the tuber, and then—with brute strength—they break it free of the rootlets.

The labor-intensive qualities of the plant are not finished yet. It is a species related to Polynesian taro, which contains enough calcium oxalate (an agent that can cause anaphylactic shock in humans) that it should never be eaten raw. All parts of arrow arum are full—*very* full—of calcium oxalate that has to be neutralized. (Not having callused hands, we had to wear rubber gloves when handling the tubers.) John Smith, interested in plants that could be put to use to feed his soldiers, wrote that there were two ways to do the neutralizing: peel and bake the tubers in an earth oven for twenty-four hours, or peel them, slice them, and sun-dry them. The slices will then taste like flour-and-water paste and can be eaten like potato chips. But to make bread, which was apparently preferred by Indian people, the slices had to be pulverized in a mortar (by women, of course). The result is lumpy. Our chef friend found that even the most sophisticated food processor in his kitchen would not remove all the lumps. The flour can then be made into cakes and baked—after which it has no taste at all. But it's filling. And the women making it understandably developed arthritis young.

case of plant stems, the stems would be peeled and the long, lengthwise fibers extracted. Properly cleaned, silk-grass fibers really do feel like silk.[28] In late seventeenth-century Virginia, John Banister described its special preparation: "They peel [fibers] when dry and beaten becomes a very fine shining something between hair & silk; the Indians dye it of several colors, weave it into baskets & cohobs [tump lines; one is shown in figure 3.2]."[29] Before dyeing, the fibers would be hand-twisted together, with more fiber continually added in for greater length. This was a job women could (and probably did) do at any time when their hands were not otherwise busy. Still more cordage was needed for trussing up things for transport: freshly killed carcasses, dead wood for firewood, and so on. Baskets were made of various things such as reeds from the marshes, wild grape vines from the forest edges around fields, and splints of various kinds of wood. One way of working on a basket, rather than holding it in one's lap, was to start the bottom with vertical ribs sticking up and to hang that upside down from a tree limb; then, with both hands free, to weave in further horizontal pieces, working downward until the inverted basket's top was reached.[30]

Women's work included processing animal carcasses. Deer were especially prized, not only for their size but for their many uses: a deer carcass yielded meat and entrails for stews, hides for clothing, brains for tanning those hides, sinew for thread, antlers for boiling down into glue, and bones for making a variety of tools. Tanning, with or without the hair left on (in which case the hide was soaked and scraped) was done in a solution of water and deer brain—which is an excellent tanning solution, rather than being a stopgap—until the hide absorbed the liquid. The hide was then stretched on a frame and dried while being scraped with an "oyster shell" or a wooden scraper until it was both dry and pliable.[31] There were loincloths and moccasins to be made from tanned deerskins, as well as purses for carrying powders and small valuables: these were long affairs whose tops were looped over a cord belt when being worn, as shown in figures 4.2 and 5.2. A very heavily embroidered one, using shell beads and called "the Virginia Purse," is in the Ashmolean Museum in Oxford, England.[32]

Pottery making went on at intervals: gather the fine clay, wherever along the riverbanks it was available; save and grind up oyster shells for the temper; mix both with water to make a paste; hand roll the paste into fillets; and add the fillets in an upward coil to the hand-formed bottom of the pot, smoothing them into one another along the way. Let the finished pot dry out for several days. Gather the firewood, place it over and around the pots to be baked, and make a blazing fire, keeping it going for at least an hour. Let the pots cool, and begin using. Before European kitchen influences began to be felt (with indoor hearths, trivets, and flat-bottomed cooking pots), Indian pots were made for specifically Indian outdoor-hearth cooking. Pots had conical bottoms so that they could be wedged down in among the burning logs and propped in place with a few rocks.[33] With fire around a good-sized part of their bottoms, their contents could be brought to a boil in about two-thirds of the time it would take with a comparable-sized flat-bottomed pot.[34]

Women also provided their families with a certain number of wild plant foods, which supplemented or took the place of the domestic plants they were raising. The only reliable source of sugar in the people's diet came from wild berries (mulberries, raspberries, blackberries, wild raisins, for instance) and wild fruits (wild cherries, persimmons, and so on).[35] These had to be gathered in the proper season where they were growing and taken home on foot, using baskets held to the women's shoulders with tump lines around their foreheads. The same was true for the quantities of nuts and acorns gathered on the major camping trip the family took each fall. The burden of nuts plus venison and deer hides had to be humped back to town, with or without men's assistance.

All these jobs that women handled were carried out in sociable groups, with children helping (or just running around and making noise). It did not matter if any wild animals nearby were scared away; with dangerous predators around, such as bears and wolves, that was a good thing. Staying in groups became a sensible proceeding when traveling in the forest, in case of accidents, and groups were a necessity in propelling the heavy dugout canoes and digging tuckahoe tubers. It is safe to say that Indian women were almost never alone; even when staying in the menstrual house they were succored by other women.

Women's business was so varied and so continual that it kept them very physically fit for pregnancy and delivery. Working right up until delivery contributed to their having "very easy travail with their children."[36] They then would suckle their children "till they are well grown," meaning three or four years old if another baby did not come along. If a woman had difficulty producing enough milk, there were two alternatives: another woman in the town who was lactating might be able to feed that baby as well as her own. Otherwise, among people who lacked domestic animals like cows, a temporary substitute for mother's milk had to be made and used until a lactating woman could be found. European records say little about such matters, since nearly all the record makers were men. But one account does mention a milk substitute. Though it comes from the eighteenth-century Abenaki, Algonquian speakers far to the north, the Powhatans and probably the Carolina Sounds people had the ingredients at hand: it was *powcohicora*, or "nut milk."[37] Nuts were pounded up and mixed with water to make a milky liquid. The Powhatans used that as a high-prestige drink at feasts. Abenaki Indian women mixed cornmeal into it, boiled it, and fed it to their babies if they were away from other families and their own milk was insufficient. Although the mixture provided calories and water, it was deficient in protein and seriously lacking in calcium and B vitamins. Thus it was not a long-term solution but only a stopgap while the search for a wet nurse went on.[38]

The English recorded very little about naming practices among the Native people they met, so we must use data from the related Virginia Algonquian speakers to the north. Babies were given two names to start with. One was public and the other was a secret, very personal name that was to be bound up with the holder's future welfare (see chapter 4). Various nicknames were given a child thereafter, often teasing ones. Pocahontas got her best-known nickname, which essentially means "you bawdy, mischievous little brat," from her high-ranking father, the paramount chief Powhatan, probably when she went too far in tormenting that busy man to get his attention. Meanwhile, her secret name was Matoaka (meaning unknown), and she revealed it only after converting to Christianity and getting a new name, Rebecca. Boys, especially, were expected to earn new names periodically, as they demonstrated their growing proficiency as hunter-warriors. Chiefs took new names upon rising to power. There are two instances from Virginia and one from the Carolina Sounds of chiefs taking a new name when they expected a successful change in their status: Wingina became Pemisapan in 1586, Opechancanough became Mangopeesomon in 1621 before a major military effort, and Oitchapam became Itoyatin when he succeeded his brother Powhatan in 1618.[39] (The real reason behind Wingina's change will be surmised in chapter 6.)

Babies could be left behind when mothers left the towns to work, because mothers belonged to extended families, and there were grandmothers and other women available to do the babysitting, probably on a rotating basis. When children were toddlers, too big to carry conveniently and not yet old enough to keep up on the trail, they would have been left behind like that. But while they were still small, their mothers could "carry them to work" in a cradleboard, which could be hung from a tree branch or propped up against a tree trunk while the mother labored. The cradleboards made by Mid-Atlantic Algonquian speakers were extremely basic affairs compared to the elaborately embroidered ones we can see in museums of the Plains Indians. All that was required was a flat board, about one by two feet, with buckskin laces

FIGURE 3.2 Returning from nutgathering (painting by Karen Harvey, based on John White's painting of a woman and her toddler and an idea of the author's).

attached. The baby was placed on its back on the board and then laced "down very close, having, near the middle, a stick fastened about two inches from the board, which [was] for the child's breech to rest on, under which they put a wad of moss" that acted as a diaper. A cord was tied onto each upper corner of the board, "whereby the mother [slung] her child on her back" or hung the apparatus on a tree limb.[40] When she shielded herself from the rain, she threw a deerskin or mat over both herself and the child on the cradleboard.[41] Basic as this arrangement is, the babies would have loved the security of it.[42]

It would have been only older toddlers, having outgrown the cradleboard, who were carried by two hands and one leg on their mother's back, as shown in the White painting and de Bry engraving.[43] One suspects that this uncomfortable method encouraged the toddler to resume walking soon afterward (figure 3.2). Endurance and hardiness were prized virtues in the Indian world.

In line with other traditional Native Americans, the Carolina Algonquian speakers used only very loose discipline with their children. A century later John Lawson wrote, "To their children they are extraordinarily tender and indulgent; neither did I ever see a parent correct a child."[44] Children were expected to watch adults quietly and learn from them what proper behavior consisted of and how to do various tasks. They learned such expectations very early in life. Getting called down for a mistake would have been extremely embarrassing for a child, and no conscientious parent would have done it. Parents were rarely tempted, though, because children over the age of two or so had already caught on to how to behave properly.[45] And in any case, there was no "kids' culture" that postponed maturity; the adult world was what the children aspired to join as full members. Girls therefore learned the women's role in society by accompanying their mothers and other female relatives as they worked. Gradually they would build up the computerlike memory for plants, locations, and seasons that their elders had.

The Men's World

Men's work in England was normally away from the house, or in the case of craftsmen and merchants in towns and cities, away from the family's eating and sleeping quarters. But the Indian setup was both different and hard for the English to appreciate. For starters, all Indian men except priests were expected to have a major occupation: hunting animals and, as warriors, hunting people (same weapons, same techniques) (figure 3.3). Hunting was a deadly serious, very intensely focused job, as we shall see. Even if a man did not have to chase a deer for miles after failing to make a clean kill, he would return home, lugging a carcass, thoroughly tired out. Around the house he would need to rest up, consult with other men about where deer were to be found, and make any necessary repairs to his hunting equipment before going out again. English visitors to the towns saw Indian men at such slack times and concluded that they were lazy, a misapprehension that has continued in the public mind down to the present day.

While they rested, if it was not harvesttime, men could also talk politics, visit with their sons, and make things for themselves and their households: using a stone scraper to grate deer bones down into projectile points and fishhooks, and knapping stone into knives (used by both sexes) and more projectile points. Other jobs that took longer fell to men who were not proficient hunters, perhaps because of poor eyesight or else advancing age. These men were the ones who helped the women bear burdens and who would have done

FIGURE 3.3 A man with hunting gear (painting by Karen Harvey, based on the John White portrait).

much of the lengthy burning-and-scraping required to hollow out canoes. They also made wooden platters and dishes and spoons.[46] All able-bodied men were probably expected to cooperate in making fish weirs, because that job required a great deal of very heavy labor while either holding a canoe steady or wading in the water, depending on the tide (see chapter 2).[47]

Boys were expected to grow up to be superlative hunters like their elders, but the hunting itself was too important and the stalking too delicate an operation for their fathers to take them along until they neared the end of childhood. Boys therefore listened to their fathers talk in town but otherwise practiced and honed their skills on their own. When they were proficient enough to be taken along, and had accumulated more experience yet, they were formally initiated into adulthood by being "huskanawed."[48] Young men were put through this grueling process every year or two in the early winter. Only the most promising young hunters qualified, and boys competed for the honor of being chosen. A man who had never been a good enough hunter to be chosen, being passed over year after year, would never be considered a real man. The first stage was both a public recognition of the boys' prowess and a symbolic killing of them, which led John Smith to call it erroneously a "sacrifice of children."[49]

A huge concourse of people assembled adjacent to the chief's town, consisting of all the members if the tribe were large, or all the people in two smaller tribes putting on the ceremony cooperatively. First, there was a feast for everyone and also a formal community dance, with people wearing their best clothing and paint and jewelry and moving four abreast in two big circles around a fire, one circle going clockwise and the other counterclockwise. Dancing in the center were several men wearing blackened horns on their heads and carrying green boughs (meaning uncertain). At two points in the dance they suddenly acted violently crazy—probably in imitation not only of how violent the boys' caretakers would be toward them later, out in the forest, but also of how strangely the boys would act under the treatment. The "crazy" men shrieked, threw down their boughs, burst out of the circles, and ran over to a small tree while clapping their hands. They then tore the tree to the ground, after which they resumed their place in the center of the two circles. When everyone had danced themselves into exhaustion, the candidates were brought into the circle, their bodies painted in white to contrast with the black worn by the "violent" men. The boys were seated together, after which a gauntlet of two lines was formed by the older men, who were armed with reed bundles (*bastinadoes*). Five young men, previous initiates, then led each boy through the gauntlet, protecting them while the older men tried to beat them, as if furious about the "abduction" of the boys, who were still technically children. Once all the boys had been through the gauntlet, another gauntlet was formed and the procedure was repeated, and then repeated again. All the while, the women and girls were crying and mourning loudly. They had brought a great deal of firewood along with them to the ceremony.

The candidates were then taken to another spot, where the chief waited, and another feast for the people took place over the next two to three hours. But suddenly the older men, still clutching their reed bundles, jumped up and made another gauntlet, through which the boys had to pass a fourth time (four being a mystical number in Native American religions). This time the boys had no help and did not "survive," being "killed" and their bodies laid aside. The older men danced around the pile of "corpses," then sat down in a circle around them. The chief then had the women bring over the firewood, stack it up high, and set it afire (although cremation of real corpses was not actually practiced in the region). At that point, when it appeared that the boys' bodies would be burned, the public phase of the huskanaw ended and the people were sent home.

As with so many male initiations the world over, the essential part of it was done in secret, away from all females and uninitiated males. In the Indian world, that meant being taken far out into the forest, well away from human habitations or hunting activities. For five or six weeks, the candidates were confined in a large, bent-wood cage—potentially uncomfortable in itself if "Indian summer" had ended and the inmates could not move around actively to fight off the cold. The ordeal did not end there; the boys were given a concoction—ingredients not recorded—to drink, and it made them into violent maniacs who *needed* to be confined. It is possible that overdoses and physical accidents in the cage could occur. In Virginia, the Powhatans told several English writers over the years that most times not all the boys lived to return home. Their mothers would be told that one of the deities had chosen that boy as a sacrifice.

At length, the boys were brought off the medicine and back to their senses—but they no longer "remembered" anything about their lives as children. When taken back to their villages, they did not even recognize their own mothers. (Any boy who slipped up and showed otherwise would be taken back and re-huskanawed, which in his already weakened state he would not survive.) Now the last and crucial stage of initiation was reached: the candidates would be retrained *by men as men*. They had now entered a world set apart from that of women and children, and though they would marry and have children of their own, they would never entirely leave the men's world again. No wonder they were so magnificently focused on hunting.

The English in the 1580s saw little hunting going on—probably because it was taking place away from the towns they were visiting—so that important as it was to Indian hosts and foreign visitors alike, they wrote little about the methods of doing it.

Hunting of deer and many other animals had to be done all year, in all types of weather. It was not just a sport, though the men enjoyed it to that extent; it was a necessity. Finding the prey might mean a long walk from town and then a long stretch of stalking before firing off an arrow. Merely wounding the prey would mean chasing the animal until it dropped, perhaps miles away from the shooting site. Men had to be proficient cross-country runners, with that kind of runner's lean, wiry build (and probably not the stocky, bulging-muscular look suggested in the White paintings and made conspicuous in the de Bry engravings). Then the heavy carcass had to be brought back home on foot. And if the Carolina practice was like the Virginia one, there would be no gutting before the carrying, because the entrails—rich in vitamins—went into the stewpot along with the meat.[50]

Boys and men trained hard to become expert stalkers. They probably used rituals and physical aids like smearing on something to disguise their scent, but the English records from the Sounds region say nothing about it. John White noted that on Roanoke Island hunters would ambush deer among "high reeds, where oftentimes they find the deer asleep." Those would be fairly easy kills compared to hunting in the forest. Priests, on the other hand, went after birds with their bows and arrows.[51]

In the fall, when families went out in large camping groups, there were more personnel available for deer drives. Women and children joined in making plenty of noise, and men set fires in the woods near where the deer were. If a herd were being surrounded and slaughtered, the fires and noise in a circle around it would be drawn in until the animals could be dispatched. At other times, the noise and fire was on one side of the herd, which was driven out onto a neck of land and into the water, where men stationed with canoes could make easy kills.[52]

For men outside the chiefly families, the road to personal prestige lay in being expert hunters of both animals and people. John Lawson said it best: "He that is a good warrior, is the proudest creature living; and he that is an expert hunter, is esteemed by the people and himself. . . . Several of the Indians [of Lawson's time, 1709] are possessed of a great many [trade goods], yet such an Indian is no more esteemed amongst them, than any other ordinary fellow, provided he has no personal endowments [i.e., outstanding abilities]."[53]

Besides building fish weirs, men went shellfishing, taking whatever kinds were available in the waterways. This was done intensively, along with the fishing, in the spring and summer when the anadromous fish runs were on (shad and alewife in the spring, sturgeon in the early summer) and the field crops had not yet come in. It went on later if the summer were dry and the crops were late in ripening.[54] The only limitation on how much shellfishing people could do was the water depth involved: where people could walk at low tide, wade at high tide, or dive to the bottom and back in one breath, then shellfish could be gathered.[55]

Although the de Bry engravings show men in the distance "fishing" with bows and arrows, the engraving titled *Their Manner of Fishing*, as well as the original John White painting, shows men wading and spearing fish with something that looks like a javelin. White's text explains that it was "a small forked stick" that was used on crabs. But Hariot's caption to the de Bry engravings says that it was "the hollow tail of a certain sea crab" whose description matches that of a horseshoe crab.[56] This kind of fishing was done mainly by men, thanks to their greater height and upper body strength and also to the uninterrupted time (which mothers of children rarely have) that they had to walk slowly in the water waiting to encounter fish. No English account mentions angling for fish or shooting tethered arrows into them, which the Powhatans to the north are known to have done; angling could have been done by both sexes and most ages of people.

One last kind of fishing was fire-fishing, shown in the sixteenth-century illustrations with some artistic license.[57] In reality, of course, it was done at night. In addition, fish were attracted by the fire's light, so the fire had to be visible to them, not hidden down inside the canoe. While one person poled the canoe through shallow water, a second person held the fire, if it was a portable hearth, at the canoe's head; or the second party lit pieces of lightwood (very resinous pine wood, quick to catch fire) and held them like candles "within two inches of the edge" of the canoe's gunwale.[58] When fish approached the boat, curious about the light, they were speared. If the shallow water were clear, fish could also simply be spotted on the bottom and speared there.[59]

Still other activities took men far away from their towns: warfare, diplomacy, and trading (see chapter 5). The English records are too sparse to tell us if women went along on these expeditions; some women did so in other tribes.[60] There was, after all, nothing physical about traveling on foot or by canoe to keep those athletic, hardworking mothers at home, unless they were in quarantine after giving birth. Otherwise, they could take their babies along in cradleboards and keep at a distance during menstrual periods, while the other women in the extended family looked after their older children left behind.

Men and Women Together

After the day's work was done, evenings were spent in recreation, and men and women usually spent them together, not segregated. There was singing and dancing around a fire most nights, accompanied by gourd rattles of various sizes.[61] Other musical instruments, attested in Virginia, included reed flutes, blown into as one does with a recorder (not as with our familiar transverse flute) and requiring a great deal of air pressure to make a sound. There were also frame drums (usually handheld, with a stretched-hide drumhead on only one side). The Algonquian speakers' version sounds as if it was large and too heavy to hold in one hand (it would have rested on the ground), for John Smith and William Strachey described the frame as "a great deep platter of wood"—that is, a wooden bowl, with its mouth covered with a hide. Walnuts had been tied onto the four corners of the hide, after which the drummer "twitched" them together near the bowl's bottom and, once the drumhead was stiff and taut, secured them with a cord.[62]

The people also had gambling games, the most common one involving fifty-one small sticks, about seven inches long and evenly cut and polished. One player would rapidly throw some to an opponent and as fast as possible have to guess correctly how many sticks remained in his hand.[63] Losers were expected to remain good-natured about it—another instance of self-control being valued. Competitive games similar to tennis and soccer were recorded for the Powhatans in eastern Virginia,[64] though not for the Sounds folk, but nothing like the ancestor of lacrosse seems to have been observed among the Algonquian speakers in either region.

At all times the people in the towns kept in mind two main principles in dealing with one another: reciprocity (help them, and they will help you) and keep up good relations with everybody, at least superficially. To live by the first principle, you share food and goods when you have them, especially with relatives, including distant ones. Help your relatives and neighbors with big jobs like building houses and canoes, not to mention large-scale hunting and nutting in the fall. Don't steal from fellow countrymen (but foreigners had better look out!).[65]

To live by the second principle, you remain calm, deliberate, and non-threatening, even in aggravating situations.[66] (That was not easy to do in small towns and camps where there was no sonic privacy and not much visual privacy.) Don't cause offense by telling other people what they should do, or how to do it better.[67] Don't scold anyone, and don't get into fisticuffs.[68] As we shall see in chapter 5, chiefs in the Carolina Sounds were not very powerful leaders outside of diplomatic meetings and wartime, so they could not always resolve conflicts; therefore people took care to prevent conflict from erupting in the first place. Active community singing and dancing after a hard day of work would leave people tired, euphoric (prolonged dancing raises one's endorphins), and less likely to air disagreements. But even without those palliatives, people were expected to practice rigid self-control at all times. John Lawson saw the result: "They are a very wary people, and are never hasty or impatient. They will endure a great many misfortunes, losses, and disappointments without showing themselves in the least vexed or uneasy."[69] Smooth interpersonal relations were to be kept up at all times. Before the coming of Europeans with their alcohol, one of the very few approved outlets for anger and aggression was war and its aftermath, as we shall see in chapter 5.

CHAPTER FOUR

Religion and Medicine

Religion (and medicine when it is intertwined with religion) comprises the
most difficult parts of any culture for an outsider to understand. There is so
much that is intangible and has to be explained to visitors who may have next
to no command of the local people's language. Outsiders may be forced to
rely on young people (like the youth Manteo) as interpreters, and young
people may not understand the more subtle aspects of the religion they were
raised in. That is the situation which confronted the English of the 1580s in
the Carolina Sounds region, and as a result, we cannot be sure they recorded
the people's beliefs accurately. We cannot draw too much on John Lawson
either, because although he had good interpreters, he wrote over a century
later, when the Indians had long been in contact with the highly evangelistic English. By that time in North Carolina, as in Virginia, the Native people
had become unwilling to discuss religion at all with Englishmen.[1] Thus in a
book aimed at presenting reliable, accurate information, this chapter must
focus rather more upon what people were observed to make and do, rather
than upon what they believed.

By the early 1700s the Native people believed (or said they believed) in two
gods, a good one and a bad one.[2] But in the 1580s, the Algonquian speakers
of the Carolina Sounds were polytheists, with a belief system that seems to
have resembled the Powhatan one: they believed in a great god (name not
recorded; the Powhatan name was *Ahone*) who was distantly neutral, rather
than being actively friendly or hostile to mankind. They also believed in a
host of lesser, tutelary powers who often had human shape (in Powhatan belief, also the shape of forces of nature, dangerous things such as English
firearms, and large, dangerous animals); these were called (in plural) *mantóac*. That word is a cognate with the word *manitou* among other Algonquian
speakers.[3] The human images of these deities, which were kept in the
temples, they called *kiwasowok* (singular, *kiwas*), a term applied by the Powhatans to the deities (called *okeus*) and the priests, as well as the images.[4] The
Powhatans additionally believed that the *kwiokosok* (in their dialect) moni-
tored human behavior and punished any failure of respect toward themselves.[5] When presented with unfamiliar pieces of English technology,
such as compasses, "spring clocks that seem to go of themselves," guns, and

books and reading, especially of the Bible, the Sounds people initially considered those things to be the works of gods, or at least things taught the English by deities. Thomas Hariot found the people he visited to be eagerly "receptive" to his evangelizing, though more likely his hosts hoped instead to partake of the power that Hariot (being able to read) and his book had. He observed that "many would be glad to touch it, to embrace it, to kiss it, to hold it to their breasts and heads, and stroke over all their body with it."[6]

The great god first made other important gods, then the sun, moon, and stars, who were lesser gods doing the bidding of the important ones in creating still more things in the world. The waters were made first, and from them all other earthly things proceeded. As for people, woman was made first and then impregnated by one of the gods, after which her children and their descendants populated the earth. All of this happened long ago; nobody knew how long.[7] There may have been other creation accounts among the people of the Sounds; their relatives, the Powhatans, told the English three different versions in the early years of the Jamestown colony, one of which (a regrettably sketchily recorded one) from the James River area matched the Carolina one just described.[8]

The people of the Sounds also believed in an afterlife that sounds suspiciously as though the English misunderstood it: there was—somewhere—a heaven of bliss, and to the west there was a hellish, burning pit called *popogusso*. John Lawson recorded beliefs about an Indian-style heaven and hell 120 years later, but whether his informants really believed that or were merely saying things they thought he would like and find no fault with, we cannot know. We do know that the people's linguistic relatives to the north, the Powhatans, believed as of 1607 in an afterlife consisting of a heavenlike place to the west (not the east), where souls went and spent one "lifetime" before being reincarnated back in this world. Other Powhatans believed that only chiefs and priests had any afterlife at all.[9] Orthodoxy was not a sought-after state in the Indian world; multiple beliefs were tolerated.

These two matters, creation and afterlife, were as far as the English of the 1580s were able to penetrate into the local people's beliefs. There must have been much more; John Lawson heard so much a century later that he was overwhelmed, while remaining prejudiced: "They have thousands of these foolish Ceremonies and Beliefs, which they are strict Observers of. Moreover, several Customs are found in some Families, which others keep not." The few he cites, such as not letting a "big-bellied" (pregnant) woman eat the first fish taken from a newly built weir, for fear of small catches ever after, may belong to the Tuscaroras rather than the Secotas he met.[10]

Plainly, though, religious beliefs and rituals permeated Indian life. In better-recorded North American tribes, there were many rituals, large and small, that surrounded hunting and warfare, both being essential parts of survival that required men to focus totally upon them and also to expend tremendous amounts of energy. Both were also potentially hazardous to a man's health. Men therefore not only underwent rituals they believed were necessary for success, but they also often practiced sexual abstinence for varying periods before setting out. The abstinence could be extra insurance, given the women's careful withdrawal from town during their menstrual periods, to keep the men from carrying any faint smell of blood, a smell that is known to frighten away any deer that senses it. But there would be another result as well, whether the men practicing it were aware of it or not: abstinence on the part of the husband, even if his wife were not in the menstrual house, would further reduce the time for a couple to conceive children. That, in turn, helped to limit population growth among the tribes, a useful thing if the carrying capacity of the land, given how the people got their food, was not very productive—or undergoing a drought. Further, it could put a brake on population growth, which might otherwise lead to hostile expansion into neighbors' territories. A by-product for the women would be more time between births, which made their lives easier.

There were potential misfortunes inherent in many activities the Sounds people pursued in order to survive. Dugout canoes are not easy to maneuver, so strong winds, especially sudden, very violent squalls, could blow them far from land and tip them far enough over that paddlers fell overboard and were likely to drown before they could swim home. Women gathering roots or reeds in a marsh, or men hunting water birds, might step into quicksand or sink into an underwater mudhole and drown before they could be rescued. Forest sojourns risked numerous mishaps: snake bites, falling tree limbs, meeting a bear, tripping and breaking a bone, even getting a deep briar scratch that turned septic afterward. Hunting in the forest did not always result in meat for the stewpot and clothes for the family. Ranging too far from home, people could meet raiding enemies, with disastrous results: death for a man, captivity for a wife and children who would never see home again. There were also thanks to be given after a safe return home, not to mention bringing down a deer or finding a good crop of nuts or tubers.

In or out of the town, illnesses lurked that were caused by agents (viruses and bacteria) that no humans in the 1580s understood as yet. People worldwide turned not only to whatever they believed about the human body and its ailments but also to the Supernatural, which presumably did understand all ailments. Avoiding various menaces required propitiation of the gods and giving thanks afterward for being spared. Once the English came visiting, they became an explanation for all sorts of mishaps: "There could at no time happen any strange sickness, losses, hurts, or any other cross unto them, but that they would impute to us the cause or means thereof for offending or not pleasing us."[11] (That kind of thinking is very hard to shake. Some modern people, presented with the germ theory of disease, will say, "All right, germs caused it—but who sent the germs?")

Some rituals would have been carried out daily; we have to rely on Powhatan information to reconstruct it. Bathing was done every morning before dawn and at sunset, by people ten years old or more, in the nearest stream, even if it were salty water. Afterward, they dried themselves on the bank as the sun rose or set and offered some shreds of tobacco by tossing it on the ground or into the water, in order to honor the sun.[12] They were free to eat the first or last meal of the day afterward. Thanks were given before meals; William Strachey heard the prayer recited in 1611 with an interpreter present, but at the time he did not record either the words or a translation.[13]

Other rituals were conducted irregularly, when the need arose, the people not having a custom of keeping a sabbath every seventh day. Tobacco was always included, whatever the power being invoked. Thus Thomas Hariot wrote, "Sometime they make hallowed fires and cast some of the powder therein for a sacrifice: being in a storm upon the waters, to pacify their gods, they cast some up into the air: also after an escape from danger, they cast some into the air likewise, but all done with strange gestures, stamping, clapping of hands, holding up of hands, and staring up into the heavens[, at the same time] uttering and chattering strange words and noises."[14] The "strange words" may have been in a religiously preserved archaic Algonquian dialect. John Banister wrote of Virginia Indians in the late seventeenth century that "their languages at their sacrifices is like the Roman mass [said in Latin] . . . not understood by the common people." Robert Beverley clarified it further: "They have a sort of general language, like what Lahontan calls the Algonkine, which is understood by the chief men of many nations, as Latin is in most parts of Europe."[15]

Larger-scale thanksgivings after surviving great dangers, from weather or in war, were celebrated by men and women alike. A big fire was made, and around it the people sat, men and women together, "holding a certain fruit [probably a gourd rattle] in their hands."[16] Some of the thanksgivings were several specifically family-oriented rituals. As discussed in chapter 3 using

Powhatan data, each child got two names soon after birth. One name, usually kept within the immediate family, was extremely personal.

Anyone who wanted to harm the person could perform a sorcery ritual using the name; not knowing the name would prevent the effort being made. Pocahontas's personal name was Matoaka, and she revealed it only after being baptized and given the new (and in her mind, powerful) name of Rebecca. Before her baptism, she and her family feared the English might learn her personal name and do the sorcery on her.[17] The naming—or rather, the nick-naming—of a baby, on the other hand, was a public occasion, to which relatives and neighbors were invited. The father held up the baby and announced what the child's name was to be, after which the rest of the day was spent in dancing and eating the feast the parents sponsored.[18] Personal names, especially for boys, would be changed as they grew up and accomplished feats of prowess; outstanding performances during raids also earned new names for adult men. At each of these, there would have been a ritual (undescribed in the English records); the local chief conducted the ones honoring the adult men.[19]

Weddings and funerals were another occasion for formal celebration, probably with a strong religious component. We know some of the outlines of funerals from Virginia sources, but even they say nothing about who presided over the ceremony or what was said over the corpse. Chiefs' funerals and burials set them apart, as we shall see, but commoners were dressed in their jewelry and wrapped in mats and deerskins before being buried fairly simply in a grave lined with sticks. Meanwhile, the women in the family mourned loudly for twenty-four hours, with their faces painted black.[20] People were apparently buried near the place they died: no cemeteries are mentioned in the records, and the graves found by archaeologists are scattered. John Lawson wrote, perhaps not about the Algonquian speakers, that women's corpses were treated differently, but he was a man, and nobody would tell him how; apparently, it was women's business.[21] Ralph Lane mentioned an additional custom (which Virginia writers did not) among the Roanokes; he called it a "month's mind" because it resembled something his people did at home. A month or so after someone's funeral, the family would hold a second, perhaps smaller-scale one, as a formal commemoration of the deceased.[22]

Still other rituals were performed seasonally. The huskanaw, or initiation of boys into manhood, occurred in the early winter, as described in chapter 3, and it must have had very serious religious overtones when carried out. There was also a firstfruits celebration, though we have few details about it

FIGURE 4.1 John White painting of townspeople dancing.

from either North Carolina or Virginia. John White saw a late summer green corn dance—held "at a certain time of year" and after sundown "for avoiding of heat."[23] In his painting of the celebration, three young women dance while embracing one another, while others—men and women both—put on a very active dance. Around the dance grounds were posts topped with faces, but the meaning is unknown (figure 4.1). Other parts of the ritual— and there would have been much more, based on better-recorded tribes in the Southeast—went unrecorded.[24]

There were probably other rituals conducted in the wintertime, to give thanks for the safety and food granted to them in the previous year, as well as to ask for safety for any war parties setting out. Yet another ritual was very probably held by the Carolina Sounds people, though the English records do not mention it. In the spring (according to Powhatan usage) Indian men purged themselves by drinking quantities of "black drink." This was an infusion of the dried leaves of yaupon holly (*Ilex vomitoria*) in water, which tastes like old rubber boots and whose caffeine is the agent causing the nausea.[25] The yaupon trees grow on and near the Outer Banks; it is hard to imagine that the local people traded all of them away without making use of their power for themselves.

As we have seen, the places at which rituals were conducted were various places around town and out in the foraging territory. Given the English silence about special places for curing the sick, we can assume that curing rituals took place in or around someone's house in town. Other rituals would have taken place at holy places, which Indian people did not mark the way Europeans did (i.e., take a holy spot and build a chapel over it); instead, they left it in its natural state and passed down oral tradition about it to the next generation. Such places were, of course, not recognizable to non-Indians, if they ever approached them, so they do not appear in the English records. On the other hand, there were holy buildings, which the English called temples and the Native people called *matchicomuck*. Priests may have been involved in many kinds of the rituals conducted in public, in front of ordinary folk, but Hariot tells us that nobody (except possibly the chief) was allowed inside the temples to watch what the priests did there. He himself had to guess: "They worship, pray, sing, and make many times offerings unto [the gods]."[26]

The temples the English saw were located in the center of the towns; there may have been more out in the forest, as in Virginia. In a village where houses were scattered and there was enough space around the temple, there would also be a ceremonial dance ground like the one in figure 4.1.[27] Temples were built in the same way as houses: bentwood frames covered with mats or bark sheets. As in other houses, the only light came from the door, the smoke hole, and the hearth in the center of the floor. The layout of partitions, however, differed from that of a dwelling house. One end—the west end among the Powhatans—was a storage place for the bodies of past chiefs and for the wooden "idol" particular to the town. These items were placed on a scaffold built nine to ten feet above the ground; underneath lived a rota of priests saying prayers "night and day" and sleeping on deerskins. Because of the venerated relics inside them, temples always had space left around the outside, even in crowded palisaded villages.[28]

"Idols" were wooden images of a god, but not the god in person, and as Hariot heard it, the images rather than the gods were called *kewasówok* (plural of *kewasa*, cognate of Powhatan *kwiocos*). This is the opposite of how the Jamestown colonists heard it—that is, the term being applied to the god; either one or both sets of foreigners got it wrong. Each image was about four feet long, with a human-looking head painted in Native flesh color—which may mean it had been anointed with puccoon. The body was painted, the chest in white, the rest in black, with white spots on the thighs. Copper and shell bead necklaces were hung around the neck. Hariot noted that there were up to three idols in a town, which lends weight to the people believing in a polytheistic system.[29] The White painting and de Bry engraving of a temple's interior show the building fairly realistically in cutaway, as well as a priest tending the fire, but artistic license marks the rest of the picture.[30] "Idols" actually came in pieces and had to be put together before being viewed in public. They were taken out of the temples and displayed on special occasions, including being taken along when a raid on enemies was planned.[31]

The reason we know that these "idols" were kept bundled up in pieces most of the time is because an English writer in Virginia committed sacrilege (in Indian eyes) and broke into a temple over a century later. Robert Beverley chose a day when he knew most of the town's people would be away at a conference with English authorities. He and his companions examined three bundles on the temple's shelf; the first two contained human bones.

> In the third mat there was something, which we took to be their Idol, tho of an underling sort, and wanted putting together. The pieces were these, first a Board three foot and a half long, with one indenture at the upper end, like a Fork, to fasten the Head upon, from thence half way down, were Half hoops nail'd to the edges of the board, at about four Inches distance, which were bow'd out, to represent the Breast and Belly; on the lower half was another Board of half the length of the other, fasten'd to it by Joynts or pieces of Wood, which being set on each side, stood out about 14 inches from the Body, and half as high; we suppos'd the use of these to be for the bowing out of the Knees, when the Image was set up. There were packt up with these things, red and blue pieces of Cotton Cloath [definitely post-Contact valuables], and Rolls made up for Arms, Thighs and Legs, bent to at the Knees. . . . We put the Cloaths upon the Hoops for the Body, and fasten'd on the Arms and Legs, to have a view of the representation: But the Head and rich Bracelets, which is usually adorn'd with, were not there, or at least we did not find them.[32]

Chiefs' corpses eventually wound up as bundles of bones—not the laid-out naked bodies in the Hariot and de Bry illustrations—which had been wrapped up in deerskins and placed on the shelf in the temples. Nothing about the ceremonies that must have accompanied each stage of the process was recorded; we know only the barest outline. Preparation involved removing a body's skin and sun-drying that, disposing of the entrails, and cleaning the bones of their flesh, probably after leaving the corpse for some time in a charnel house. The removed flesh was carefully dried. The skeleton, held fairly intact by its dried ligaments, was then wrapped up in deerskins, in a humanoid shape (contradicted by Beverley, who found only a bundle of bones). Lastly, the bundle was laid on the shelf in the temple, with the dried-flesh bundle at its feet. Writers of the 1580s say nothing about any jewelry or other treasure of a chief stored with his remains, but Virginia ones do, and the second bundle Beverley opened contained several swordlike tomahawks, perhaps having been the chief's favorite weapons.[33]

Holy men were important people in their towns, but regrettably, nothing was recorded for the Algonquian speakers in North Carolina or Virginia about what families they came from or what their training had been like. We know only about their appearance and some of their duties. All of them seem to have been male. There were at least two kinds, or rather specialties, among them, priests and conjurers, and their appearance reflected which sector they belonged to. Priests wore a short fur cloak, the fur worn outward; their head was shaved except for a roach and a visorlike ridge over the forehead; and they wore copper earrings.[34] Conjurers, apparently because their duties were far more active, did not wear cloaks but instead only an apron, with a leather purse draped over the belt for it. The purse's contents were never described; they could have been herbs for remedies or perhaps special objects with great meaning only for the man who carried them as an amulet. Conjurers' heads were supposedly shaved, but there must have been tendrils left because they managed to stick on various things, such as a stuffed bird.[35]

Priests took care of temples and their contents, made offerings, and presumably saw that a fire was kept going in the hearth at all times. They probably also led public ceremonies of thanksgiving, as in the Green Corn rites, and of asking the gods' protection for a war party leaving on a raid. They may or may not have been diviners, as the conjurers were. Conjurers did other things, which involved invoking the spirit world in a public and physically active way (figure 4.2). Among Algonquian speakers to the north, they were extremely important as diviners, able to tell the outcome of various endeavors, so that they were major participants in war councils.[36] They may also have been able to find things that people lost (a common ability among Native American shamans). They were known to put on displays of magic, both to entertain the townspeople but also to retain their respect, if not awe. John Lawson recorded one instance, which he saw in the early 1700s among the Chowanokes. A conjurer named Roncommock took a two-foot-long reed in

FIGURE 4.2 Conjuror's trick (painting by Karen Harvey, based on John White's portrait of a conjuror and an idea of the author's).

his mouth, and keeping it there, he stood at the edge of a creek about a quarter-mile across and called out two or three times. Finally he flung out his arms and "fled over the creek," running on top of the water.[37]

The most urgent job that conjurers (and perhaps priests—the accounts are not clear) did was to cure the sick, if they had not been able to shake off their maladies in other ways.

People followed a regimen that kept them well most of the time, using a method common all over North America and attested for their Powhatan relatives: they took sweat baths in a saunalike hut called a sweat lodge, for continued vigor, to combat tiredness after hard work,[38] and also when they had "dropsies, swellings, aches, and such like diseases."[39] Located at the edge of the nearest waterway, it was a round, low building with a heavy, impermeable cover of mats or skins (removable or not) and a central hearth inside. John Banister's account from late seventeenth-century Virginia (copied by Robert Beverley) is the most detailed one we have:

The Doctor gets 3 or 4 big stones, which heating red hot he places in the middle of the stove, laying on them some of the inner bark of white oak beaten in a mortar; this done they creep in stark naked, 6 or 8 or as many as can sit round, & close up the hole or mouth (for it is usually made like an oven in some bank near the water side) then to raise a steam he pours cold water on the stones, & now & then sprinkles the men to keep them from fainting: having sweat as long as they can well endure it, they get out, & tho' it be in the depth of winter, forthwith plunge themselves in the water, which instantly closes up the pores, so that they take no cold. The heat being so suddenly driven from the extream parts to the heart makes them a little weak and feeble for the present; but they instantly recover their strength, & their joints are limber & supple: as tho' they had never travelled or been ayling.[40]

The daily taking of "black drink" (the decoction of boiled yaupon holly leaves) as a tonic if not also as an emetic was also considered healthy.[41] The Powhatans did not do it daily; there is no record about how often their Carolina relatives did it.

There were numerous herbal remedies known to priests and conjurers, and possibly some of them were known to ordinary people (table 4.1). (Among the Powhatans, most of the herbal knowledge remained firmly in priestly hands.) Called *wisacon*, a general term for "medicine" rather than a specific term for one type,[42] three examples were recorded by Thomas Hariot. A refined clay called *wapeih* was used on sores and wounds, and some people performed bloodletting on their chests when sick.[43] When wounded by poisoned arrows, they applied a medicine made with what was probably *Euphorbia maculata*, ground milkweed (which Hariot called "a kind of Asclepias [the genus name of common milkweed]) or swallowwort."[44] *E. maculata* is one of several plants with the common name of "swallowwort." Puccoon, already mentioned as a source of red dye, was widely considered—at least elsewhere in North Carolina—to have other useful properties: when mixed with bear oil and worked into one's hair, it killed any lice lurking there.[45]

But still, there were times when these remedies were not enough—or when men were wounded in war or when people of both sexes were injured while doing their daily work or simply "came down with something."

Diseases, in our modern terminology, are hard to identify from old records—harder yet from records about utterly different cultures—because the terms that sick people and their families use are hardwired into their

TABLE 4.1 Sample of native wild medicinal plants (widely used among Eastern Woodland Indians, including twentieth-century Powhatans)

Plant	Habitat	Remedy
Acorus calamus (sweet flag)	freshwater marshes	root tea for indigestion
Asclepias syriaca (common milkweed)	abandoned fields	milk to remove warts
Cicuta maculata (spotted cowbane)	wet old fields, swamp	strong poison
Cornus florida (flowering dogwood)	deciduous forest	root-bark tea as tonic
Diospyrus virginiana (persimmon)	many habitats	bark in sore throat cure
Hedeoma pulegioides (pennyroyal)	old fields, open woods	menstrual difficulties
Phytolacca americana (pokeweed)	old and new fields	skin ailments, rheumatism
Prunus serotina (wild cherry)	woodland edges	tonic, cough medicine
Sambucus canadensis (elderberry)	old fields, thickets	skin problems
Sassafras albidum (sassafras)	thickets, open woods	root tea for tonic

Taken from appendix C of Rountree and Davidson 1997.

beliefs about what has made them sick in the first place. Thus we are trying to learn about diseases the Roanokes and others had (phrased, through Manteo, according to their theory of disease), as told by Englishmen who believed in the old European four-humor theory of disease. Neither understood the other, and all too often we can't understand from either source what the Native folk actually suffered from. All we have are brief descriptions of what the "doctors" actually did to the patients in the brief time the English were in the region in the 1580s. The accounts speak of bloodletting, which left scars, and of sucking an illness out of a patient's body in "strings of blood."[46] The latter sounds like the widespread shamanistic "disease" of "object intrusion," in which the object was magically injected into someone's body and therefore had to be magically sucked out (all without breaking the skin). Two other shamanistic "diseases," which the Roanokes and others *may* have believed in, had their own logical cures. One was "ghost possession," in which the ghost of a recently lost loved one possessed a person, causing him or her to go into a decline and eventually die, thereby joining the ghost; the cure was driving the ghost away. The second was "soul loss," in which one's soul became somehow detached from one's body, usually because of some disease or trauma; the soul then traveled to the afterlife, and the body left behind was in danger of dying. The cure was for the doctor to go into a trance (helped by smoking the strong native tobacco) and send his or her soul to fetch back the patient's soul, a proceeding that was understandably dangerous to the doctor.[47]

Compared to the incredibly rich fund of knowledge and memorized ritual to be found among better-recorded tribes in western North America, we know next to nothing about the religion and medicine of the Carolina Algonquian speakers when the English first met them. That is a pity; they must have known about whole worlds that we cannot touch.

CHAPTER FIVE

Trade, Politics, Diplomacy, and War

Of all the Native peoples' social (as opposed to physical) lives, we know more about the subjects covered in this chapter than in any others, for the simple reason that all written records about the Carolina Algonquian speakers were made by foreigners who encountered them in these four contexts. Those foreigners traded with them, negotiated with them, warred with them, and were affected by their intertribal politics.

Indian townspeople and Englishmen exchanged corn and the labor needed for building fish weirs for European "trinkets" (in the English view) made of metal and glass, two substances the Indian world all but lacked.[1] What Indian people traded among themselves is much less well documented. We know that the Indian towns were pretty much self-sufficient, so that trade items would mainly have been what the people considered to be luxury (i.e., nonessential) goods; the recorded observations bear this out. Native people exchanged special things they had but other tribes didn't for things they themselves didn't have. If the things were colorful or shiny, so much the better. Unfortunately those records say nothing about the timing of trading expeditions (in some better-attested groups, young men went far afield every spring for trading), much less about whether the trips were male-only affairs (in some of the same groups, women went along to cook the animals the men hunted along the way).[2]

Native copper—the soft, nearly pure copper the Carolina Sounds people used in their jewelry[3]—came from far up the Roanoke River, where there were probably middlemen connected ultimately with the Great Lakes, where most of it is known to have been mined in prehistoric North America. Another extremely valuable substance widely traded among the Indian peoples in the east was puccoon roots (*Lithospermum caroliniense*), from which a valuable red dye was made. Almost the only place it grows in the Mid-Atlantic region is the sand hills of southern South Carolina, well outside the Algonquian speakers' area.[4] Various Indian people, notably the Tuscaroras, had tried to grow it themselves but without success; the soils were wrong for it.[5] So for coastal people, puccoon, like copper, remained extremely expensive to acquire.

The Sounds people also appreciated pearls for jewelry, which were usually imported. Pearls are found rarely in Mid-Atlantic oysters and freshwater mussels. The shellfish that produces the most pearls, however, is the freshwater-loving eastern river pearl mussel (*Margaritifera margaritifera*), which today reaches no farther south than the Little Schuylkill River in Pennsylvania. (It may have reached a little farther south during the Little Ice Age.) The Chowanoke chief showed a large quantity of these pearls to Ralph Lane, saying he had "bought" them two years before from a chief to the north (possibly the Nansemond chief), accepting only copper, itself imported, in exchange.[6]

Coastal people, however, had a couple of things that inlanders wanted but lacked: yaupon trees, whose leaves were used to make "black drink,"[7] and whelk and hard-clam shells for making jewelry. The jewelry was not described well in the 1580s, but we have later accounts to fill in the gaps: John Lawson in North Carolina and John Banister and Robert Beverley in Virginia.[8] Whelk (colloquially called conch) shells were made into large disk-shaped pendants called "gorgets" (Lawson's "gorge"). The columns of the shells were also made into fat cylinders (called *runtees* in Virginia) and long pipe beads. Hard-clam shells, with their white interiors and dark purple spot where the muscle attached, were made into cylindrical beads about a third of an inch long; purple ones, coming from a smaller part of the shell, were more valuable. Both were called *peak* or *wampumpeak*, later shortened to *wampum*. There is no mention in any seventeenth-century Mid-Atlantic account of weaving belts of wampum with designs in the purple beads; that was a northern, Five Nations Iroquois custom that spread southward in the eighteenth century. Hard-clam shells were also made into disks one inch wide and one-third inch thick, "drilled edgeways." Those clams are a salt- or brackish-water species, unavailable in freshwater areas. Whelks are strictly saltwater shellfish, and their shells do not wash in great quantities into the Carolina Sounds or, for that matter, the Chesapeake Bay. It was mostly ocean-side people who could collect them for jewelry making (the Nanticokes of the Maryland Eastern Shore were famous for it). Producing such beads and pendants is a difficult, chancy business; even for modern workers using diamond-tipped drills, there is a high shatter rate. For people using stone drills for the holes and abraders for the polishing, the process would have required phenomenal skill and abundant patience. And therein lay yet more of the value of such items in trade.

There is one more exchange, hinted at in the Virginia records, that may have been practiced in the Carolina Sounds. Oysters are salty- and brackish-water creatures; deer are forest animals that live in swamps but prefer deciduous forest such as that around the western end of Albemarle Sound and well up the Pamlico River. People who had oysters in the Sounds region had fewer deer available, and thus a trade was possible: dried oysters for dried venison and cakes of deer suet.[9]

For trading, as well as diplomacy and war, Native American people were willing to travel great distances, by canoe as far as rivers would take them and after that on foot in a far-flung network of trails throughout eastern North America.[10] Where very long distances were involved, as in the copper trade, people could have traveled the whole distance or, more likely, have used middlemen—we don't know which. Given the itineraries of traders and warriors recorded in later times, the former option was entirely possible for the Algonquian speakers in the Sounds region.

When foreigners, European or North American, came to call in the Sounds, whether the issue be trade or peace or war, each town's chief played a central role. Thus at nearly all the times that the English met Native people, they dealt with them through the local chief, who was surrounded for the occasion by some very stately protocol. Any visitor who tried to bypass the chief was promptly steered back to where he belonged.[11] How much power chiefs really had on ordinary days, without foreigners around, is hard to say. But judging by the records about their Powhatan relatives, they were probably not, in reality, the powerful "kings" that the early English visitors imagined them to be. They were more likely the official representatives of their people, on both political and religious occasions.[12] Therefore they could not be considered absolute rulers any more than the "subject" towns they "controlled" constituted hard-and-fast, long-enduring "tribal" territories. In most aspects of life, towns were autonomous entities. People's loyalty to chiefs depended upon how effective the chiefs were believed to be in diplomatic and military matters, beliefs which might not last indefinitely. For instance, by the summer of 1586 Okisko, chief at the town of Weapomeoc, found himself and his townsfolk at odds with the other towns previously under his influence. The latter were willing to join an intertribal alliance against the English invaders—which was within their rights—and he was not. The English commander, hearing this, wrote that militarily, at least, Weapomeoc was "deuided into two parts."[13]

Belonging to a chiefly family gave a person the possibility of becoming chief, but in a world that utterly lacked a police force or a standing army, a candidate also needed great personal integrity (at least among one's own people), a gift for smoothing ruffled feathers, and real savvy about conducting guerilla warfare to make the possibility a reality. A dignified carriage, maintained even under difficult circumstances, was an additional prerequisite.

Inheritance of the position of chief was by lateral matrilineality, a technical term with no equivalent in colloquial English, which was a far cry from the way European monarchs succeeded to their thrones.[14] All chiefs were the children of females in chiefly families; there may have been further kinship qualifications, but the English records are silent about them. That requirement in itself reduced possible strife among half-siblings, for a woman's children came out in a definite order, and there would be no bother about the identity of their male progenitor, however many wives he might have. Let us assume that a town's last chief of the older generation has just died. That person's eldest sister's children became the next generation to produce chiefs, with the eldest son of the sister going first unless unfit for the job, then the brothers in order of age, and then the daughters in order of age. The next generation after that would be the eldest daughter's children, and so on. Women thus could be chiefs—several of them appear in the Virginia Algonquian speakers' much more extensive records—but when that happened, they would be well on in years and experience and would have lacked firsthand knowledge of warfare. They and their brothers were trained, before their promotion if it happened, by being delegated to rule satellite towns, outside the chief's town. Succession was not automatic, however. Small polities like those of the Mid-Atlantic could not afford chiefs who were mentally deficient; there were no bureaucracies to take up the slack and carry on the business of government. So a brother or sister, like Paramount Chief Powhatan's next brother, the "decrepit and lame" Opitchapam, would be passed over in favor of the next in line, which happened to be the very formidable Opechancanough. The system was not immune to jealousies and intrigue, but it seems to have worked very well on the whole, at least in Virginia.[15] This was probably also true in North Carolina, though the brief time capsule of English records there does not tell us.

Neither in North Carolina nor in Virginia do English observers tell us clearly whether or not chiefs acted as judges in the English sense. In fact, they tell us little about the specific laws that must have existed among the Algonquian speakers. (John Lawson's text may be mainly from the Tuscaroras, so we don't use it here.) All we can be sure of is that there were laws the English found sensible: there was "punishment ordained for malefactors, as thieves [from their own people], whore-mongers, and other sorts of wicked doers; some punished with death, some with forfeitures, some with beating, according to the greatness of the facts." There may have been priests involved: Hariot hints that they and the chiefs were adept at detecting wrongdoing. Virginia observers tell us that in Powhatan towns, the people seldom stole from one another, "lest their conjurers should reveal it and so they be pursued and punished."[16]

On ordinary days, chiefs and their families very probably lived the same way other people did: the men hunted and fished, and the women did the many jobs described in chapter 3. But on extraordinary days, when chiefs and their entourages represented their people to outsiders (and remember, every day that the English visited automatically became extraordinary), they had to stand out from other people and offer lavish hospitality to visitors, just as European monarchs did.

Chiefs had more puccoon paint, jewelry, and fancy cloaks to wear than commoners did.[17] They *looked* more important on dressed-up occasions, and so did their wives and children, brothers and sisters. They—and even their wives in the chief's absence—traveled with an entourage.[18] They lived in larger houses, with space to accommodate overnight guests—and the guests' entourage. The houses also needed to accommodate more wives, who would serve not only as more sexual partners for the (male) chiefs but also would provide the much greater labor needed to carry out the prodigious feats of hospitality to impress guests.

Here is what went on when foreigners arrived in a town.[19] When visitors were expected, people had to shift from working for their families to working for the chief. The chief and his retinue had to get dressed up for what was going to be a formal diplomatic occasion, while the rest of the towns-people, knowing that the visitors should be fed, began the preparations for a feast. For the women, that meant hauling water and pounding corn and nuts from the chief's store; for the men, it meant some of them immediately going hunting and others fishing, to provide fresh meat. All this meant that a truly friendly visit to the town should not be a matter of "dropping in," but of giving notice well in advance.

When the guests came ashore, the chief and his entourage of councilors, wives, and commoner "servants" walked—"their gait sedate and majestic"— over to meet them.[20] Some commoners spread large mats on the ground in the form of a square. The chief seated himself on one side of the square, sit-ting alone and cross-legged; his councilors sat on the two sides adjacent to him; and the visitors were seated on the fourth side, facing the chief (figure 5.1). All of this was done in silence, with the utmost decorum being maintained. In silence also, a pipe of tobacco would be passed around, with each person, beginning with the chief, taking only a puff or two. After a pause, the chief, followed in turn by several councilors, delivered orations of welcome with expansive gesticulations, while everyone else listened

FIGURE 5.1 Diplomatic meeting (painting by Karen Harvey, based on an idea of the author's).

politely. It was then time to exchange presents, and protocol dictated that the guests give everything to the chief, who would then distribute things to his followers. The English leader, receiving Indian goods, was expected to parcel them out to *his* followers.

Eventually the feast, or the first part of it, would be ready for the dignitaries, who were still seated on their mats. (If the hunting took too long, the feast would stretch out to multiple installments.)[21] There would be fish from the weir if necessary, but fresh venison, boiled and then roasted (double-cooked), was much more prestigious to serve guests. Likewise, the bread served had to be made from corn, no matter what the season, and there had to be plenty of it. Instead of water, there should be nut milk to drink. Commoners served the courses in silence and with great dignity, on behalf of the chief. And the quantities presented, if we may use Virginia data here, were aggressively generous, partly to show off the wealth of the chief and partly because all the onlookers knew that they themselves would get to finish off the leftovers afterward.[22] (For instance, while he was a captive, before he had learned this bit of protocol, John Smith was given so much food that he feared he was being fattened before being sacrificed.[23]) Following the meal there was entertainment, in the form of more orations by elders and then the townspeople's music and dancing to honor the visitors.

After all of these preliminaries, the chief and guests could begin to parley—or try to, in the absence of interpreters. If the hour were late and people were too tired for something as important and delicate as parleying, it would be put off until the next day.[24]

When the time came to retire for the night, the visitors would be shown to houses in the town where beds were ready for them. The highest-status visitor got special treatment: if he were a male, he would be given a woman to keep him company for the night.[25]

Hospitality to friendly foreigners was exceedingly generous, even when it took place at short notice. In late July 1585, when the garden crops had begun to come in, Philip Barlowe and some other Englishmen paid an impromptu visit to the Roanoke town on Roanoke Island and found the chief absent. The chief's wife, however, knew what was due to important foreigners. It was a rainy, blustery day, so she had some of her people help the English to land their barge (large rowboat)—which included carrying them ashore bodily. She took them to her and her husband's house, where she had their clothing washed and dried. Meanwhile she had food prepared, and then in another room fed them to bursting with venison, fish, "melons raw and [boiled], roots of divers kinds, and divers fruits." Her husband did not return by evening, and the English were afraid to stay in town, instead electing to sleep in their boat at the shore. So the wife—whose name Barlowe did not bother to record—therefore sent along with them the half-cooked supper, "pots and all," and detailed "divers men and thirty women" to sit near the boat all night long (possibly to keep it from drifting away at high tide).[26]

It was chiefs of whom the English took enough notice to learn their names. Except for Manteo, Wanchese, and two other Roanoke commoners, all other Carolina Sounds people—even the wives and children of chiefs—are anonymous in the English records. Here is the list of chiefs and the chiefdoms they governed:

Croatoan: No chief was named, which is more evidence of its being a camp within some other chiefdom. Manteo and Wanchese came from here.[27]

Chowanoke: The chief was Menatonon, but we cannot be certain whether he was that group's overall chief or only chief of the upriver towns, while Pooneno was chief of downriver ones.[28]

Pomeioke: The chief there was Piemacum.[29]

Roanoke: The chief was Wingina, who changed his name to Pemisapan after his brother died (before April 1586). The brother, who governed in his absence, was Granganimeo, and his father's name was Ensenore (who, by the rule of chiefly inheritance, was not himself a chief).[30]

Secota: No chief's name was recorded.

Weapemeoc: The chief was Okisko. The satellite town of Chepanoke was governed by an unnamed woman, so the English called it "the woman's town."[31]

The Carolina Algonquian speakers were by no means all friendly with one another. A shifting pattern of alliances and enmities was the norm for them. As of 1584, the Chowanokes, Roanokes, and some Secotas were allied with one another,[32] and the Pomeiokes and the (possibly Iroquoian-speaking) Neuseocks made up a rival alliance.[33] The Pomeiokes and Roanokes had been allies until a few years before, when the Pomeiokes had turned on some Roanokes, ambushing them and breaking the peace.[34] Before that happened, around 1582, both groups had made a mistrustful peace with the Secotas, but their new "allies" continued to dislike and stage raids upon the Roanokes.[35]

The making and keeping up of alliances would have required official visiting, present-giving, and probably also the exchanging of women as wives.

Enmity, caused by insults such as disrespecting a chief or stealing one of his wives (recorded in Virginia), resulted in guerilla warfare.[36]

Tribes with small populations do not have people to waste. Therefore, warfare took the form of ambushes and raids rather than open-field battles. Long deliberations were required beforehand, with the chief consulting a council consisting of priests (useful as diviners) and hunter-warriors, both older and up-and-coming, who had earned outstanding reputations—the only way for nonchiefly men to become prominent.[37]

War was waged at least annually in the Carolina Sounds and, for that matter, the whole of the Eastern Woodlands of North America. Much of the men's self-image rested upon it; they were great hunters of people as well as animals, and they were powerful defenders of their families. War was undertaken not for territory, as in Europe, but for revenge for past wrongs and for capturing women and children, who were not harmed but instead were taken home,[38] treated warily but kindly, and eventually adopted into the captors' families, swelling the population of useful laborers. Thus enemy men were humiliated as warriors and lost their families in the bargain. Those men, considering themselves newly wronged, plotted violence in return. And so it went, back and forth, generation after generation. All men grew up in that vicious circle, as their male ancestors had before them. They could not imagine any other way of being: John Lawson wrote that "they cannot live without war, which they have ever been used to; and that if peace be made with the Indians they now war with, they must find out some others to wage war against; for, for them to live in peace, is to live out of their [male] element, war, conquest, and murder, being what they delight in, and value themselves for."[39] Similar things would be written about the Iroquois (direct quotes from their leaders, in that case) and the southeastern tribes later in the eighteenth century. John Lawson also began to perceive a dichotomy that was, in fact, built into the system: constant war and violence for enemies, constant restraint and respect for allies and one's own family and townspeople. Tensions that built up too high in the latter could be released by being even fiercer toward the former. They could take it all out on enemies, especially captured male ones.

Peace could be made, and it *was* made from time to time, new enemies being found elsewhere. The English reconnaissance expedition to the Carolina Sounds encountered this situation in 1584. They made friends with the neighboring Roanokes, which immediately put them at odds with some Secotas (who became more or less allied with the Roanokes later on). The English were careless that summer and did not erect a stockade around

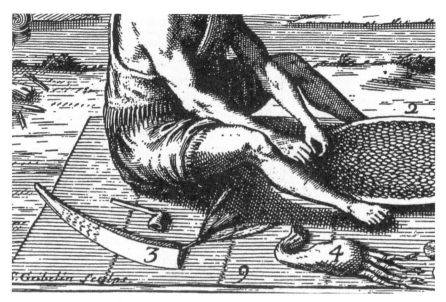

FIGURE 5.2 Detail of the Gribelin engraving of a couple eating: the man has laid down his purse ("4"), his tobacco pipe, and his swordlike wooden tomahawk ("3"). The latter two were important symbols of peace and war, respectively, and much later in the West they were combined into one ceremonial object to present to strangers, who had to choose which side of the pipe bowl/hatchet end they wanted used.

their cabins. After one of the supposedly friendly Secotas called a couple of Englishmen outside, an apparently friendly meeting turned lethal, and only a few Englishmen escaped.[40]

Fights with enemies usually took the form of ambushes on people taken unawares at meals. Given a preference, male guests kept their tomahawks within easy reach (figure 5.2). The Pomeiokes broke the peace with the Roanokes by inviting their supposed allies' chief and important men and "thirty women" to a feast during which the host and his men "came suddenly upon them, and slew them every one, reserving the women, and children."[41] The Roanokes, for their part, could be on the giving end as well as the receiving one. By mid-1585, when they had turned against the English, they planned an intertribal feast to commemorate the death of Wingina's father, which had happened a month before. They invited their English "friends" to come, and they asked some of the other attendees, Weapemeocs and others, to be ready to attack. After the English guests had gone to bed in Indian houses, with Roanokes outwardly acting friendly, the other Indians were to set fire to the houses and then club the Englishmen to death as they tried to escape.[42]

The plan fell through: the Indian guests, wanting at that point to remain on good terms with the English, declined to cooperate.

Women and children were not harmed if captured; neither were male members of chiefly families, who might serve useful diplomatic purposes later.[43] Other men were expendable; they could be killed during the attack, or they could be taken back home and tortured to death by slow burning. Complete stoicism was expected on the part of the victim, who could regain some of the lost honor of his people if he "died well."[44] All males grew up knowing they could face that ordeal, so from early boyhood onward, they practiced enduring the vilest conditions while hunting for their families. They may also have done what Choctaw Indian boys did, testing their ability to suffer self-induced pain in order to harden themselves to it.[45]

The English saw both allying and warring behavior in the Sounds region, sometimes with the same Native people going back and forth between the two.[46] They were probably aware that the Indians' reactions to their own behavior varied with distance: after an initial period of friendliness with everyone, the chiefdoms closer to the English fort turned against them, while more distant chiefdoms remained friendly. That factor, which operated as well in the early Virginia and Maryland colonies, certainly would have determined where they could take refuge after their own people (apparently) abandoned them in 1587.

PART II | A More Complicated,
Faster-Moving World

CHAPTER SIX

Dealing with New Foreigners

The Algonquian speakers of the Carolina Sounds had been dealing with "foreign" Indians for centuries, because Indian people were no less adventurous and curious about other places than were other peoples in the world.[1] Previously they had had contacts—trading, war, and so on—with other Eastern Woodland peoples whose way of life resembled theirs in many ways, so that the behavior of strangers was fairly predictable. However, in the mid-1500s they had sporadic encounters with itinerant Europeans, who were much more "foreign" to them than anyone they had known before. They discovered early on that such strangers could be either friendly or hostile, sometimes for reasons that were apparent and sometimes not. Wary yet lavish hospitality and careful observation were called for from the outset.

This chapter describes those encounters, as far as possible, from the Native American side, not the European one. Although we have to use the records made by those Europeans, the Native people's society being nonliterate, the picture that will emerge here does not closely resemble the one previously drawn by historians. Several scholars, such as Michael Oberg (2008) and Karen Kupperman (2000), have tried to approach a view that is both balanced and fine-grained for detail, which is admirable, but they still get most of their details from the English records, with the result that their work inadvertently remains unevenly weighted toward the thoughts and actions of the English. This chapter tries to reconstruct only what the Indians would have perceived about the English during those four years, even with the help of good interpreters like Manteo and Wanchese, and accordingly, the chapter is coarse-grained and rather short. It also emphasizes geographic, diplomatic, and military matters, to set the stage for the chapter that follows.

First, though, for purposes of clarity, we need a brief, schematic summary of the Roanoke "colonies" (though not all of them were actually attempts at a colony), along with which Native people they contacted.

First set of English: July and August 1584; reconnaissance; men only; met Roanokes; took two youths back to England to train as interpreters.

Second set of English: June 1585 to June 1586; attempt at initial settlement; men and livestock; met people of Croatoan (friendly), Roanoke (became hostile), Pomeioke (friendly), Aquascogoc (became hostile), Secota (became hostile), Weapemeioc (friendly), Chesapeake (friendly), and Chowanoke (initially hostile, then friendly). Another fifteen men left by tardy extra ship; they were later killed by people from Secota and Roanoke.

Third set of English: July and August 1587 (and beyond, when rescue did not come); attempt at permanent settlement; men, women, children, and livestock; met people of Croatoan (friendly) and Roanoke (hostile).

As far as we know, the first people in the Sounds to see Europeans were the Secotas, who in the late 1550s rescued some castaways they met on Ocracoke Island. This oral account, probably among the neighboring Croatoans and passed along later to the English by Manteo, states that the Secotas helped their visitors to rig up two boats with sails and then saw them off. But they were soon wrecked again, likely within Croatoan territory, since it seems to have been the Croatoan man Manteo who passed along the story to the English.[2] Nothing further is known of them. Given the date, if it is accurate, the castaways would have been Spaniards, because Spain claimed to own the whole region at the time. Another Spanish ship visited the Outer Banks about the same time. This was the expedition that took aboard a visiting Powhatan (actually, Paspahegh) man who was later christened "Don Luis."[3] The ship's captain was so focused on what this man could tell him about the Chesapeake Bay, which was already known by the Spanish to be more desirable than the Sounds region for colonizing purposes, that he recorded nothing about the people "Don Luis" had been visiting. The skimpy records do not indicate hostilities arising between hosts and visitors. But the visitors would have been armed and on their guard, and the hosts would definitely have taken note: foreigners could be hostile as well as friendly, dangerous as well as advantageous to trade with.

The next strangers the Sounds people are known to have met arrived some two and a half decades later (July 13, 1584), and they were anything but castaways; they were there because they wanted to be. They appeared at what later generations would call Gunt Inlet, just north of modern Oregon Inlet. They came in two huge vessels, to Native eyes, propelled not by long-handled paddles but by something else—masts with sails attached—that looked utterly strange to those seeing European ships for the first time. There were many people aboard, elaborately dressed in clothing far too heavy for mid-summer at a latitude nearly twenty degrees south of their own country, and all of them were adult males. That was suspicious: all-male parties could be war parties. Accordingly, none of the local people, who were commoners out foraging on the Banks at that season, showed themselves for some time. It was not their place, after all, to deal with new arrivals: that privilege belonged to their chief and any emissaries he chose to send.[4]

This was Roanoke territory, and as it happened, its chief, Wingina, was laid up with serious wounds he had received in a skirmish with a neighboring enemy, probably Pomeioke people.[5] During the month that the visitors stayed in his country, he was never well enough to meet them, delegating the task to his brother, Granganimeo. And Granganimeo was sufficiently cautious, not to mention mindful of protocol, that he sent carefully chosen emissaries to the first meeting with the new arrivals. He did so in a way that clearly showed peaceful intentions.

Two days later, three unarmed Native men went outside the inlet and beached their canoe. One man, probably a councilor of Wingina's, got out, walked down the beach, and halted at a spot opposite where the foreign ships were anchored. Taking the hint, the newcomers unshipped a large rowboat and loaded in some trade goods; four dignitaries and several rowers then went over to the beach for a parley. According to proper diplomatic usage in the Indian world, Granganimeo's representative began with a long oration, the content of which is unknown since there were as yet no interpreters. The strangers then invited him aboard their ship and presented him with "a shirt, hat, and some other things, and made him taste of our wine, and our meat." He seemed to like the latter, strange though it was to his palate, although he may simply have been acting polite. He was given a tour of both vessels, after which he went ashore again.

Granganimeo's representative had grown up in a world in which people believed very strongly in reciprocity as a matter of propriety, so he and his companions promptly launched their canoe and "fell to fishing" (method unknown), which brought in a great number of fish. They presented them to the newcomers, some fish to each ship, and then they went home. No one was in anyone's debt for now.[6]

The report they brought back to Granganimeo was favorable. They probably had not yet seen soldiers in armor, holding firearms; in later meetings ashore, they would see both. The firearms made a horrific blast of sound, which frightened all the Native people who heard it, but since those early demonstrations, during the meet-and-greets around parleys, probably involved only blanks and not metal objects spewing out of the barrels, it is unlikely that the local people made the connection between the noise and people dying. That would come later.

The first report, then, would have told Granganimeo that the foreigners were friendly, though the gifts they gave to people were odd, and that they did understand fair exchanges. Assuming that the gifts included metal knives and hatchets, even though of poor quality by European standards, Granganimeo's people would have quickly discovered that those particular items kept an edge longer than the Native version did, and thus they were very desirable. They concluded: let us, by all means, continue to cultivate such people's acquaintance!

Accordingly, the next day, Granganimeo himself and his entourage of "forty or fifty" men paddled down to the inlet,[7] through it, then to the ocean-front beach opposite where the foreign ships remained anchored. The strangers, seeing so many men ashore, went to the meeting in armor, as if they were ready to be attacked. Their precautions proved unnecessary. The meeting involved a chief and therefore had to be done slowly and formally, according to protocol (see chapter 5). The meeting went smoothly, though neither side understood the other except in general terms, and because of that, the chief took no offense when the newcomers made a faux pas.[8]

It was gift-giving time. The visitors began handing things not only to the chief but also to the councilors sitting with him. That was improper: on occasions like this, the chief was the sole representative of his people. Politely but firmly, Granganimeo took the things away from his men and put them in his own collection basket, explaining why (in signs) as he did so.

The present that pleased him most that day was a "bright tin dish." He had a hole punched in the rim, a thong inserted, and began wearing it around his neck, pointing out its "similarity" to the foreigners' breastplates. (He may have been acting overly polite at that point.) He was also very taken with a copper kettle, and he handed over fifty furs (deerskins?) for it. From what archaeologists have found in the Mid-Atlantic region, that kettle would not have been used for stewing back in the village. It would have been cut up into squares and rectangles, drilled through, and hung around people's necks as pendants.

Granganimeo was glad to get metal knives and hatchets, but disappointed when he was not allowed to buy any swords. In Indian minds, swords were not necessarily weapons; they could also be used as machetes, and both sexes in the Indian world did slashing work (clearing ground, cutting reeds) in which long, sharp metal implements were desirable. The people may still have had a few metal "edge tools" that they had gotten from the castaways two decades before, but in any case they had entered the meeting knowing the tools' value. Granganimeo offered a great many freshwater pearls for the swords, without result. In the days to follow, he sent game and fruit and vegetables to the newcomers, apparently hoping to put them enough into his debt that maybe then they would part with a sword or two. When that did not work either, he may have felt some disenchantment with his guests. Nevertheless, he considerately established and continued a procedure for letting the English aboard the ships know how many canoes to expect on future visits: he had that many fires lit on the beach—which meant that besides collecting food for visitors, some of his people had to spend time and labor collecting firewood each time before any trading could begin.[9]

It is safe to say that people from the satellite village of Dasemenkapeuc, on the mainland, attended these sessions. The draw of quaint strangers to gawk at and metal cutting tools to buy would have been irresistible. The Roanokes probably did some of the same things during these days that Philip Barlowe recorded about the Secota people later: they stared at the size and complexity of the boat (a small pinnace) used by the exploring party in shallow water; they were badly scared at first when an English firearm was shot off as a demonstration; and they marveled at how pale the foreigners were and wondered if they were that way all over.[10]

Before many days had passed, a party of the visitors began going farther afield than Gunt Inlet. This was the stage at which they first visited the Roanokes' village, where they violated protocol by simply showing up, rather than sending notice to the chief (figure 6.1), and by treating their hosts with suspicion that night (described in chapter 5).[11]

After they left, they went farther around the Sounds, visiting people who were both friends and foes of the Roanoke Islanders.[12] Visits to the latter must have created unease in Roanoke minds, but if the English had any interest in such feelings, they did not record them. (They also did not record how vulnerable, in the face of larger Indian numbers, they themselves often felt.) It did not yet matter very much, though, because the strangers had made no attempt as yet to establish a settlement within the Roanokes' territory.

The foreigners departed on their ships after about one moon's stay, and two young men went with them: Manteo and Wanchese. Wanchese seems to have come from Roanoke Island, but Manteo's mother's people lived at Croatoan.[13] Everyone apparently blessed their going. Not only were they to experience life in London and report back about it, but everyone, both Indian and English, wanted the youths to learn English and serve afterward as

FIGURE 6.1 The English dropped in (painting by Karen Harvey, based on John White's portrait of a wife of Wingina and an idea of the author's).

interpreters. Both sides would have recognized that there was a "spying" factor involved. Both sides, but especially the Indian one, wanted to know much more about the other's country, especially its intentions toward their own people. Allowing the youths to go also shows that Granganimeo had understood the Englishmen's signs indicating that they intended to return. It is less likely, though, that he comprehended as yet the English intention ultimately to settle among his people, not merely as neighbors but as conquerors. That enlightenment would come later.

The next year (1585), the strangers in their ships arrived—again, well into the growing season (in early July),[14] when Indian families moved back and forth between their fields and their foraging territories. There was visual evidence from the outset that this batch of foreigners intended to stay longer, if not permanently; the young interpreters they brought back with them could soon confirm that impression. They had more ships this time, bringing many more passengers. Those passengers were once again all males, but this time, besides the seamen and soldiers, there were others whose occupations would become clear only with the passage of time: farmers and fort builders.[15] The ships' cargo was also much more varied this time. Besides the usual armor, weapons, and food supplies, there were plants which would not get cultivated that year and—the greatest surprise—animals that were completely new to the local people: "horses, mares, kine [cattle], sheep, swine, &c. [chickens?]." There was at least one mule, for one was found somewhere on the Outer Banks by English visitors in 1587. And there were also very probably several large guard dogs, like the mastiffs the later Jamestown colonists are known to have had.[16] Altogether, it was a fascinating but worrying arrival in the local people's eyes.

There was another hitch as well: it was only a partial arrival, as Manteo and Wanchese soon told their people, because the main cargo ship in the fleet had grounded near Ocracoke and lost some of its supplies.[17] The foreigners would therefore not be able to remain self-sufficient for as long as they had hoped, and that in turn would mean pressure on the local population's food stores if they stayed around too long.

That pressure would come sooner than the locals thought, because the two peoples had very different attitudes toward farm animals. The Indians had no concept of animal husbandry. Animals were simply there to be hunted and eaten as need arose; they were not for doing work for people or for selective breeding. Native people would expect the foreigners to slaughter and eat up all their animals, except the dogs (Indian dogs were not eaten), and they would prefer that the visitors would do it in a series of feasts put on for their hosts. The newcomers, of course, were not prepared to do anything of the sort—unless they absolutely had to. Hard feelings were bound to arise down the road, when the "stingy" aliens tried to get Native men to hunt for them while keeping alive some of their livestock. Not only that, but if the livestock were to survive—all of them being herbivores except for the dogs—there had to be pasturage somewhere. (Only the omnivorous pigs and the seed-eating chickens could thrive in a forest.) At best, it meant foreigners having to clear extra acreage, besides gardens; at worst, it meant formidably large animals raiding the Roanokes' cornfields. That sort of thing became a major bone of contention between Indians and non-Indians in the seventeenth century; Ralph Lane's account says nothing about whether it started up in 1585–86, but it could have.

Something else happened that would have far-reaching consequences for Native people and foreigners alike. The two young men returned from their months-long stay, over the winter, in England. The experience plainly had affected them in different ways. Manteo returned feeling both impressed by what he had seen and well disposed toward the English. He reported favorably back to Wingina and thereafter lived among the English, willingly serving them as an interpreter; in August 1587 he accepted baptism into Christianity.[18] His people, at Croatoan, would remain pro-English in spite of all the ugly incidents that happened later.

Wanchese, on the other hand, seems to have returned to his people with relief, and he had little to do with the foreigners afterward.[19] He had found his London hosts to be arrogant, hungry for territory and riches, and dismissive of any of the good things about the Native way of life. (He was not the last Native man to have that experience: the Powhatan priest Uttamatomakkin had the same reaction in 1616–17.)[20] So he hastened to warn his chief, Wingina, about them. The chief's reaction to the two different accounts would become clear before much longer.

The foreigners arrived in two contingents a couple of days apart. The main ship, which went aground for a time, sent out small boats to explore the Pamlico Sound area before it managed to reach Gunt Inlet. Those boats' passengers went to see the people at Secota and Pomeioke, the latter being enemies of the Roanoke Islanders, who may or may not have heard about it later. At the town of Aquascogoc there was a nasty incident. The English missed a silver cup they'd had, and when they returned for it and found the village deserted—possibly because it was still the season for serious foraging by Indian families—they assumed the townsmen had fled, fearing retribution, so they burned the houses and also the field of nearly ripe corn. That exaggerated (in Indian eyes) vengefulness must have left a sour taste in the mouths of any Native people who heard about it, though nobody moved to help the victims take revenge. Soon afterward Wingina, Granganimeo's brother, now recovered, assigned—but did not give, in the European sense—some currently uncultivated land for the "visitors" to build on and use. Most of the ships, once the 107 people and their surviving livestock were unloaded, left for Europe.[21]

During the next several months, the strangers sent out expeditions for exploration, this time farther yet afield, to nations still friendly with the Roanokes: Weapemeiocs, Chowanokes, and Chesapeakes.[22] A party actually wintered among the last-named. Still more distant tribes like the Mangoags would have had some of their people travel to gawk at the newcomers. There is no firsthand record of the Roanokes' and nearer tribes' feelings about these activities, or about the strain, which they must have felt, of having to help support so many foreigners close at hand, especially in the hungry time of the spring and early summer (of 1586). Either Ralph Lane avoided writing about relations with the locals going sour because he knew his writings would become promotion propaganda for colonization, or he and his followers may have been too intent on their ultimate colonizing goal to notice. There is strong indirect evidence, however, showing not only that relations had become very strained with the Roanokes, but also that that impatience with the foreigners was beginning to spread outward from Roanoke Island.

Wingina's people had definitely become hostile to their difficult neighbors by that spring. The first indication was subtle. The foreigners learned that Wingina had taken a new name, Pemisapan, upon the death (cause unknown) of his pro-English brother Granganimeo, but the name change seems to have meant nothing to them. In the Algonquian speakers' world, however, a chief taking a new name could mean either that he had a new status, having achieved something remarkable politically or militarily, or that he was planning to do something that would greatly enhance his reputation. Making a serious move against his former English allies could qualify. It is an exact parallel to events among the Virginia Algonquian speakers after Powhatan died in 1618.[23]

The second indication was not subtle at all, although it was indirect and typical of a Native military leader who did not want to risk his own men unless he had to. It was easier to be indirect and convince more distant chiefs that the English were dangerous enough that they should be given a strong hint, in the form of an ambush, that they should leave the region. Hints of that kind, involving the killing of relatively small numbers of enemies, were sufficient in the Indian world, with its lower population density than Europe, for responsible leaders to preserve the rest of their people by packing up and withdrawing before another hint came. That would be Opechancanough's thinking in 1622 and 1644,[24] and it did not work any better for him than it did for Wingina/Pemisapan. English people did not respond "correctly" to hints of that kind. They stayed around and struck back.

In March 1586, an exploring party went westward up the Albemarle Sound and up the Chowan River, with four Roanoke guides (Manteo as interpreter, plus Tetepano, Wingina's brother-in-law Eracano, and Cossine). Reaching the Chowanoke chief's town, the aliens once more neglected to send notice ahead. That was just as well, because they found the chief, Menatonon, in conference with his neighbors, the Moratucs. Suspecting a conspiracy (correctly, as it turned out) and becoming aggressive, they broke up the conference and took the chief and his son prisoner, after which they sent the son to their fort on Roanoke Island as a hostage.[25] They also made peace, as they thought, with the Moratucs, although hostilities resumed within a few days, mainly in the form of denying food to the explorers when they tried to go up the Roanoke River through Moratuc territory.[26] So much for the first English visit to the Chowanokes and their neighbors!

Ralph Lane, leader of the party, interviewed the chief under those conditions of duress, receiving the impression that Menatonon was telling him more about the region "than I had received by all the searches and savages" previous encountered.[27] It may be significant that Menatonon's information, including the riches of the Nansemonds to the north, was exaggerated in order to produce a desirable effect from everyone's point of view: leave the Sounds people alone and go north. That may well have been the catalyst for Lane to begin to shift his colonizing interest northward to the huge natural harbor of the Chesapeake Bay. The report of the party wintering among the Chesapeakes—the records of which have since been lost—seems to have clinched the matter.[28] If that change in interest had been followed through upon, the Roanokes would have been far happier and Wingina/Pemisapan would have lived longer.

Meanwhile, Menatonon told Lane, through Manteo, that it was Pemisapan of Roanoke who had advised him repeatedly that the foreigners were enemies, urging him and his western neighbors, the Mangoags, to join forces with him and stage a massive assault on the fort on Roanoke Island. The intent would not have been to kill everyone, but rather to drive the aliens away. That scheme was now thwarted for the time being. But the enmity behind it remained—and grew.

Back on Roanoke Island, Pemisapan started a rumor among his townsmen that Lane and his exploring party had been wiped out. Since that would presumably leave the men in the fort without a leader, and because it was spring, the hungry season for both peoples, the townsmen then felt free to begin disparaging the "useless" aliens to their faces, threatening to withdraw altogether from the island and leave them to starve. (It is safe to say that all the foreign livestock had been eaten up by then, except for any animals that escaped into the forest.) The rumor died only when Lane and his men and guides returned to their fort.[29] A counter-rumor then began among the Native people to the effect that the strangers had supernatural powers, stemming from their being "dead men returned into the world." In other words, the Chowanokes had killed them, all right, but they had risen again. That belief may not be so far from what the Virginia (and perhaps Carolina) Algonquian speakers believed about themselves, with their version of reincarnation.

Soon afterward, Pemisapan's rumor was refuted, and the foreigners' standing improved on Roanoke Island. Menatonon sent an emissary to visit his hostage son and also to inform his captors that he had convinced Okisko, the Weapemeoc chief, to become a subject like himself of the English queen. In conjunction with that message, Okisko had sent two dozen of his men to Pemisapan to affirm the truth of that new allegiance. This was not long before Ensenore, the chief's father, died, but in his last days he convinced his son to keep the peace and have his people plant gardens especially to feed the aliens in their fort. He also persuaded the chief to set aside a plot of fallow ground for the aliens to do their own kind of gardening in. That created a truce, albeit a shaky one. The gardens of both peoples would not begin producing vegetables until early July, and in the meantime the foreigners would remain hard up. Pemisapan may or may not have known that they expected a relief ship from England that spring, although it was running very late.[30]

Then Ensenore died in late April, which left the chief and all his councilors free to take action against their no-longer-welcome guests.[31] Not surprisingly, one of the councilors urging Pemisapan to resume hostilities was Wanchese. The local people thereupon refused to share wild foods from their foraging activities. They also broke up the fish weirs they had built for their "visitors," denying them food from that source. The foreigners responded by doing what they had learned from the Native people, up to a point: they split their personnel into groups and sent them out along the Banks, to live on oysters and whatever roots they had learned were edible.

Besides hoping to reduce the aliens' numbers through starvation, Pemisapan resumed his efforts to get more distant peoples—this time the Weapemeoc towns, the Mangoags, and the Chesapeakes—to help him carry out a large-scale ambush. They were all to gather at Dasemenkapeuc on the mainland for a great feast commemorating the death of Ensenore—Lane called it a "months mind," for it was analogous to the English custom. At a signal, all the warriors, who would have come to the feast by canoe, were to get into their canoes, go to the Roanoke Island, and attack the fort. The foreigners would be outnumbered and slaughtered.[32]

Pemisapan moved over to his mainland town, partially to avoid the daily begging of fort people for food and partly to be able to dispatch messengers to his hoped-for allies without being readily observed. The replies, though, were less than he had hoped for. The Chesapeakes sent no answer at all. Some of the Weapemeocs, under Okisko, refused the summons and went out foraging as usual, coincidentally taking themselves out of reach of the foreigners. Only some Weapemeocs and the Mangoags agreed to participate. The date set, by the European calendar, was June 10, 1586.

It was a Native person who leaked news of the plot to the foreigners: Skiko, Menatonon's son from Chowanoke. He had escaped briefly, making contact with local Indian people on the island before the aliens caught him again, and he had heard about the plot while he was free. Once retrieved by his jailors, and treated kindly, he revealed what he knew. So the foreigners were now on guard.[33] Not only that, but their leader, Ralph Lane, cannily sent word to Pemisapan that ships from his own country had been sighted near Croatoan (which was a lie), meaning that reinforcements were on the way to the fort; he added that he intended to go to meet them. He then informed the chief that he now wanted to buy food for the four-day trip and borrow some Indian men to fish for those of his men who would remain in the fort. That must have been galling for the Roanoke leadership.

The chief politely sent word that he would visit the foreigners' fort, presumably to bring the needed provisions and fishermen. But he kept putting off the visit in order to wait for his Weapemeoc and Mangoag allies to arrive—the assault date having been put off by eight days. Meanwhile, he ordered his own Roanoke and Croatoan people to begin assembling at the Roanoke village on the island, as if they were getting ready to comply with the foreigners' request. (The Croatoans obeyed, but they did not fully participate in his enmity.) To Pemisapan's chagrin, however, Lane fooled him. Before all the villagers had assembled there, Lane staged a sundown raid on the town and captured not only canoes but the people in them, two of whom he had beheaded in full view of their relatives. A skirmish followed, which the foreigners won; the next day they came over to Dasemenkapeuc to confront Pemisapan. The chief temporized and allowed the aliens to come ashore and meet with him. But shortly after, the aliens turned on them with their pistols, wounding several men including the chief. Managing to escape, he and his people fled, but he was overtaken by one of the aliens, killed, and beheaded, the head being taken back to the fort.[34]

Killing a chief was an unforgivable offense in the eyes of all the Algonquian speakers up and down the Mid-Atlantic coast. Chiefs were supposed to be taken prisoner and perhaps ransomed, but as privileged people they were never to be killed. By itself it amounted to a declaration of war by the foreigners, and unremitting raids by the Native people would be in order thereafter.

The foreigners seemed not to grasp this fact; their definition of "war" was much more drastic. They went on about their business as if very little had happened. A few days after the skirmish, a fleet of ships (under Sir Francis Drake) did in fact bring them supplies, and to the Native folk it looked as if those ghastly aliens would manage to stay on and on. But after a slow-moving mid-July hurricane blew through, the aliens changed their minds, carried their goods from their fort to the ships, and abandoned Roanoke Island.[35]

That was not the end of the matter, however. Not long after the fort was abandoned, it was reoccupied again, this time by a couple of dozen or so foreigners from a different ship, whose commander idiotically left them there and sailed away.[36] The surviving local people and their neighbors had avoided the ship's commander (Richard Grenville) and his soldiers, but now that they had gone, the Natives felt free to eliminate these stragglers, which they and their allies did.[37]

News of the Roanokes' difficulties with the foreigners would have spread far and wide in the Sounds region and beyond. Horror at Pemisapan's fate, which went far beyond Ralph Lane's taking the Chowanoke chief prisoner, would have convinced the Native people that foreign visitors were just as dangerous as they had suspected all along. Even people like the Weapemeocs, who had not directly had trouble with the aliens, would have hoped never again to see their like.

Such hopes were dashed a year later. Once again, a fleet of ships arrived toward the end of the usual growing season—which in that year of drought (1587) was running late. People out foraging for their families saw deposited, once more, a large party of soldiers, would-be settlers, and their goods and livestock. This time, however, the newcomers included women and boys.[38] Perhaps, then, this load of aliens might be less threatening—militarily, at least, though another threat might still loom in their obvious intention to make a permanent settlement, uninvited this time, on Roanoke Island. The Native people would not learn until later that the settlers did not want to be there at all: they had been intending to go and live in the Chesapeake Bay region, but their lead ship's pilot refused to guide them that far.[39]

Trouble was not long in coming. The foreigners went straight to the site of their old fort, which had been all but razed by the local people, and began repairing the few houses left standing. Within five days, the new Roanoke chief (name unknown) sent some men to the island to hunt deer and also, from out among the reeds, to view the aliens—some of whom were wholly new to the "New World" and took no thought for any danger. (John Smith would write in 1608 that some newcomers to Jamestown were utterly obtuse about "straggling," "which mischief no punishment will prevent but hanging.")[40] Seeing a foreigner "wading in the water alone, almost naked, without any weapon, save only a small forked stick, catching crabs withal, and also being strayed two miles from his company," the hunters proceeded to kill him with multiple arrow shots, after which they took their hardened-wood swords and beat his head in.[41] Thus was the welcome mat laid out.

The people at Croatoan had remained fairly friendly, since their man Manteo was still among the foreigners. But when those foreigners went with him to visit his people, there was an initial standoff, with the townspeople acting hostile and the aliens marching "with our shot [firearms aimed] towards them" and making the people flee, so that Manteo had to call them back and assuage their fears. The harvest so far that summer had been poor—and would remain poor—and they asked the newcomers not to take any of their corn. The newcomers agreed and were taken into the town, where, of course, they had to be feasted.[42] Thus they got some of the locals' precious corn anyway.

The Croatoans then agreed to approach some of their neighbors—people from Secota, Pomeioke, and Aquascogoc—about forging an alliance with the newcomers. It is significant that the folk from Roanoke, Weapemeoc, and Chowanoke were omitted, but it is also a little puzzling: the Croatoan leader told their guests that it was a mixed party from Secota, Aquascogoc, and Dasemenkapeuc that had attacked the stragglers on Roanoke Island the year before. Not surprisingly, the invited chiefs never showed up, and no conference took place.[43]

The foreigners took great offense at not getting their way, and very shortly they went to Dasemenkapeuc and ambushed the people there just before dawn, killing both men and women; this was not, Manteo said, because they wanted to kill both sexes, but because when the locals ran unclothed out of their houses, men and women looked alike in the dark. That was bad enough, but even worse was that the victims proved to be friendly Croatoans come to harvest the crops left behind by the Roanoke chief's followers, who had killed that one foreigner early on and promptly fled the area to escape reprisals. The foreigners ceased fire, shamefacedly gathered up their surviving friends and the abandoned ripe crops, and took them all back to their refurbished fort for safety.[44]

And there things rested for a while. The aliens finished moving into their fort on Roanoke Island, the island now being abandoned by its former owners, who with their neighbors and allies kept out of sight. In a very few more weeks, the ships loaded up what they needed for the ocean voyage and departed.[45] Ninety men, seventeen women, nine boys, and two newborn babies remained behind. They were now at the mercy of the Native people, most of whom—with good reason—were wary of them at best and actively trying to kill them at worst. The people in the fort, and probably also the Indian nations around them, expected ships to return later with more supplies and, if necessary, to evacuate them, as had happened the year before.

But the ships never came. The foreigners were entirely on their own. And while they were not in immediate danger of starving, they were seriously outnumbered.

CHAPTER SEVEN

Foreigners Merging In

The English people left behind on Roanoke Island became known as the "Lost Colony," thanks to the uncertainty of their fate after August 22, 1587, when John White took leave of them and sailed back to England in quest of supplies. What concerns us now is the aftermath, as it affected the people native to the region. There is a strong likelihood—not merely the possibility—that those English families were *not* completely wiped out by the hostile Algonquian speakers nearest them. Instead, at least some of them would have managed to take refuge with more distant, friendlier Native people. Those refugees would not have stayed for long in only one place, either: even in a good crop year, which 1587 was not, no one Indian town's food supplies could possibly have supported a hundred or more extra people. So the "lost colonist" refugees would have had to split up. Some would have been split off involuntarily, by being captured and taken home by hostile Native people. Given how Indian warfare handled women and children, any English women and children captured by the hostile neighbors would have been kept very much alive for as long as possible. On the other hand, English adult men, who were as touchy as the warriors they faced, may not have survived for long as captives or even as guests. But if they avoided sickening from the local "bugs" to which they had no immunity, English females and pre-adult males had a good chance of living a long time and gradually assimilating into the Indian world. Early eighteenth-century traveler John Lawson was of this opinion too.[1]

Concrete evidence of their having done this merging is scanty and downright tantalizing, ranging from an alteration to John White's map hiding what may have been a planned new English fort at the west end of Albemarle Sound, to sightings of an Indian with yellow hair and pale skin in the Appomattox River area in the early 1600s.[2] Many other scholars have written about this subject, and most agree nowadays that the colonists were not simply wiped out. They disagree about the details, however, and we shall leave it all to them, with only one parting shot: English-descended Indians in the early seventeenth century could very well have existed in *many* places in eastern North Carolina. Because of how war captives were treated, *any* of the Indian nations in the Sounds region, friendly or hostile as of 1587, could have added English people to their population. Not only that, but intertribal wars continued at least into John Lawson's time, the early 1700s, so that English captives and their descendants could have been recaptured and thus distributed all over the place. Scholars should therefore not just look toward the friendly Croatoans, for instance, as having English-descended people among them. Everybody probably did, after a decade or two.

This cultural anthropologist is more interested in reconstructing how the assimilation process would have played out. In the 1580s, it would have been the English minority merging into the Indian majority, whose culture was then the strong, well-established one in the region. Part 1 of this volume has reconstructed what that culture apparently was like, so the job is partly done. But there is a second matter to keep in mind: the English of the 1580s were Tudor English, whose culture in some ways was almost as different from ours today as the Indian one was from either theirs or ours.

Some Indian practices that we modern people would have found to be stumbling blocks would not have been hard at all for Elizabethans to adapt to. So for each aspect of life in the Indian towns, we shall have to do a certain amount of description of Tudor English ways before engaging in educated speculation about how their practitioners, formerly the Roanoke colonists, would have fared when having perforce to learn their Indian hosts' version of "human" behavior.

Thomas Hariot, who tried to record the Roanokes' language, had gone home to England, and no one knows how long Manteo, who had been to England and back, stayed with his English friends. So for many, if not all of the former colonists, the language barrier between the two peoples may have been fully in force. Therefore, just like the English who were now arriving in the Indian towns, as guests or captives, we must begin not with parleys but with smells, sounds, and sights.

The dominant smell in the Indian towns was that of wood smoke, and the ex-colonists would have been very familiar with it. Even though there was a shortage of firewood in England by the 1580s, most houses were still heated with it.[3] Missing from the Indian towns, on the other hand, was any smell or sound made by domesticated animals, whether mammals like cows or birds like geese, and also missing was the noise of wheeled vehicles drawn by draft animals. Not only that, but the ex-colonists would have missed a major noise common to English towns and cities: the calls of vendors hawking their wares. The Indian world was a lower-tech one, as well as an unspecialized one, and therefore it was quieter. When visitors arrived, the dogs in the town sounded the alarm by howling, for they could not bark.[4] Most of the time, the main noises to be heard in the Indian towns were those of children playing and their elders talking and joking with one another. That in turn might impress the new arrivals in another way: the talk stayed pleasant and good-natured; it was not punctuated by arguments or scolding, as often happened in England.

The initial sights greeting the ex-colonists would have been largely unfamiliar to them and, in their eyes, not impressive in the least. Given the descriptions of Indian technology in chapter 2, the fields would have looked messy and the houses flimsy and "carelessly" sited (i.e., no lining up along streets, however crooked). And this was where they were expected to live! Further experience with Indian houses would have shown them a couple of familiar aspects, though. English houses back then were almost as dark as the Indian ones, even though the former had windows. But few of those windows had glass in them in Tudor times; instead they were covered, when shut, with a frame with oiled cloth stretched onto it, making a translucent barrier to drafts.[5] Glass windows were for the wealthy. Another point of familiarity for any English people who lived in really old-fashioned houses at home would have been the central hearths that heated the Native people's houses. In England, hearths in the wall with chimneys to vent the smoke (and some of the heat, unfortunately) came into fashion during the 1500s, and an ever-smaller number of central-hearth houses remained un-"modernized."[6] Indian houses had hard beds, but only the wealthiest English people had beds that were soft. Lastly, the fleas in the bedding and the lice attacking one's body were familiar, though detested, by both peoples.[7]

English families getting accustomed to Indian houses would have noticed something good about them within a few months of John White's departure: Indian houses were wonderfully warm when cold weather set in. Two decades later, John Smith was to write admiringly of the "dry, warm, smoky houses of Kecoughtan."[8] Not only did a central hearth warm more people— no hierarchy of privilege in getting to stand next to a chimney—but there was plenty of firewood for building big fires. No need to freeze to death on *this* side of the Atlantic!

Right from the beginning the English families would have noticed—and been embarrassed by—how scanty their hosts' clothing was. An apron worn in front of the groin area left a lot of skin showing. English men and women, on the other hand, covered up all their skin except for the face and hands, and the women, if married, bound their hair up and out of sight, as many observant Muslim women do today.[9] Not only did the English wear a lot of clothes, but their garments were tremendously varied, even on a daily basis, according to the wearer's wealth, social standing, occupation, and so forth.[10] There were even laws to regulate such matters. Nothing like that was to be seen among the Native people, whose society was not truly stratified and contained no full-time specialists except priests. On ordinary days, one could not tell a chief from a commoner, something that would go against the grain in anyone who had grown up in Tudor England. The foreigners would have to adjust, of course, to what was normal among their Indian hosts. And they would eventually have to adopt that style themselves.

Sooner or later, the ex-colonists' clothing would wear out or be outgrown — with no possibility of getting more. The Carolina Algonquian speakers' world did not have woven cloth (baskets, yes; cloth, no), let alone all the people required to make even one English outer garment. If that garment were of wool, then going from sheep to garment involved shearers, carders, spinners, weavers, washers, fullers, tuckers, dyers, cloth merchants, and tailors or seamstresses — all of whom were full-time specialists who worked by hand.[11] No one English person, male or female, knew enough to do all that was needed to make English-style clothes completely from raw wool, and there were no domesticated sheep in the New World anyhow. So ultimately, everyone who wound up in the Indian towns and lived long enough would have had to "go native" in the matter of dress. By the time it happened, fortunately, their concept of modesty had probably long since changed over to the Indian one, which was more behavioral (how they moved) than it was simply covering up certain body parts.[12]

Both peoples believed strongly in personal hygiene, but they went about it in exactly opposite ways. Indian people cleaned their skin daily by bathing in the nearest waterway; for that matter, they deliberately opened their pores when using the sweat lodge. The English believed that open pores let in disease, so most of them avoided bathing except under doctors' orders.[13]

Instead, they wore linen underclothes next to their skin and changed those daily; they also had daily rubdowns, with more linen cloths. Made with fibers from another Old World domesticate, flax, linen readily absorbs body oils as well as dirt.[14] But when used in these ways, it required constant laundering and thus was high-maintenance compared to the Indian way of doing things — especially for all those working mothers in the Indian towns. Linen also wears out, so eventually the English families would have had to adopt Indian practices of hygiene as well as clothing.

One immediately visible aspect — to us — of the Indian towns would probably not even have been noticed by the ex-colonists, either early on or later, because they came from the same situation at home: the Indians' ratios of adults to children (many more children) and to the elderly (relatively few elders). In both societies, infant mortality was high and so was the birth rate to compensate for it. And thanks to less-than-effective medicine and ignorance of antiseptic procedures, most adults in both cultures did not reach old age, which was well underway at age fifty.[15]

Within a very few days, the English newcomers would have noticed—and had to adapt to—a difference in telling time. Both peoples took notice of the seasons, the moon's phases, and approximately what time of day it was. But though the Tudor English were not quite the slaves to clock time that their descendants became, they took more account of the time of day than the Roanokes and others did, and they had much more help in doing it. Back home, many of them kept chickens in the yard, even in cities, and the roosters would begin crowing in the early dawn, waking people up to a new working day.[16] But there were no chickens in the Indian towns and so no reveille from that source. The larger English towns and all the cities had large, elaborate church buildings, whose furnishings included equally big and elaborate mechanical clocks. (Few tabletop-size ones existed yet.) The bells in the churches' high towers were rung on the hours shown by the clocks, and everyone within earshot knew what hour it was.[17] Some people also had sundials. Meanwhile, for the Indian people of the Carolina Sounds, observing the sun and noting how high or low in the sky it was sufficed; they were not bound, like Europeans, to scheduled meals or to set hours for prayer.

Both peoples expected to begin the day with prayer, but the Indians combined it with bathing, while the English, already rubbed down with their linen cloths, held family prayers, reading theirs out of books.[18] The books the English brought with them into the Indian towns would have mystified their hosts, as John White had observed in 1585; the Indians would have viewed each book as a talisman, at least for a while.[19] The prayers themselves, and the theology behind them on both sides, would have remained obscure until the language barrier broke down, unless Manteo or Wanchese were present to explain things.

Most of the food ways of the Carolina Algonquian speakers were unfamiliar to the foreigners. Both peoples said grace before meals, and both had menus that included stew ("pottage" to the English) and mush ("frumenty" to the English).[20] Both considered game, especially venison, to be a very desirable part of the diet, with the Indians in their sparsely settled region partaking much more often than the English could, back on their crowded island.[21] Both peoples had bread as a standard component of the diet, though the English had more domesticates (multiple kinds of wheat, besides barley and rye) from which it was made.[22] The Indians had their rather delicate corn, but their grains (wild rice, little barley)[23] were native wild ones and therefore drought resistant. Both peoples liked something oily on their bread: butter (from domesticated cows) or deer suet (a by-product of all those deer carcasses).[24]

But there the similarities ended. The other foods available were different. The only domesticated animals the Indians had were dogs, which they did not eat, so the Native people's diet lacked beef, pork, mutton, chicken, eggs, and any dairy products. Potatoes were expensive luxuries at that time in England, and being a South American domesticate, they were unknown in North America at that time. The other root crops familiar to Europeans, like turnips, were missing here, and the gatherable roots (arrow arum, groundnuts) on this side of the Atlantic were new to the English.

Native people ate when they were hungry, a sensible proceeding with all the coming and going from town that they did. The English were accustomed to scheduled, formal family meals, the meals being considered analogous to Holy Communion.[25] Indian cooking was also extremely bland, no spices or salt being used. The English of the 1580s, surprisingly enough, were used to much more spiced-up meals if they could possibly afford it—with recipes not so different from the cuisine of France that survives to this day. British cooking did not become so notoriously bland until the 1800s, with the advance of the Industrial Revolution.[26] The two people's ideas of proper liquids to drink with meals were also in opposition. Where the Indians were able to drink pure water, the English recognized that their available water supply was often polluted—they knew not how—and thus whenever possible they drank low-alcohol ale, and later beer, that had been brewed and its water content purified. The English newcomers to the Indian towns must therefore have been very uncomfortable at first with the idea of having water with a meal, not to mention wishing that the food would have more taste. In one last matter, though, both peoples of the 1580s differ from us in the twenty-first century: they were accustomed to seeing the late spring and early summer, before the crops came in, as times of shortages, when people could go hungry. However, the Indians did have one big advantage at such times: they could turn to wild sources like freshwater tuckahoe that were available all year. In the lower Tidewater, they could harvest oysters. Actual famines were more rare here than in Europe—although by 1607 the Mid-Atlantic region would be heading into one.

One last area of life in which ethnic differences would have presented themselves even before the language barrier began fading was the everyday work done by men and women in the Indian towns. These English people, if refugees, would not have remained waited-upon guests for long, especially with the crop failure that fall. If they were captives, they would have been put to work immediately. And the ex-colonists would have had very different experiences, depending on whether they were men or women.

Men's work in the Indian world consisted of a few very intense jobs, in which a much higher proficiency was expected than English men were prepared for: hunting and war expeditions, with resting up and preparing for the next occasion, both physically and mentally, being important "work" between times. Staying focused on hunting helped them stay focused for war, and vice versa. Indian men had been in training for these few jobs almost since infancy, and their attitude toward poor performers was contemptuous to say the least. Very few English males were brought up to hunting and war, because frequent hunting and occasional leading of troops into war (of a different kind) were reserved for the upper levels in the social pyramid. Not only that, but in England the weapons used in the two activities overlapped only a little: pikes were not used in hunting, and falcons were not used in war. It is safe to say that few of the men of the "Lost Colony" would have been proficient with firearms, because they came from other social levels and had learned other trades, skills that were necessary to building a fort and a town and cultivating foods for the inmates. Initially their possession of firearms and metal tools would have given them some cachet in Indian eyes, and perhaps some tolerance of early mistakes. But once the ammunition ran out and the tools were traded, lost, or broken, the necessary learning of the Indian version of hunting would have been a long, drawn-out, excruciating process accompanied by ridicule, spoken aloud or not. Meanwhile, English men would have been deemed analogous to the semi-men in the Indian towns, who mostly helped with women's work. The frustration inherent in being treated that way might well have made some men explode in anger — English people were prone to angry outbursts anyway, as we shall see — and that could have gotten many of them killed, even if they had not been war captives to begin with. The English men in the Indian towns were definitely in a precarious position.

The English women would have been in a far better place for surviving and adjusting. Not that they were meek and lowly; they, too, engaged in arguments and even brawls back home, which would have been frowned on in Indian society. But they were already trained, in a general way, for much of the work they were given to do. Cooking, hauling water, child care, gardening, and dealing with clothing and household furnishings have always been women's work in human cultures, leading one anthropologist to speak of "the free-masonry of women."[27] The work that was familiar to them at home but missing among their new neighbors was caring for domestic livestock and the food preparation arising from it.[28] That did not mean less work to do, of course; the Indian women's very extensive, unspecialized job list made up for it. The work least familiar to the failed colony's women would have been all that collecting of wild plants, because the plants themselves were new to them. They would have been expected to learn the botany that Indian girls began learning as toddlers—and do it through the remnants of the language barrier (figure 7.1).

Foraging for wild plants to eat would have been a more pressing necessity than usual as the three-year drought set in. It is too bad that the least familiar work for the English women became so urgent just as they were settling in among Indian families.

The English who were refugees probably brought their remaining supplies with them, but when those ran out, they became dependent upon the hard-pressed Indian families. Among the women of both peoples, as they tried to learn to work together, there must have been a good deal of frustration and resentment.

At this point, we need to look at what the English "national character" was like in the 1580s, for it was not a promising one for long-lasting, peaceful relations with the Native people they were forced to merge with. As the language barrier wore down, the two sides would get to know even better the workings of each other's minds, and that created even more potential for strife. Both peoples were ethnocentric and, probably, downright xenophobic; the English were certainly the latter, according to foreign Europeans who lived among them.[29] The Indians had long assimilated captive people, but those people were other Eastern Woodland Indians, whose ways were not nearly as distant from their own as the English ones were.

The English of the 1580s were not the dignified, stiff-upper-lip stereotype of Victorian times; any acquaintance with Shakespeare's plays will demonstrate that. They were, in fact, volatile—and proud of it. They belonged to a nation of people trying to rise socially and economically, in whatever ways they could.[30] Their religion, Christianity, had several variants, and within the previous century their country had been involved, like other European countries, in bloody squabbles about which variant was "right." (Yet they all agreed that non-Christians were scarcely human.) In the sixteenth century, England had produced mariners who sailed around the world in small, clumsy ships, as well as adventurous people who had tried—so

FIGURE 7.1 Indian hemp (*Apocynum cannabinum*).

far, unsuccessfully—to establish colonies on other continents, with or without the permission of the locals. At home, among themselves, the English believed firmly in authoritarian hierarchies in both society and the family; the higher the position, the greater the power to give orders. They also had a great tolerance for loud arguments between equals and for physical violence, especially toward inferiors such as children, in order to maintain those hierarchies.[31] Even within the nuclear family (husband, wife, children), one's position in the hierarchy usually outweighed all other considerations. One historian, Lawrence Stone, has written this of them:

> Such personal correspondence and diaries as survive suggest that social relations [among the English] from the fifteenth to the seventeenth centuries tended to be cool, even unfriendly. The extraordinary [compared to 1970s America] amount of casual inter-personal physical and verbal violence, as recorded in legal and other records, shows clearly that at all levels men and women were extremely short-tempered. . . . Alienation and distrust of one's fellow man are the predominant features of the Elizabethan and early Stuart view of human character and conduct. . . . What is being postulated for the sixteenth and early seventeenth centuries is a society in which a majority of the individuals who composed it found it very difficult to establish close emotional ties to any person.[32]

Ian Mortimer writes of "the bold abrasive character of the people." He adds, "It is the self-confidence of youth that gives Elizabethan society much of its arrogance and determination. . . . The Elizabethan character is an amalgam of rashness, boldness, resolution, and violence—all mixed in a heady brew of destructive intolerance."[33] And that was how they treated their fellow English! Convinced that their ways of life were right, and prepared to be openly aggressive about it: this was not the kind of character to make absorption, however gradual, into a different, especially a non-Christian, culture a smooth process for the "Lost Colonists." That would be even truer as the language barrier broke down and the two peoples became aware of a new set of differences between them.

Respect and deference toward elders and social superiors was highly valued in both cultures; it has been described as "a bulwark of Tudor life."[34] Not unexpectedly, though, it took different forms in each society. The English had such an elaborately stratified society that books of instruction on proper behavior were a popular read, and open discussions of "proper behavior" were common. The Indians' society was simpler and less scheduled, and parents expected children to learn the rules—at their own speed—by quiet observation. Native people rarely explained "propriety" in words. For instance, hardly any of the ex-colonists' hosts would tell them, when they gave offense, that "good" behavior among Native people involved avoiding even a hint of aggression. If the Algonquian speakers were at all like the traditionalists in western American Indian tribes today (and John Lawson does make them sound so), then they took nonaggressiveness farther than any European would have believed possible. One example of the differences in "politeness" will suffice. According to Hugh Rhodes's *The Boke or Schoole of Good Manners* (1577)—and according to most Anglo-Americans today—it is proper to keep up a good deal of eye contact when conversing with someone, to indicate polite attention.[35] By Indian standards, however, that much eye contact means pure aggression; good manners require looking away the whole time while listening carefully.[36] The potential for either side to annoy the other one—all day, every day—should be obvious.

So now we move into the areas of life where intangibles such as attitudes and beliefs are crucial to understanding people's behavior: family, child-rearing, politics, and religion. Needless to say, the Carolina Algonquian speakers and the Tudor English were different, if not poles apart, in their understanding of what was "normal," "acceptable," "proper," and so on in relating to other people and also to the higher power(s).

Family, in both societies, was supposed to be primary in one's life and to consist of people who could be trusted to be on one's side. Early observers say little about the structure of Indian families (see chapter 3) and only tantalizing bits about the relations between the various members. Parent-child relations were very warm, indeed, at the same time that husbands and wives seem to have been fairly autonomous from each other in their working partnerships. Among the English, on the other hand, we know from contemporary records that relations between even closely related family members were often cool, hierarchical, and repressive.[37]

Women in England were servants to their husbands—by law. The husband held his own property and also that of his wife, and he could do anything with it that he wanted without consulting her. She, on the other hand, had to get his permission even to draw up a will, much less sell anything. She could not let any nonfamily members into the house without his consent. "She [could] be chastised or beaten with impunity by her husband as long as he [did] not actually kill her. . . . And many men [did] beat their wives, whether because of [the husband having] a violent nature, [or] a disagreement, or an act [on her part] of disobedience." She had more autonomy if she were a spinster or a widow, but her rights still would not approach those of a man.[38] The English women who merged with Indian townspeople in the Carolina Sounds may soon have gotten used to the easier-going, more independent ways of Indian wives and husbands. On the other hand, the English men would have expected far more obedience and also deference from Indian wives than they would ever get. They would have been nonplussed at the children of divorce staying with their mother, and they would have been appalled by the tolerance shown in the Indian towns to adulterous wives. They had been reared in a patrilineal and patriarchal culture that kept the children with their father and blamed an adulterous wife, not her lover.[39] In joining the Indian world, English men would have lost many of their privileges around the house. And if they became too violent about it, their Indian in-laws would have taken action, possibly lethal action.

The attitudes of the Carolina Algonquian speakers and of the English toward children and child-rearing differed widely and would have caused conflict as soon as English women began helping Indian mothers with babysitting and vice versa. There would also have been serious conflict between spouses over how to rear the children in any interethnic marriages that occurred in the first generation or so after 1587.

Indian children learned at their own pace by observing; everyone assumed that children are reasonable beings, in need only of being shown an example. No physical correction was used. Adults simply waited until their children caught on and conformed, of their own will.

English children underwent an entirely different process, for the adults around them assumed that "immature children were . . . regarded as mere animals lacking the capacity to reason, and [were] therefore to be broken in just as one would break in a puppy, a foal or a hawk."[40] Among the English, the Puritans in particular looked to the doctrine of original sin, which led them to think that children were inherently sinful until trained to be otherwise.[41] Since sinful beings were expected to resist changing, their will had to be broken not only by scolding but also by whipping and beating to teach them respect for authority.[42] Such punishments became ever more common, as the Puritan movement gained momentum, until by the seventeenth century "caning" was frequently dealt out even to university students.[43] English children were reared in a culture that had strict hierarchies both socially and within the family, and children ranked low in both cases. Making them learn and practice deference to their betters was a major goal in child-rearing.[44] Looking for "misbehavior" and "correcting" it, rather than controlling it by expressing affection and winning children over, were common for some, but not all, Elizabethan English people who dealt with children.[45]

English children were taught—lectured at—by their parents only in their early years. By their early teens they were handed over to others, who were assumed to be not only knowledgeable but also unlikely to "go soft" with youngsters who were not their own offspring. Thus many English children left home and were apprenticed to workmen to learn trades, and meanwhile to earn their keep as boarders. Higher-echelon parents "fostered out" their children, sending them to live with (and work for) families of yet higher status in hopes of their children later rising to that level. Meanwhile, those parents were taking in other people's children from socially inferior families, and so on. This "musical chairs" game with children was very widespread in England, and it appalled continental Europeans who watched it.[46]

The reaction of the Carolina Algonquian speakers to hearing of such things may be imagined. Who would want a woman with those attitudes babysitting their precious little ones? The English, for their part, called the Indians "indulgent" parents, which was not a compliment. And the instances of "wrong" or "foolish" behavior of the adults toward children on one side, in the eyes of the other side's adults, would have increased the longer the ex-colonists lived among the Indians—until (if ever) they adopted Indian ways. The English youngsters who had been brought to the Indian towns probably liked the Indian way of dealing with children, and as they grew up and became parents themselves, they may have clashed with surviving ex-colonist parents about how to raise their offspring "properly."

The Native people's ideas of good government differed sharply from those of the Tudor English who tried to settle on Roanoke Island. Chiefs were moderately powerful leaders who led partly because of personal ability and influence and partly because of belonging to a chiefly family. People exercised a great deal of self-restraint to prevent quarrels from occurring, since when that happened, there were no justices of the peace or police to intervene. On the other hand, coming from an extremely hierarchical society with hereditary absolute rulers and an elaborate legal system to enforce "the Queen's peace," the "Lost Colonists" must have felt very unsettled when they realized how informal the culture was that they now had to merge with. Their aggressiveness and quickness to take offense and become physical about it would have put them in daily jeopardy of causing their Native hosts terrible offense, at the least, and of getting them killed, at the worst. Nobody from the Indian side could have intervened, even in an Indian-English squabble, for it was not their business. Somebody on the

English side would probably have tried to interfere, for being one's brother's keeper was perfectly acceptable back home. But to the Indian onlookers, the interference would have been just as appalling as the original quarrel. There was probably much more interpersonal strife breaking out into the open once the English arrived in the Indian towns. Any inveterately quarrelsome English people would initially have been shunned and later would have been told to leave (or worse).

Both peoples believed in superhuman power and had rituals for invoking it, as well as individuals with special ability to communicate with the supernatural. But there the resemblance ended. The Algonquian speakers were polytheists and, if they were like their Powhatan relatives, they were easygoing about which deities other people chose to emphasize in their prayers.[47] The English, meanwhile, were monotheists who insisted that everybody should believe—in detail—in the "right" form of Christianity. Their disagreements about which form was the "right" one (variants running from Catholicism to Puritanism) only made the arguments more virulent, and blood had been shed in their home country within living memory. Religion and the controversies surrounding it were never far from English minds. Pressuring people—which could extend from arguing with them in public up through royalty issuing compulsory edicts backed up by capital punishment—was an integral part of the situation. Of tolerance, there was little in Tudor England. Many people from such a background would not easily have adapted to the polite, restrained laissez-faire practices of the Carolina Sounds people, who followed their belief in good manners and did no evangelizing whatever. There must have been eruptions at times, at least on the part of the English newcomers, which would have strained relations for some time afterward.

When people get injured or become sick, they feel vulnerable, and their first impulse is to get help in the way their own culture provides. Only later, in desperation after "their" medicine fails them, do they turn to other kinds of cures. That is what the ex-colonists from Roanoke Island had to do eventually. Their medical beliefs about the causes of disease were different from those of their hosts, and so, therefore, were their cures. European medical beliefs were not based upon science but upon a theory of four substances in the body that had to be kept in balance. Historians often say that the cures did more harm than good, for they often involved substance removal, such as bloodletting to restore the "balance." American Indian beliefs were not based upon science either, being supernatural cures based upon supernaturally caused maladies, but they could do wonders for patients' morale, thus helping the patients to cure themselves. Regardless, the English newcomers and their offspring would ultimately have had to put their trust in Indian medical practitioners, if for no other reason than that their own medically educated persons had died out. Fortunately, back in England they had had their own informal tradition, more or less underground, of going to local herbalists and charm-makers—who ran the risk of being accused of witchcraft—and also to their priests, whether Catholic or Church of England, for healing that the "doctors of medicine" could not or did not provide.[48] That tradition would have made the transfer to Indian doctoring easier for the "Lost Colonists" than it would be for most modern Americans.

We often hear of European diseases like tuberculosis, even the common cold, carrying off New World people after first contact. That worked both ways. There were "bugs"—unidentified disease vectors—in the Mid-Atlantic region up through the seventeenth century, and they carried off so many English immigrants who had no immunity to them that Virginia colonists spoke of one's first year in the region as "the seasoning," analogous to seasoning wood. The ex-Roanoke colonists must have lost some people that way, and even Indian medicine would not have prevented it. We have no way of knowing how many of the ex-colonists got "seasoned" and lived long enough to encounter the difficulties with their hosts that are described in this chapter.

It would have been a very rocky road that any surviving ex-colonists had to travel to fit into the Carolina Algonquian speakers' world, yet when no English ships managed to rescue them, that was the only road open to them other than starving to death. They had to learn some new skills to become useful neighbors in the Indian towns, and that would have been challenge enough. But simultaneously with all the work, it would have been very hard indeed to have to change their lifelong attitudes toward "proper" behavior to adults and "right" treatment of children—across the language barrier, no less. Some of the English would have been better at it than others, but even they would have taxed the forbearance of their hosts. The three-year drought must have made things worse, because everybody had to work harder to collect wild foods in order to stay alive. Even Indian tempers would have been shorter than usual. But their treatment of foreigners who tried to get along was generally kind, and as we know from the stories of European captives of the Indians of later centuries,[49] the captives not infrequently bonded with their captors over time, some of them so strongly that they refused rescue when it finally arrived. Some of the "lost" colonists must have succeeded in finding a new life and new family ties among their Indian hosts.

On many fronts, the children among the Lost Colony English would have become "Indianized" and at ease in the Indian towns to a greater extent than their parents could manage, due if nothing else to their learning the locals' language at an earlier age, being more fluent, and taking in more of the culture as participants from childhood onward. The children of Indian-English unions would also have been better at negotiating the differences between the two worlds. That would, of course, have caused a "generation gap" of major proportions between them and their English parents. That is still happening in the families of immigrants the world over.

In later times, such "between two worlds" children frequently grew up to become intermediaries between their townsmen and visiting Europeans, because they were bilingual as well as to some extent bicultural. But there is no record of such a person who might be a "Lost Colonist" or the child of one in the Sounds region. We have only those tantalizing hints of mixed-blood people sighted by English visitors some decades later. And with that, we shall have to be content.

The tragedy was that the Carolina Algonquians' way of life, so strong in the 1580s, would be seriously threatened when late in the next century many more English arrived, took up the people's land with or without their cooperation, and treated them with increasing hostility. The Native people, if they wanted to appease those neighbors and survive, would then have to change their ways to conform with English ones—another rocky road.

CHAPTER EIGHT

Merging in the Other Direction

BY WESLEY D. TAUKCHIRAY AND HELEN C. ROUNTREE

The decades following 1587 in the Carolina Sounds are largely a closed book to us, because the Native people had no writing—they didn't need it—and because the English, who did have it, were not yet moving into the region in any great numbers and leaving records. Nearly all the records we have in coastal North Carolina after 1587 date after the 1660s. Immigrants from Virginia probably began filtering in during the 1630s, and patents for land along what is now the Virginia–North Carolina border south of Hampton Roads began to be recorded in the 1640s.[1] More immigrants came from South Carolina as well after that, and by 1670 there were enough settlers in the region for formal, English provincial governments to be established. Even then, northeastern North Carolina retained the atmosphere of a "border region" for many more years, with a European population that was relatively classless and reluctant to adhere to any strong government.[2] Yet they were almost as land hungry as their more "loyal" compatriots.

The region's Algonquian speakers, in spite of the admixture of English genes and perhaps some inherited memories of European ways, still practiced an economy that relied heavily upon wild sources of food, which meant that they traveled over large tracts of territory to where the sources were, collecting them. The English relied much more on domesticated—and through hybridizing, more productive (for people)—species of plants and animals, and because they planted or herded them intensively and spent much labor on protecting them, English families could subsist on much smaller tracts of land than Indian families could. However, there were many people in England who, encouraged by their government and their evangelistic religion, decided to migrate to North America. That was especially true once tobacco was established as a cash crop to get "rich" with. It did not matter that each English family needed less land; there were too many families crossing the Atlantic. As those immigrants began pouring into the Sounds region, the Native people were crowded onto an ever-shrinking land base, and their rights to their own homeland were ignored, making it harder to live in their age-old manner. The men, whose whole identity was that of hunter-warriors, suffered more than the women, who were already part-time farmers.

In the face of pushy English people flooding into their territories, the North Carolina Algonquian speakers went through a process of culture change (the anthropological term) very like that of other Indians in North America in more recent centuries. The end result was a way of life so drastically altered that most outsiders no longer recognized them as Indians. Some of them, for that matter, no longer considered *themselves* to be Indians. For most people, the word "[American] Indian" conjures up an image of someone who is frozen in time, the time being back when Europeans first met the local people, who were wearing different clothing, speaking a different language, and so on. Real Indian people, of course, are not fossils, but the stereotype persists.

The cultural changes in eastern North Carolina happened gradually; there were no "praying towns," no missions for Indian children to be forced into, unlike seventeenth-century New England and the western United States in the nineteenth and twentieth centuries where the aim was complete Anglicization within a generation or two. Instead, in eastern North Carolina (as also in Virginia), the changes were slow and led gradually to still other changes.

The first things Native people adopted were things that fitted easily into the way of life they already had: cutting tools, weapons, and things that could be used as jewelry and status symbols. We have already seen that beginning to happen in the 1580s.

A subsequent change was for higher-status people in the Indian towns to acquire (by gift) some English clothing and to begin wearing it at formal meetings with English leaders. Old-style garb on ordinary days remained the fashion for much longer. In some cases Native chiefs had an English-style house built in their towns, both as a status symbol and also as a concrete expression of an alliance with the English. In Virginia at least, such houses often had fruit trees, especially peaches, planted in an orchard nearby. In Virginia, where records of early decades are better, this kind of change occurred within fifty or sixty years of the arrival of the first permanent European settlers.

Ordinary Indian people began acquiring European livestock, but for many years they did not practice confining and breeding it. Instead, they turned it loose in the woods and then hunted it. Before long, only the hogs were left, being the only large domesticated animal that was able to thrive without pastureland being cleared for it (brackish-marsh grassland sufficed, if available). Later on, when Indian people's hunting territories were diminishing and they began fencing in both their cornfields and their animals, the variety of livestock they kept increased again, as did, now, the number of English-style buildings (log cabins at first) to house people as well as animals.

In the early days of having the English as neighbors, interpreters were a necessity. It is possible that enough English speech had been passed down in some Indian families with Lost Colonist ancestors that family members could slip easily into that role. Regrettably, no records were made in those decades to confirm or disprove the idea.

In the years when English traders were the primary people the Indians met (i.e., in the mid-seventeenth century), there were real economic rewards for being able to work closely with such visitors. But as more foreigners moved in as settlers, more Indian people learned some English, often because the settlers, who wanted the Indians to give up their land, saw no good reason to learn the language of a people who (they hoped) were going to leave. The Indians, of course, had no intention of leaving, but they had perforce to learn English, if nothing else in order to be able to complain effectively to the English colonial officials. By the early 1700s, the surviving documents show Indian leaders who not only spoke a fair amount of English but who also had adopted English personal names, though they probably still used their Indian names and language at home.

Some Native people died of maladies we can identify, some of them English in origin and others that were already among the people. There are very few records of epidemics (an example is a sketchy mention of one hitting the Pamlico River area in the 1690s), but smallpox and alcohol are known to have taken a toll. Though John Lawson was likely exaggerating, since he was in many ways writing a propaganda piece to encourage further English colonization, he wrote in 1709, "The small-pox and rum have made such a destruction amongst them that, on good grounds, I do believe, there is not the sixth [one-sixth as many] savages living within two hundred miles of all our settlements, as there were fifty years ago."[3] Rum could make those otherwise carefully restrained people lose their inhibitions and fight among themselves, sometimes to the death; others, losing their coordination, fell into the open hearths and burned to death. There were still intertribal enmities that caused raiding on other Indian towns,[4] though rarely on English settlements. And lastly, among those beleaguered, crowded-together, Indian people there was often personal strife that led to poisoning one another. Indian people had known about several vegetable poisons before Europeans ever arrived. One mentioned specifically by Lawson grew in "the fresh marshes" and was probably water hemlock (or cowbane; *Cicuta maculata*), an extremely strong poison (a walnut-sized bit can kill a cow) that was also known to the Powhatan people in Virginia.[5]

Facing the loss of their land and a decrease in their population, the Indian communities no longer followed hereditary chiefs or, a bit later, their priests. Those chiefs and priests had not, after all, been able to staunch the flow of foreigners into their homeland, and it is also possible that much of their knowledge had died with them if an epidemic occurred and they were its victims. (In a nonliterate society, elders' memories, passed on orally with dignity and respect for the supernatural powers [i.e., slowly] are the only way of preserving knowledge.) Priests as curers probably lasted longer than chiefs, for people still got sick or injured. By the early 1700s leadership positions seem to have gone to the men—in North Carolina, unlike Virgina, we hear of no female leaders—who regardless of family affiliation were best able to handle the often difficult relations with aliens who looked down on Native people and wished them gone.

In eastern North Carolina, many of the above changes did not occur until well after 1700, and even then there were people in the towns who did not want to participate. Where enough of the people's land remained in their possession, one or another faction budded off into a separate town. Where there was not enough land, the two factions lived unhappily together, as is the case on many western Indian reservations today. The internal conflict, and the feeling of being a tiny minority in a land that was once theirs, led some individuals and some families to do what social scientists call "spinning off"— that is, giving up and leaving altogether for another place, gradually merging with other people. They might or might not keep up with the relatives they had left; later generations might or might not remember that they had ancestors from a certain tribe, or even that they had Indian ancestors at all.

Thus the Indians in the Sounds region did not vanish; they only became harder to distinguish from other ethnic groups in the region. Many people "spun off" into English society, where their descendants live today. Others moved in with friendly but more distant tribes, to get away from the English; the Secotas may have served that purpose for a time. Still others held on for a long time as communities that identified themselves as Indian. Few Algonquian speakers died in a war with the English, because other than the Tuscarora War of 1711–15, there were no major English-Indian wars in North Carolina. During that war, of course, there were losses, no matter with whom the Algonquian speakers sided. But for a very long time, Indian-descended communities who remembered their antecedents survived in eastern North Carolina.

By 1709, John Lawson reported that the people who were conservative enough that he recognized them as Indians, and who were descended from

Algonquian speakers, were living in only ten towns, with reduced populations and, in most cases, different names from those the Roanoke would-be colonists had encountered. They were, in fact, self-identifying by the names of their towns, and the English were following suit.

Formerly Roanoke: Hatteras, one town on the Sand Banks near
   Cape Hatteras, with sixteen men.
Formerly Pomeioke: Pamptico, one town at the "island,"
   with fifteen men.
Formerly Secota: Machapunga, one town, plus Mattamuskeet,
   one town, for a total of thirty men; Bear River, one town, plus
   Raudauqua-quank, one town, for a total of fifty men.
Formerly Weapemeoc: Jaupim (Yeopim), only six people still living
   together; Paspatank, one town on the river of that name, with ten
   men; Poteskeet, one town on the North River with thirty men.
Formerly Chowanoke: Chowan, one town on Bennett Creek,
   with fifteen men.

Using Lawson's estimated ratio of two men to every three women and children gives us a population of only 283 Indian people still living a tribal existence. We should note that the more populous groups (former Secotas, former Weapemeocs) were those more distant from areas where the English were settling more actively. Those groups may, then, have experienced fewer European diseases, or less temptation to "spin off" away from Indian society, or they may have received dissident Indians from elsewhere.

By 1731, the governor of North Carolina knew of only four communities remaining: Hatteras, Mattamuskeet, Poteskeet, and Chowanoke.[6] The Moseley map of 1733 shows much the same thing, though once again we should note that the map was part of a campaign for further English settlement. We shall follow the histories of these groups in the order given in the list above. The histories will be about the groups, not about individuals descended from them after they broke up (which would be tens of thousands by now, and legally merged with non-Indians).

One last matter: for as long as possible, Native people clung to their age-old ways. Nearly 120 years after the Roanoke colony failed, the Indian trader William Gale wrote to his father (on August 3, 1703) about the Indians of the Carolinas and Virginia: "They live in small towns and bark cabins, palisaded with 2 or 3 rows of stakes; every town or nation has its particular king and different language; they have some notion of the [Biblical] Flood, but very obscure. They offer the first fruits of every thing they eat to the devil, by whom they cure diseases and act several strange things, as laying [quelling] the wind, etc."[7] The Native people may have been flooded out in their own region and hard for visitors to find amid all the immigrants, but for them the real merging into English culture would come only in the eighteenth century, if not later.

Croatoan

We need to look at this sixteenth-century group because of its famous association with the Lost Colony. The settlement of that name was one of three towns along a ridge running west from Cape Hatteras (shown on Theodor de Bry's map but not John White's), and as detailed in chapter 2, the English records are not clear about whether it was a year-round town or a seasonal camp. The name "Croatoan" does not appear at all in any post-sixteenth-century records, indicating that the people, who were already allied with, if not part of, the Roanoke chiefdom, appear in those later records under another name, probably "Hatteras." Correspondingly, the name Hatteras, applied to people rather than to the Cape, only begins appearing in the later records.

Roanoke, Later Called Hatteras and Part of Mattamuskeet

In the 1580s, the Roanoke paramount chiefdom under Wingina occupied Roanoke Island, the Outer Banks down at least to Cape Hatteras, and much of the south side of Albemarle Sound in what are now Dare and Tyrrell Counties. The incoming English saw more of the Roanokes than of any other Algonquian speakers because they chose to build their fort within a stone's throw of the chief's town. Not surprisingly, they also alienated those neighbors earlier than almost any other Indian group. The main published source on the Roanokes' subsequent history is a short piece by Dunbar, to which the senior author of this chapter has much to add from his research.[8] An article by Brooks has added considerably to the picture.[9] Yet more research needs to be done, however, because there is at least one modern organization claiming to be a "tribe" descended from that chiefdom.

The map in John Lawson's book shows the town named "Roanoke" located inside the elbow of Cape Hatteras[10]—where a Croatoan town was in the 1580s (map 8.1). Lawson wrote that he talked with the "Hatteras" Indians of his time, who told him that they used to frequent Roanoke Island, which by 1700 was firmly in the hands of the English. They added that "several of their ancestors were white people, and could talk in a book [i.e., read] as we do; the truth of which is confirmed by gray eyes being found frequently amongst these Indians and no others. They value themselves extremely for their affinity to the English, and are ready to do them all friendly offices."[11] It is likely that given their coastal situation, other people from across the ocean, besides the "Lost Colonists," added their genes to any that those colonists had contributed 120 years before.[12] Baylus Brooks has suggested that by the end of the seventeenth century, there were two towns on the cape—a more Anglicized one closer to Buxton, whose men may have participated in English whaling expeditions, and a more conservative one on the site of the sixteenth-century town near Frisco.[13] That would be in keeping with the culture change and the differences of opinion about it that were then going on among the people.

In 1714, the Hatterases' alliance with the English during the Tuscarora War brought trouble, for they had to take refuge on an English plantation for a time, after enemy Indians (Tuscaroras and perhaps others) had attacked them.[14] They were paid in the next year, apparently for fighting alongside the English, and in 1720 the colonial government provided them with ammunition.[15] The 1733 Moseley map shows two Indian houses at their old town site near the cape, indicating two towns.[16] A report on Indians in the colony, probably dated in early 1755, listed them as having eight or ten people.[17] If that meant eight or ten men, then their population would have been about twenty-five people.

By then there were English settlers moving in near them. Their leader, Thomas Elks, complained about it to the colony's governor in 1756, but his allegations of multiple encroachments were disproved. The Hatteras group in that year had only three male members, one of them being "a small boy." Three years later, in an attempt to protect their remaining lands, a patent in the name of William Elks, the other adult male besides Thomas, was issued to them for two hundred acres at "Currituck including the old Indian town." That could indicate a move northward, but the patent seems to have done them no good. Within two more years, the missionary Alexander Stewart was writing of them as living at Mattamuskeet, on the mainland.[18] We will pick up their subsequent history below in discussing the Mattamuskeet Reservation.

Some members still owned the group's land on the cape. In 1788, two sisters named Elks sold that 200-acre tract to an Englishman; its boundaries indicated that it was the land granted the Hatterases back in 1759.[19] "By then," says Brooks, "being an 'Indian' may merely have been an understanding, rather than being an observable trait."[20]

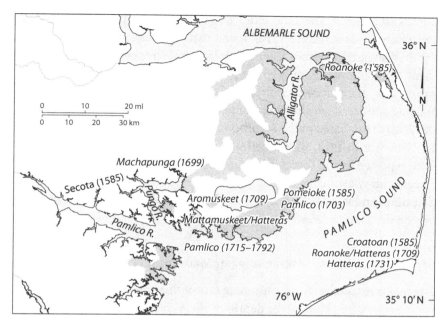

MAP 8.1 Historic period locations of the Roanoke/Hatteras, Pomeioke/Pamlico, and Secota/Mattamuskeet Indians. Light gray areas are wetlands.

In succeeding decades, their descendants mixed with their English neighbors on the island, and they have traceable descendants living there today. Brooks concludes, "Indians remained on Hatteras Island throughout the eighteenth century and perhaps remain even today. Past speculation about Hatteras, however, has favored migration away from the island to explain the 'missing' Indians, or the absence of Indian phenotypes [physical appearance]."[21]

Pomeioke, Later Called Pamlico or Pamptico

The sixteenth-century Pomeiokes occupied territory from the mouth of the Pamlico River northeastward to include Lake Mattamuskeet (which the Indians called Paquip), in what are now Beaufort and Hyde Counties. Some scholars have considered them to be part of the Secotas or Roanokes, though the eyewitness accounts are vague on the matter.[22]

Seventeenth-century accounts of the group, now called Pamlicos, are few. In 1695–96, a former governor of North Carolina wrote about hearing of "a great mortality that fell upon the Pemlico [sic] Indians," possibly being due to smallpox.[23] The Gale letter of 1703 mentions them, calling them Pampticos. A deposition of 1707 stated that they were hostile enough that the English nearby went in fear of their lives and were considering capturing them, once and for all, to keep the peace.[24] From the beginning of the Tuscarora War, they made the mistake of going against the English, with devastating results when the Tuscaroras withdrew to their own territory and the English retaliated in the Pamlico River area.[25] The last mention of them by name was in 1718, when the Indians of their area—a weak remnant—were reported as still threatening the settlers.[26]

Taukchiray estimates that only seven or eight of them remained alive at that time, and it is likely that those individuals joined the refugee community on the Mattamuskeet Reservation thereafter.[27]

Secota, Later Called Machapunga or Mattamuskeet

The major researcher for the ultimate fate of this chiefdom is archaeologist Pat Garrow, who plumbed the depths of the records of Hyde County, where the community had its last pieces of reservation land.

The Secotas occupied the Pamlico River area in what is now Beaufort County. Next to nothing was recorded about them in the seventeenth century, though John Lawson may have seen enough of them that he included Secota data in his account of "Indian" culture. He was told that they had successfully ambushed their enemies to the south, the Corees, at some time before they acquired firearms from the English.[28] By the early 1700s the name "Secota" had faded away, and they were known by the names "Machapunga" (two towns on the Pungo River named "Bear or Bay River" and Raudauqua-quank) and "Aromuskeet" (two towns on or near Lake Mattamuskeet named Machapunga and Mattamuskeet). The first pair of towns had thirty fighting men and the second pair fifty, suggesting that their total population was around two hundred people.

They made a formal peace with the colony of North Carolina on September 23, 1699, at which time their chief was a Bear River man named Sothel (an English planter's name). Any quarrels they had with English people were henceforward to be handled by an English court, and people shipwrecked in their territory were to be rescued and handed over to an English planter. They were to pay a tribute of ten skins to the governor every year. A copy of the treaty was to be kept at Raudauqua-quank, rather than at Bear River, indicating that people were leaving the latter.[29] By 1709, the Bear River site had been deserted; 125 of the people lived at

Raudauqua-quank, and 75 more lived over at Lake Mattamuskeet in the two settlements there.[30] As we shall see, the migration was a result of English settlers moving in, at least some of them being purchasers rather than squatters.

The Native people were taking on English names by then, though they probably retained Indian-language names for use within the family. The great men who signed the treaty along with Sothel were Matheny, Edmund, Captain Gibbs, Luis, and George Higher (later Hiter). In spite of this apparent drawing closer to the English, with the personal names and the treaty, relations between the two peoples remained distinctly uneasy, partially because the Indians were not at ease among themselves. The records from 1701 through 1704 show more than one chief: a "King Charles" at Machapunga and "King Luther" at Bear River; the Lake Mattamuskeet and the Pungo River sectors were autonomous from each other. The people, both sexes of them, were having trouble with alcohol, something that afflicted the other surviving tribes. The Machapunga chief's wife upbraided their son for drinking too much—a public scolding that was still unthinkable among her own contemporaries—and the young man, aged about twenty, told her that he "would have her satisfied." He went out and shot himself, in a suicide that said, "See what you made me do?"[31]

Trouble with individual Englishmen was also occurring. A deposition of 1701 describes some Machapungas turning hostile weapons on English passengers they were transporting by canoe; one of the Englishmen grabbed an Indian and pretended to kill him, so that his fellows fled the scene. There were also petitions from English settlers complaining of Indian "insolence" and hog killing. The English of North Carolina were doing what the Virginia English were engaged in: playing cheapskate and letting their hogs run free in the forest, where Indian hunters, taking no account of earmarks on the animals, hunted the pigs as if they were wild game. In the present complaint, an Indian man named "King Charles" had visited by night and warned his English neighbors that some of his people had moved to a "wilderness" place into which they could take refuge (meaning elsewhere around Lake Mattamuskeet?). Warrants were therefore issued to capture the Indian men from the canoe incident.[32] In October 1704 another Englishman made a deposition that stated that sixteen Bear River (now Machapunga) men under "King Luther" had raided and robbed his house, threatening to burn it and uttering obscenities in English. They had also stolen another Englishman's fishing gear, axe, and clothes at Drum Inlet. The next month, there were several complaints about Indian people threatening the English in Pamlico Precinct, as well as charging the English too much for land.[33] Some Indians, at least, were selling out and withdrawing.

In the Tuscarora War, the former Secotas sided with the Tuscaroras, for which they paid the same heavy price that their allies, the Pamlicos, did.[34] In January 1712 the North Carolina governor reported that among others, his army had killed many "Bay [Bear] River people" and Mattamuskeets, with about fifty men and two hundred women being taken prisoner (probably an exaggeration, remembering John Lawson's numbers). The governor estimated that only about fifty-five, plus or minus ten, people from four tribes (including the Corees and Neuses) were still living free on their own land.[35] The next month the colonial council decided to sell the "Bay River" captives as slaves because they had attacked English plantations, and a month later the order for selling was given.[36]

In August 1714, an English militia captain was ordered to go down the Outer Banks to make peace with "Pagett and the rest of the Indians," who were probably a Hatteras-descended sector of the Mattamuskeets. The militia contingent had a Poteskeet Indian with them, perhaps to be an interpreter if needed.[37] On February 11, 1715, the colony of North Carolina made peace with the Indians. The remaining Machapungas, Mattamuskeets, Neusiocks, and Corees all agreed to settle at Mattamuskeet town on the lake, thereby creating a multitribal refugee settlement. In 1717 a formal reservation was created there. The Corees were in need of refuge: their main town on the south side of the Neuse River had been lost in a 1714 land grab.[38]

In March 1716, Francis Lejau, an Anglican missionary, wrote to the Society for the Propagation of the Gospel that an English eyewitness had seen "Maramoskeets" sold as "slaves to be transported abroad." Caribbean islands like Antigua were being used by the Virginia colony for things like that.[39] The Mattamuskeets were now "dispersed, many killed or sold; yet there is a remnant of it settled somewhere not far from Renoque."[40] John Lawson had already heard of the two families so settled.[41] Three years later, when they were still peacefully settled, the colony gave ammunition to them for hunting.[42]

The people on the Mattamuskeet Reservation, whose leader was known as "King Squires," were granted land in 1727 between the lake and the Pamlico River; the Mosely map of 1733 shows their settlement just southeast of the lake. The land was to be held in socage (from an overlord, conditional upon performing certain services) rather than in fee simple (unconditional ownership); a quitrent of one shilling per hundred acres was to be paid for it on September 29 of each year.[43] The Indians were going to have to come up with a good many shillings annually; the reservation included an area about five by nine miles, from modern Englehard on the north to below Eyesocking Bay on the south.[44] It was, however, a big enough tract that Indian people who wanted to live there could do so while following their age-old economic practices. Not all of them did want to stay, however. The population was a small one, consisting mainly of Corees and Machapungas, who had formerly been enemies. The Corees seem to have left soon after the grant went into effect, moving in with the Tuscaroras—who were in the process of moving north to become the sixth nation of the Iroquois Five Nations. That left only people from the former Machapunga sector of the former Secotas, and their population was declining. In 1731 they had well under twenty families; in 1755, they had only "seven or eight fighting men." A deed made in 1761 was signed by only six adult males. Their surnames were Squires, Mackey, Long Tom, and Russell.[45]

The people's political structure had become much less formal than it had been with the chiefs of Thomas Hariot's time. John Squires was the leader (not called "chief") on the Mattamuskeet Reservation from 1718 to 1746, with at least two advisors, John Mackey and Long Tom, to assist him at one point. Squires's son Charles succeeded him—showing that the lateral matrilineality of the sixteenth century had ended by then—but he seems to have lost most of his power in 1752–60. The 1761 deed was signed by six heads of household, with no leader of any kind mentioned. Even John Squires probably had not had anything like the power, status, and exalted lifestyle of the old-time chiefs.[46] From evidence in the deeds, discussed below, the families were living scattered out along the creeks, in the old-fashioned way of Indian towns; John Squires's 150 acres were in the center, for travelers by water. Since none of these people left wills, which would have required estate inventories in the Hyde County records, only archaeology will tell us what their houses and furnishings and farm implements were like. They were probably in transition toward English material culture.[47]

The Mattamuskeet Reservation people began selling land even before they got their grant in 1727, and their sales continued until 1761, when all the land was gone.[48]

The now landless Squireses must have left the county, since no subsequent records in the area mention them. A missionary, Alexander Stewart, made two visits to the now-former reservation in 1761. In November he established a school for four Indian boys, four Indian girls, and two black boys; he also baptized six adults and fifteen children. The population, after the Squireses had left, had been augmented by some Roanoke/Hatteras people, he said, and a Christianized "northern Indian" was living there too. He wrote that the residents were mixing with whites, but it is uncertain whether he meant by marriages or by living in a checker-board pattern among white landowners.[49]

After 1761, with one exception, the Hyde County records are bare of references to Indians—by that label. A woman of unspecified tribe named Cati Collins—not a Mattamuskeet surname—was being held as a slave, and a neighbor tried to help her gain her freedom.[50] Hatteras Indian–descended people still bearing the name Elks appear as "free persons of color." Though they had "mixed" with the English, perhaps in marriage, in the 1760s, nineteenth-century Carolinians considered them to be nonwhite, possibly indicating that outmarriage was going in a different direction. In 1843 in Hyde County, there were two "unlawful" marriages (with whites) involving women named Elks. By 1850, Hyde County had only one Elks left: a fourteen-year-old girl living in a white household.[51]

The last appearance of the Mattamuskeet Reservation people as a group occurred in 1792. Seven Indians sold the reservation—again—to a white person; the county court accepted it as legal for some unspecified reason. The buyer later failed to assert his claim, but with all the earlier sales in place, it did not really matter. Several of the seven "sellers" were surnamed "Longtom" (now one word). Three of the seven were children; the adults were all women—a common pattern in tiny remnant Indian groups in the late stages of dispersal. It went along with poverty and the binding out of the children as apprentices, which the Hyde County records also demonstrate. The children's non-Indian parents were both white and black.[52]

By 1800, the Mattamuskeets could not have been properly called a tribe, and many whites did not call them "Indian" anymore either, thanks to the outmarriages, increasingly with blacks. Over the next century, most of the descendants lost even the memory of having Indian ancestry, because of the struggle to survive in poverty-stricken, broken families. Their economic woes were exacerbated by the increasing unrest around them, punctuated by slave rebellions, leading up to the Civil War. Gradually, as in other "slave" states, North Carolina stripped nonwhite people of nearly all their civil rights. Especially disruptive to Indian-descended parents in the three decades before the Civil War was Hyde County's aggressive policy of taking nonwhite children away from their parents and apprenticing them to white masters. Passing on of family memories became a sometime thing under those conditions.[53]

Family traditions of "Indian" ancestry were retained by only a few people, but the name of the tribe became lost. That was the situation that anthropologist Frank Speck would have found in the 1910s if he had focused on the Hyde County court records instead of looking only for people who still called themselves "Indians."[54]

Weapemeoc, Later Called Yeopim, Paspatank, and Poteskeet

The major researcher for this chiefdom is Whitney Petrey, who was interested in the Indians as watermen trying to keep going as such when they lost most of their waterfront property. Wes Taukchiray has also done a great deal of unpublished research in this area. The movements of the people as a group after 1585 are shown in map 8.2.

The Weapemeocs occupied the north side of Albemarle Sound in what are now Chowan, Perquimans, Pasquotank, Camden, and Currituck Counties. They were in regular contact not only with other Carolina Sound groups but also with the Chesapeake chiefdom in what is now Virginia Beach, because their foraging territories graded into one another. It was probably this group's chief who told the second English would-be colony on Roanoke Island to visit the Chesapeakes, which they apparently did in the winter of 1585–86.[55]

English visitors from the Virginia colony were coming into Weapemeoc territory by the 1640s. In 1645, during the Third Anglo-Powhatan War, a militia force went out into the Atlantic, down the coast, into Albemarle Sound, and attacked some of the chiefdoms, including "Yawopym [Yeopim] about Roanoke [River's mouth, i.e., the capital town at modern Edenton]." A physician with that force was paid for his services on the foray by Lower Norfolk County that fall.[56] The treaty between Virginia and the Powhatans, made in October 1646, attempted to set an English-Indian boundary—around the English, not the Indians. The boundary south of the James River went from "Yapin [Yeopim] to the black water [river], and from the head of the black water [near modern Petersburg] upon a strait line to the old Monkin town [Monacan, on the James River, well above the falls at modern Richmond]."[57]

The eastern extent of the boundary from "Yeopim" is uncertain, indicating that English settlers were not yet eyeing the area. That changed within a decade and a half, of course, when the chief, Kiscutanewh, began selling land. The earliest record we have of his sales is dated 1660, with another sale in 1663; on September 25 of the latter year, several Lower Norfolk County English people took out land patents with Virginia.[58] The area around modern Edenton, where the chief's town had been in the 1580s, is not mentioned; either it had already been abandoned to the English of North Carolina, or

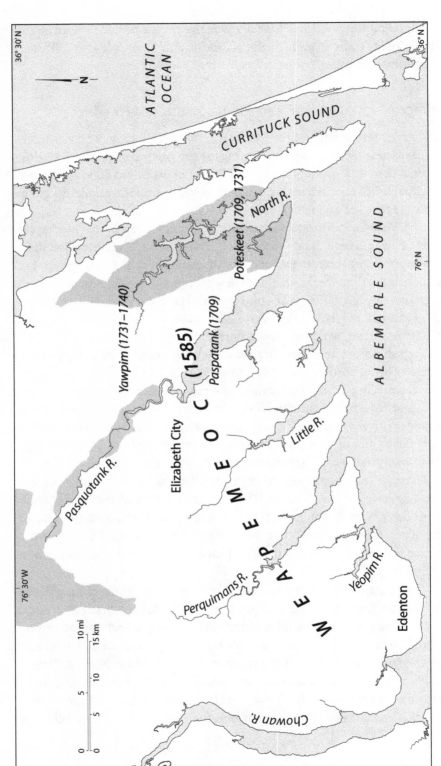

MAP 8.2 Historic period locations of the Weapemeoc/Yeopim Indians. Light gray areas are wetlands.

the records about it have not survived.[59] As they moved eastward, the Weapemeocs lost all touch with Indian peoples they had once known; by the late seventeenth century, former neighbors like the Meherrins had hardly even heard of them.[60] The surviving records show that Kiscutanewh was now selling his people's eastern lands piecemeal, disposing of tracts on the Perquimans and Pasquotank Rivers, one tract on the latter running "towards the head of the North River." One plot on the Perquimans River lay "nigh an Indian field," presumably being one still in use by Indian women (otherwise it would have been called an "old Indian field"). The Weapemeocs and the English were now definitely neighbors. It is uncertain whether or not Kiscutanewh understood that the English buyers intended to hold onto the land permanently, rather than use it and then return it to "public" use. He might have been less free in parting with his territory if he had known the full extent of the possessiveness that English law allowed.

In 1669, the lords proprietors of Carolina drew up a document setting a two-and-a-half-mile radius around Indian towns, within which no English were supposed to settle.[61] However, that same document said that land across a river from an Indian town could be taken up—and Indian towns were waterfront affairs lying on both sides of waterways, if those were creeks or rivers rather than sounds. That permission made the Native towns half-circles, not full circles, of land. (Virginia waited until 1705 to do the same thing.)

As with the other Carolina Sounds chiefdoms, we have very few further documents about the Weapemeocs in the seventeenth century, not even many English land patents. The next record about them dates from 1697, a time when one of their English neighbors wrote complacently that they were "so civilized as to come into English habits [of behavior], and have cattle of their own," though they had not yet converted to Christianity.[62] The "Yawpims," as the English now called them, nevertheless had to complain of encroachments on their remaining land that year, and an order of protection was made. The town involved was "above three miles from the northeast side of Pascotank [sic] river towards the said Indian town till they come to the head of the river."[63] The order seems to have done little good, and many of the Yeopims, as we shall call them hereafter, chose to move again.

On April 12, 1704, an order was given for four square miles of land to be surveyed for the Indians where they then lived, which was on both sides of the North River in the far eastern part of their original territory. A total of 10,240 acres was laid out for them, but the surveyor did not get paid in his lifetime; payment was finally made, half by the Yeopims themselves, in 1714.[64] This community was the one known as Poteskeet (we have found no record of any land being allocated to the other sectors of the tribe). The reservation was located near the North River's mouth, which with its access to shipping was already considered desirable by English would-be settlers. Though records on the subject are lacking, the Yeopims apparently sold off or lost that waterfront land and retained an area on the back up the river's headwaters, in Currituck County, south of Shawboro and east of Bellcross. Those headwaters of the North River are still called Indiantown Creek, and there is a crossroads called Indiantown to this day, not far south of the creek in Camden County.

For all of having so much land, the Yeopim population was diminishing, in both numbers and in distinctly "Indian" characteristics. The former chiefdom had split apart geographically into "Paspatanks," "Poteskeets," and "Yeopims." John Lawson wrote in 1709 of the Poteskeets being on the North River, as stated above; it was the largest sector of the tribe, with thirty men (and therefore seventy-five people). The Paspatank sector still lived on the Pasquotank River, but had only ten men (and therefore twenty-five people) residing there. The Yeopim "sector" had only six people, and Lawson neglected to say where they lived.[65]

There is evidence that the Poteskeets were more conservative in their ways than the Paspatanks, even retaining a chief (see below). William Gale's 1703 letter says, "Some [Indians] are civil [i.e., Anglicized] and some barbarous [i.e., traditional], they [the latter] using the Seaboard [i.e., living farther east, where there were fewer English settlers]."[66]

The Paspatanks were decidedly Anglicized, for they "did formerly keep cattle, and make butter."[67] Nonetheless, James Adams described the Poteskeets in 1710 as "about seventy or eighty Indians . . . many of which understand English tolerably well." By then, nobody was living in a sixteenth-century time warp. The smaller Yeopim community, if relations with the larger one were uneasy, would have had difficulty finding Indian marital partners, which would encourage unions with non-Indians. The children of such pairings, usually involving an Indian woman and a non-Indian man, remained in the Indian community and gradually brought further English influences into it, including the adoption of English first and last names.[68]

The Yeopims (Paspatanks and Poteskeets both) chose the winning side in the Tuscarora War, fighting alongside the English. In 1714, George Durant, "a Yawpim Indian" (community unknown), complained to the colonial governor that an Englishman had taken away "an Indian slave woman" that he had captured "when he was out against the Indian [Tuscarora] enemy"; he got compensation. In August of that year, a Poteskeet man named "Fisher" went along with a militia party to the Outer Banks to make peace with "Pagett and the rest of the Indians," who were probably Hatteras/Mattamuskeets.[69]

The next March, the Poteskeets had to get a government order against Englishmen living on Currituck Banks, which was the Indians' hunting territory. The settlers had been interfering with their necessary hunting.[70] Also in March 1715, Durant's people brought to the militia captain at Little River an Englishman charged with being in debt—for "2 years rent of their town land"; the debtor agreed to pay.[71]

The Poteskeets were not just renting land out; they were selling it—but retaining the right to hunt on it. In November 1715 the colonial government confirmed the sales but forbade any future selling.[72] That, of course, was not the end of the matter. In 1723, "John Durant, King [Chief]; John Barber, John Hawkins, Harry Gibbs, [and] George Durant, great men of the Yawpims," sold another 640 acres.[73] The men were apparently fluent in English, and the Weapemeoc language may have been on the way out. A decade or so later, however, their adoption of English dress was still incomplete. John Brickell noted (in 1729–37) that on the "state visits" the Yeopims paid to the North Carolina governor, "King Durant" wore full English dress, his much-worn waistcoat "having some remains of silver lace," while his wife wore an English skirt, a belt of roanoke, but no blouse.[74]

The rest of the Yeopims' North River land was finally sold away in 1740, at the request of "John Durant, King of the Yeopim Indians" and with the colony's permission.[75] Three years later, a land grant still showed "the Indians" as neighbors, perhaps being renters. They are absent in the 1755 report on Indians in the colony.[76] In 1767 some tracts in Currituck County were recovered in a law case; a number of them were "part of the lands called Indian Lands."[77] The people from those lands were gone. They appear to have dispersed, for no records after 1743 mention them as a group, although local memory of a "Vopim [sic] Indian town" remained at least into the 1760s.[78]

It is uncertain how long traditions of "Yeopim" or "Indian" ancestry lived on among the people's descendants, whose location and movements are yet to be researched.

Chowanoke

The major researchers for this chiefdom are Warren Milteer (2016) and Forest Hazel (2014), both of whom focus on the post-1790 Chowanokes (Hazel does so exclusively). Wes Taukchiray, senior author of this chapter, has also done extensive though unpublished research covering the whole of their history. The documents he found are in the Wesley D. White (his former surname) Collection at the South Carolina Historical Society. Supplementary articles that shed light on Chowanoke-English activities at various periods are Adams (2013), Barth (2010), Dixon (2019), and LeMaster (2006).

The Chowanokes occupied territory along both sides of the Chowan River in what is now Chowan, Bertie, Hertford, and Gates Counties, possibly extending over the line into what is now Virginia (which only archaeology can prove or disprove). In 1707, the colonial governor of North Carolina would write to the Virginia governor that the lands south of the Meherrin River's mouth had always belonged to the Chowanokes.[79]

Their border with the Weapemeocs cannot be ascertained today, but it was probably a few miles upriver from the Chowan River's mouth.

The Chowanokes had long had contact with the Powhatans to the north, via their river, then a portage northward to the Nansemond River, and through those visits they experienced contacts with the Jamestown English earlier in the seventeenth century than any other people in the Carolina Sounds region. They also met English traders and would-be settlers coming south before anyone else did.

The English in Virginia had been instructed by King James in 1606 to search for any Lost Colonists who might still be alive, twenty years after anything had been heard from them. Accordingly, upon learning that some of the southside Powhatans on the James River knew the Chowanokes, they sent a man there to ask around. He returned to report "little hope and less certainty" about there being any alive (which may have been a cover-up, on the Indians' part, for English people who no longer wished to be found).[80] On another reconnaissance mission, John Pory visited the Chowanokes in February 1622 and was impressed with how pleasant their land was.[81]

The Chowanokes remained pro-English during the Second Anglo-Powhatan War (1622–32), which set them against their northern relatives, led by Opechancanough. Sometime around then, a bloody incident occurred between the Chowanoke chief and the chief of Powhatan town, a subject of Opechancanough's. The former had "detained" one of the latter's wives to keep for himself, a deadly insult that had happened to Opechancanough himself some years earlier.[82] Feigning unconcern and friendliness toward a brother chief, even if he was a thief, the Powhatan town leader had invited the Chowanoke chief to a meeting, which was to take place on a path south of the Meherrin River that led to Tuscarora country. Opechancanough and his followers were in enmity with the Tuscaroras at that time and were planning a raid upon them, so the invitation to stop at a convenient place was accepted.

Greetings were exchanged, which involved the customary embracing and then stroking one another. When it came time for the Powhatan town chief to greet the Chowanoke chief, he carried out the ritual but suddenly whipped a bowstring around his enemy's neck and garroted him. Another feud was underway. The place where it happened was memorialized for decades thereafter among the Indians by adding rocks to two cairns some distance apart and keeping the path between them swept.[83]

By the 1660s, the Chowanokes were giving up land to the English—perhaps through sales, perhaps not. The only evidence we have is the patents (with Virginia) that were subsequently taken out. Several, for tracts somewhere on the west side of the Chowan River, were dated September 1663; one tract was bounded by a regrettably unnamed creek "which is at the lower part of the old Indian town"—meaning an abandoned village.[84] We have no way of knowing which village was meant. A few more patents came later, within a few years, but Virginia's claim on the area was becoming tenuous.[85] The Chowanokes were caught between the English and other Indians, when as a consequence of Bacon's Rebellion in Virginia, the anti-English Meherrins moved southeast to live with them temporarily, and some violence against the hosts occurred. Meherrin elders remembered later that the Chowanokes withdrew up Wiccocon River, a Chowan tributary, to avoid further bloodshed (map 8.3).[86] The Meherrin guests at length were persuaded to settle elsewhere.

When the North Carolina–Virginia boundary was established in 1708–11, with the help of the memories of elderly Indians in the region, the Chowanokes were mentioned again: an aged Meherrin man remembered them as living on both sides of their river up past the Meherrin River's mouth, up to the Nottoway River's mouth. They had fled the area, though, in 1676–77, when Bacon's Rebellion was raging in Virginia and the Occoneechees to the west were being attacked. The Chowanokes had avoided trouble by withdrawing from their too-accessible river and camping out on Wiccocon River, a tributary of the Chowan River downstream from their main town. Meanwhile, they were still in touch with the Christianized Nansemonds living in Nansemond County, Virginia; Edward Bass, brother of the Englishman John Bass who had married the Nansemond woman Elizabeth in 1638, married another (Nansemond?) Indian woman and joined the Chowanokes, dying among them in 1696, aged 74.[87]

In 1694, with English settlers still moving in on them from the south—the wider, downriver stretch being desirable for English shipping—the Chowanokes complained to the colonial government, which issued an order that no

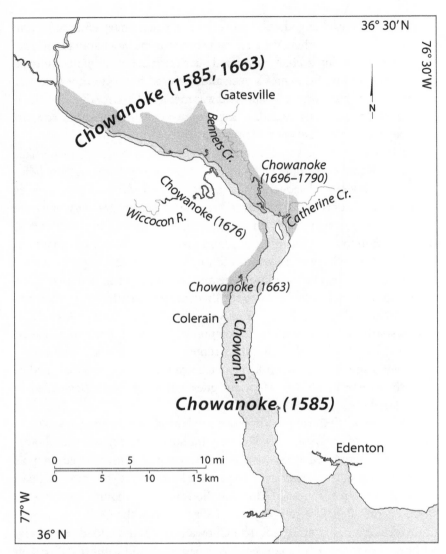

MAP 8.3 Historic period locations of the Chowanoke Indians.
Light gray areas are wetlands.

more settlers were to move upstream of Old Town Creek.[88] Within two years, a tract twelve miles square was to have been granted to them on the east side of Bennetts Creek,[89] but nothing happened. In March 1702, English neighbors reported friction with Chowanokes hunting on or near "their" farms and asked for a survey to be made. (They added that they were trying to observe a four-mile radius around the Indian town.)[90] In 1706 to 1708, the Chowanokes made a second request for a survey, this time specifying a tract six miles square on the east side of Bennetts Creek.[91] They were continuing to live in that locality, as a deed for an adjacent tract shows.[92] Yet in June 1712 the North Carolina Council, apparently in response to a third request from the Indians, ordered the issue to be taken up the following month[93]—only it wasn't. In August 1714, Chief "Hoyter" petitioned yet again for a survey, rehearsing several of the earlier attempts.[94] Once again there was no result.

Through all of this, the Chowanokes remained living together in one town, unlike the Weapemeocs.[95] They may have experienced spin-off, but they seem not to have had serious factions among themselves. They were pro-English during the Tuscarora War.[96] In December 1712, the Chowanokes had taken delivery of an apparently Indian man, hostile to North Carolina, who had been seized by Virginia Indians they knew; they handed him to the North Carolina authorities.[97]

In July 1712, an English missionary named Giles Rainsford wrote that he had talked with the chief, named Thomas "Hoyle," and found him interested both in converting to Christianity and in sending his son to a boarding school. He had a "notion of Noah's flood." Rainsford had offered to teach the son at home, but the chief declined, due to the unsettled conditions created by the Tuscarora War.[98] Chief John Hoyter was paid fifteen pounds in money, between 1713 and 1720, for scalps, presumably taken during that war.[99] But in November 1717, he had to complain yet again about encroachments, for his people's land was still not surveyed. Answering the latter complaint, yet another order for surveying was issued.[100] And yet again, nothing happened. Hoyter complained once more about encroachments in April 1720 and received another promise of action.[101] It seems to have been carried out this time.

On April 4, 1724, after the survey was made,[102] the Chowanokes supposedly got a patent for their land—though in 1735 the Indians had to notify the governor that the white neighbor who was supposed to hand it over to them refused to do so.[103] The neighbor had also neglected to register the patent at the county courthouse. Some other English people still held onto it in 1790, for they cited it in a petition of their own, and that later petition is the only evidence we have for the patent's date and the acreage involved.[104] It has been lost since; the Chowanokes may never have laid hands on it.

Now they officially (in English eyes) had land, but there were serious problems with it. It was a smaller tract than the thirty-six square miles promised them, being only seventeen and three-quarter square miles (11,360 acres). Not only that, but instead of being east of Bennets Creek and usable as farmland, it lay southwest of there, between the Chowan

River and Catherine's Creek and was "all pines, and sands, and deserts [swamps]." So the Chowanokes asked for relief.[105] There is no evidence that they got any. Prejudice against nonwhites may have been behind all this rigmarole (1696–1735), but we doubt that that was the sole cause. John Lawson's estimate of the Chowanokes' 1709 population, which comes to fewer than forty people, indicates that some of their families were spinning off into English society. Most likely the English were hoping the remaining Indians would do the same, and that the tribe, as a social group, would vanish. That is what happened eventually, though the people as individuals did not disappear by any means.

Now the land sales began. We have record of several in the 1730s.[106] The Indian signatories were variously James Bennett, Charles Besley (or Beazley), Thomas Pushon, John Reding, Thomas Hiter (or Hoyter or Hoyton or Hoyston), Jeremiah Pushing, and on one deed, Nuce (Neuse) Will, a Neusioc living among the Chowanokes. All were "great men," indicating a larger male population that they represented. A militia major visited the group in 1731, on unspecified business, and the governor of the colony listed them as one of six Indian nations in North Carolina.[107] Two years later, having apparently asked for it, they received permission to live with the Tuscaroras, pending the latter's agreement.[108] The Tuscaroras then had a 62.4-square-mile reservation on the west side of the Chowan River.[109] The move seems not to have taken place, however, for the Chowanokes remained on the Bennetts Creek land, at least for a while. In 1737, John Brickell described a visit to the colonial governor by "King Highter." Like the Yeopim chief, he wore English clothes for the occasion but old-fashioned dress at home. His entourage, consisting of his wife, his children, his great men, and his guards, all wore traditional dress to meet the governor—although the wife wore colored ribbons tied in her hair.[110]

Land sales continued in the 1740s and 1750s; the Indians had trouble getting paid, the buyers asked the government to admit Indian acknowledgments for sales, and still other English people simply moved in.[111] By 1755, a militia report noted that the group had "only 2 men and 5 women and children [who were] ill used by their neighbors."[112] The Chowan County militia commander elaborated: "Their strength is as nothing, and their condition very deplorable by the artifice and cunning of some of their neighbors. I am informed they consist of two men and five women & children which two white men [who wanted to oust them] would at any time overcome."[113]

There were more Chowanokes than that, but not many more. Their names were Freeman and Robbins. In 1737, a "commoner" (rather than great man)

Chowanoke, William Freeman, made a will in which he named six sons. The eldest would appear later as a tribal great man. The fourth son, Richard, died in 1761, leaving a will that named three children. One son, Amos Freeman, sold his fifty acres of tribal land to an Englishman in 1765.[114] Still another "commoner," James Robbins, enlisted with English forces in 1777 to fight with the Americans in the American Revolution, and he was discharged with the rank of private in 1780; he got paid for his service in 1786.[115]

Apprenticeships for Indian youth begin appearing in the records, indicating a movement further toward English society—and also poverty among the people, for otherwise the county court would not have been involved. Benjamin Robbins, aged fourteen, was apprenticed in 1779 to "learn the art of plantation business." In the next decade several more boys were bound out to become shoemakers, coopers, and so on, trades that would integrate them into working-class Anglo-American society.[116] More boys were bound out in the 1790s and early 1800s; the surnames were the same, but now they were either without a label (and therefore "white") or said to be "of colour."[117] That would be true of all subsequent Chowanoke-descended individuals, one of whom was called "a free person of color of Indian extraction" in 1811; she was also, like earlier Chowanokes, an "insolvent debtor."[118] Their civil rights were those of free nonwhite persons—that is, less extensive than white people's rights.

The Chowanokes did not always sell land; on one occasion they bought some. In 1782 a neighbor who had previously bought some of their land sold thirty acres back to them. The buyers were the eight children of Nan Robbins, but a later description of the land hints that it had never been part of the Chowanoke patent of 1724.[119]

Finally, in April 1790, the Chowanoke "Chief men and representatives of the Chowan Indian Nation" sold all the land that remained from their 1724 patent, amounting to only 400 acres.[120] However, the sale hit a snag the next October, when two of the buyers tried to get the state legislature to pass a law allowing "the said free men of mixed blood" to sell their land. (Forest Hazel correctly points out the difference in how the sellers proudly described themselves as Indians, and how disdainful was the attitude of the buyers.)[121] The buyers' petition to the legislature further stated that "since then [1724] the whole of the said Chowan Indian men is dead, leaving a parcel of Indian women, which has mixed with Negroes. And now there is several freemen and women of mixed blood as aforesaid, which have descended from the said Indians." The petitioners felt it necessary, however, in a climate of deepening suspicion against all nonwhites, to assure the legislature that "the free men alluded to in the petition, did in the late contest with Great Britain, behave themselves as good and faithful soldiers in behalf of this and the United States." Ironically, in a move to protect the Chowanokes (who wanted the sale to go through), the legislature rejected the petition because the Chowanokes themselves had not sent it.[122] Technicalities! So in late 1791, one of the Indians, James Robbins, petitioned successfully to have his people's sale of the reservation confirmed. However, several people did not sign the request, presumably the six sisters who had bought the thirty acres back in 1782.[123] They were still in possession of their acreage through 1800, though they and their descendants eventually sold out—unwillingly— in the early 1820s.[124]

The subsequent history of the Chowanoke descendants has been told in detail by Hazel and Milteer, who have located descendants of the Robbinses in Gates County (Hazel and Milteer) and adjacent counties (Milteer). The people were legally regarded as free persons of color, with all the disadvantages (compared to whites) that the status entailed. Some were farmers and others became craft workers; a few became politically active, one of them (Benjamin Robbins) voting in the U.S. House of Representatives election of 1795. The Gates County descendants attempted to live by farming, but their deeds of trust show that they were often in debt. They must have had to supplement their income, such as it was, by hunting—with firearms. That got them into trouble, since North Carolina, like adjacent states, passed very discriminatory laws before the Civil War, one of them disabling free people of color from carrying guns. Their deeds of trust—using livestock, horses and wagons, bedsteads, looms, farming implements, and so forth—demonstrate that their material culture was now much the same as that of their non-Indian-descended neighbors. There is, however, no indication in the records that they had all kept sufficiently in touch, much less gathered themselves into a church or other organization of their own, such that in Hazel's opinion (and ours), they could still be called a tribe.[125] (Milteer emphasizes instead how fully the people became respectable citizens of their counties.) Some descendants belong today to a multiple-origin entity called the Meherrin-Chowanoke Indian Tribe, which for some years has been seeking recognition as a tribe from the federal government.[126]

Afterword

The Carolina Algonquian speakers and their way of life went back many centuries in the Sounds region, and as long as they could stand up against depredations from other Indians, they expected, in the 1580s, to go on living there as they always had. They did not live in a "golden age," though later generations may have idealized the past to that extent. There were plenty of hazards and insecurities around before the Europeans began visiting, and people did not live for a hundred years, free from diseases. But their world really was their world, not someone else's, and they met the English would-be colonists with a self-confidence that impressed the newcomers.

The English came from a more complicated, much faster-changing world, where their families' getting ahead economically and socially mattered deeply. More to the point, they were convinced that they had a right to expand into other people's lands and "improve" the human creatures they found there. They soon found out the hard way, on Roanoke Island and in the early years on Jamestown Island, that that was more easily said than done. Their attempt at the former island foundered, while they eventually—at the cost of many lives—managed to hang on at the latter.

The timing of the third (and supposedly permanent) Roanoke colony was poor, with a severe drought just beginning. But for the individuals in the colony, the timing was poorer because the English nation as yet knew so little about how very expensive in people and money any successful colonizing project would prove to be. The people in the third colony were "lost," in the sense of "misplaced," by their fellow countrymen, who were unable for various reasons to rescue them. Whether the castaways became refugees or captives among the Native people, they then had to adapt in order to survive. It looked for a time as if the Indian culture had prevailed.

That situation did not last long, however, because the English had plenty of people to "spend" in establishing colonies, and they were determined to carry out their plans. The chiefdoms in the Sounds were not conquered in war. Instead they were flooded out by the settlers who so overwhelmingly outnumbered the Native people after the mid-seventeenth century. And then it was their turn to be forced to adapt to the now-dominant English culture in order to survive. In all probability, they had no easier time of it than the "lost" colonists had had a century and more before. In the process they lost their language and their old way of life, and many of them even lost their identity as Native people.

But they did not die out. We cannot speak of the "demise of the Indians" in the region for the simple reason that they went on living and adapting to circumstances that ultimately changed them greatly — so greatly for most of them that even their identities as "Indian" changed to something else. The process cannot have been comfortable for them. Culture change and especially identity change among twentieth-century people who have left records for us are often painful and fraught with insecurity for the first few generations. It was probably the same for the Indians of the seventeenth, eighteenth, and nineteenth centuries as well.

The Algonquian speakers' descendants are scattered and much changed today; most of them are not even aware that they are part-Indian. But some few of them still retain a tradition of descent from their ancestors that is very precious to them. They are increasingly active in letting the general public know about it. Indian-descended people are law-abiding citizens, useful members of society with some unique ancestral memories; they are not feather-wearing, pidgin-speaking aliens. They and we are neighbors.

Notes

Chapter One

1. Lamb 1995: 211–41.

2. Stahle et al. 1998: 566. That period was the driest in the 800-year period covered by the tree rings of very old surviving cypresses along the Nottoway River in Virginia. Bald cypress wood is extraordinarily rot-resistant, making the species the best in the region for constructing tree-ring histories.

3. A good, readable summary of the formation of North Carolina coastal lands since the last ice age is Riggs et al. 2011: 14–20.

4. For a map of known inlets, both historic and prehistoric (thanks to ground-penetrating sonar), see Mallinson et al. 2007.

5. Sawyer (2010: 50) reached the same conclusion.

6. Senter 2003: 334.

7. See, for instance, Riggs et al. 2011 and Pilkey 1998.

8. For a full list of the plants and animals useful to Indian families, complete with English and Latin names, econiches inhabited, and seasons of usefulness, see Rountree and Davidson 1997: appendix C (plants) and appendix D (fish). Most of the species on these lists occur in the Carolina Sounds region (Radford, Ahles and Bell 1968; Abbott 1974; and Lippson and Lippson 2009). I remain grateful to botanists Lytton Musselman and Donna Ware and ichthyologist Robert Lippson for checking over those lists. (Lippson did so in 2003, after the book came out, and he wrote back that catfish and largemouth and smallmouth bass were imported into coastal waters in the nineteenth century by sport fishermen.)

9. That assessment is based on personal experience, for that oak species grows where I live in Virginia. Dried and pounded up, these acorns produce a flour that has a slight cinnamon taste.

10. The English name can apply to either of two species: American hornbeam (*Carpinus caroliniana*) or Eastern hophornbeam (*Ostrya virginiana*).

11. This is the author's rough estimate, based upon watching how much twine was used in 2002, when Jamestown Settlement built one (and only one) new house for its Indian Village (Hancock and Rountree n.d.).

Chapter Two

1. Hariot 1955 [1590]: 370; 1972 [1590]: 25; 2007 [1590]: 48.
2. Hariot 1955: 417 (text only); 1972 [1590]: 66–67; 2007 [1590]: 69 (text), 159 (illustration). The 2007 translation of Hariot's text is "Since the town is quite a long way from a pond, they have dug a large ditch . . . from which they draw the necessary water."
3. Hariot 1955 [1590]: 369; 1972 [1590]: 24; and 2007 [1590]: 47.
4. David Phelps, personal communication, 1998. Phelps found topsoil beneath the sandy upper layer during his excavations at Buxton.
5. Lane 1955 [1586]: 283.
6. Linguist James A. Geary, cited in Quinn 1955: 867.
7. Quinn 1955: 862, 869.
8. Quinn 1955: 870.
9. Quinn 1955: 861.
10. Quinn 1955.
11. Quinn 1955.
12. Quinn 1955: 859.
13. Quinn 1955: 858–9.
14. Quinn 1955: 858.
15. David Phelps, personal communication, 1998.
16. Confirmed by a pre-1640 C-14 date: Phelps, personal communication, 1998. Meaning: Maurice Mook, cited in Quinn 1955: 857.
17. James Geary, cited in Quinn 1955: 858.
18. Quinn 1955: 858.
19. Quinn 1955: 858.
20. Lane 1955a [1585]: 213; 1955b [1586]: 259.
21. Hariot 1955 [1590]: 25; 2007 [1590]: 48.
22. Hariot 1955 [1590]: 378; 1972 [1590]: 28; 2007 [1590]: 50.
23. Alexander Crosby (author of *The Columbian Exchange*), personal communication, 1991.
24. Barlowe 1955 [1585]: 113. There was as yet no serious drought; that would come in 1587–89 and contribute to the demise of the Lost Colony (see Stahle et al. 1998).
25. Rountree, Clark, and Mountford 2007, totals from various chapters.
26. Illustrated: White painting: Hulton 1984: 62. DeBry engraving: Hariot 1972 [1590]: 67; 2007 [1590]: 69; and Hulton 1984: 125.
27. Hariot 1972 [1590]: 42–43, 45; 2007 [1590]: 122–23, 125; Hulton 1984: 106–7, 108. John White's map marks towns with dots (Hulton 1984: 86).
28. Overall method: Hariot 1955 [1590]: 369; 1972 [1590]: 24; 2007 [1950]: 47. This accords with the Virginia accounts of John Smith (1986b [1612]: 150 ["a Fort very wel pallisadoed and mantelled with the barke of trees"], 271, ["prettily fortified with poles and

barkes of trees"]) and Robert Beverley (1947 [1705]: 177; 2013 [1705]: 139 ["a Palisado, of about ten or twelve foot high; and when they would make themselves very safe, they treble the Pale"]. Pomeioke: Hulton 1984: 62 (John White's own caption to his painting of Pomeioke). Roanoke: Barlowe 1955 [1585]: 107. Barlowe mentioned cedar first, as if it were for the houses (which doesn't make sense), but he sometimes confused the order in which he meant things (so cedar among the poles does make sense).

29. Illustrated: White painting: Hulton 1984: 66. De Bry engraving: Hariot 1972 [1590]: 69; 2007 [1590]: 161; and Hulton 1984: 126.

30. Roanoke: Barlowe 1955 [1585]: 107. Ten, twelve, and thirty houses: Hariot 1955 [1590]: 369; 1972 [1590]: 24; 2007 [1590]: 47. Houses' occupants: Hariot 1955 [1590]: 416; 1972 [1590]: 66; 2007 [1590]: 69.

31. Lawson 1967 [1709]: 200.

32. There is only one illustration of a dog from the Carolina Sounds in the 1580s, in John White's painting of the town of Pomeioke (Hulton 1984: 62). That dog coming knee high on the man standing nearby accords with the size of the dogs found at the Hatch Site (Old Weyanock Town) in Virginia: Blick 1987, 2000, 2006. The painting also strongly resembles the modern "Carolina dog," photographs of which Karen Harvey used for her painting in figure 6.1.

33. Hunting: Winne 1969 [1608]: 246; Haile 1998: 203–4. Not pets: Strachey 1953 [1612]: 125–26; Haile 1998: 682.

34. Kept going, even at night: Strachey 1953 [1612]: 79; Haile 1998: 636. Bad luck: Strachey 1953 [1612]: 115; Haile 1998: 672.

35. Information from Indian Village interpreters at Jamestown Settlement (where I have been a consultant since 1984), most of whom have had little luck doing it over the years.

36. Smith 1986b [1612]: 162; Strachey 1953 [1612]: 115; Haile 1998: 672. Different woods, spunk: Lawson 1967 [1709]: 213.

37. Sharpening and fire hardening: Lawson 1967 [1709]: 180. Other details of house building, not mentioned by eyewitness observers, have been reconstructed by William H. Hancock, formerly head exhibits fabricator at Jamestown Settlement. See Hancock and Rountree n.d. and, for an illustrated short version, Hancock 2006.

38. Personal observation: tried successfully in a 2002 experiment by Bill Hancock at Jamestown Settlement.

39. Smith 1986b [1612]: 163–64; Strachey 1953 [161]: 82; Haile 1998: 639.

40. There may also have been food and music (work songs with instrumental accompaniment) provided; eyewitnesses are silent about that too.

41. North Carolina: David Phelps, personal communication, 1998. Virginia: the evidence is several sites dug in the 1990s.

42. Hariot 1955 [1590]: 370; 1972 [1590]: 24; 2007 [1590]: 48.

43. Hariot 1955 [1590]: 416; 1972 [1590]: 66; 2007 [1590]: 69. Hariot contradicts himself a few sentences later, saying mats could be rolled up to admit more light. Mats laid horizontally, with the reeds vertical, could not have been rolled *up*.

44. Spelman 1910 [1613?]: cvi; Haile 1998: 487.

45. William H. Hancock, personal communication, 2002, based on his experience with the Indian Village houses at Jamestown Settlement. Mats there developed rips

and holes within six months. Hancock felt that the mats would last longer if they were continually exposed to a hearth's smoke—something that could not be done overnight with safety in that museum setting.

46. Strachey 1953 [1612]: 74; Haile 1998: 632. Henry Spelman information: Purchas 1617: 954. I myself saw a menstrual house (from the outside only) among Medicine Lodge Winnebago people in Wisconsin in 1982; located in a backyard, it was a rather narrow frame building (no cooking or working space) and looked like a bunkhouse with a television antenna on top.

47. Lawson 1967 [1709]: 197 (menstruation), 196 (postpartum).

48. Data from Virginia: Strachey 1953 [1612]: 78–79; Haile 1998: 636.

49. Trees and shades: Strachey 1953 [1612]: 78–79; Haile 1998: 635–36. Camping: Smith 1986b [1612]: 164; Strachey 1953 [1612]: 83; Haile 1998: 639.

50. White painting: Hulton 1984: 75. Engraving *The Broiling of Their Fish*: Hariot 1955: 436–37 (text); 1972 [1590]: 59 (text and illustration); 2007 [1590]: 67 (text), 149 (illustration); Hulton 1984: 120 (text and illustration).

51. The shape is analogous to the V-shaped dams of rocks placed, with the point open downstream, to be closed by a reed trap, in fast-moving rivers and streams in and near the piedmont of Virginia (Banister 1970: 354; Beverley 1947 [1705]: 148; 2013 [1705]: 112–13). Remains of the dams have been found in Virginia (Bushnell 1937).

52. Experts building bays: Charles Elliot, personal communication 1984, based on his interviews with fishermen in Fox Hill, Hampton, Virginia. Text description: Beverley 1947 [1705]: 148; 2013 [1705]: 112–13. Archaeological finds: Johnson 1942 and 1949 (Massachusetts) and Cresson 1892 (Delaware). Illustrations: White painting: Hulton 1984: 73. De Bry engraving: Hariot 1972 [1590]: 56–57; 2007 [1590]: 147. The de Bry engraving, with several heart-shaped bays instead of one square one, comes closer to being accurate. Indians using them at Chepanoc: Lane 1955b [1586]: 267, 272. But the Roanokes made at least one weir for the English in 1586: Lane 1955b [1586]: 279, 282–83. In the 1880s, Chesapeake Bay fishermen reinvented this kind of weir (called fish pounds), and some of them are still being built as of this writing.

53. Personal experience, plus that of Jamestown Settlement Indian Village personnel, plus several people who made and paddled a dugout for the Mariners' Museum in Newport News, Virginia.

54. Hariot 1972 [1590]: 48; 2007 [1590]: 65–66.

55. Personal communication, Henry Bond at the Jamestown Settlement Indian Village (the canoe maker there), 1995.

56. Hariot 1955 [1590]: 421; 1972 [1590]: 68; 2007 [1590]: 70.

57. Barlowe 1955 [1585]: 105, 109 (both events took place in mid-July 1585).

58. Hariot 1955 [1590]: 341; 1972 [1590]: 14; 2007 [1590]: 40. The New England Indian Squanto learned about dropping a fish into each hole before adding corn and beans from his previous visit to England: Ceci 1975a and 1975b.

59. McIlwaine 1915: 3:349.

60. Strachey 1953 [1612]: 79; Haile 1998: 636.

61. Reclearing overgrown field: Smith 1986b [1612]: 157; Strachey 1953 [1612]: 118, Haile 1998: 676. That and cutting down large, mature trees: Spelman 1910 [1613?]: cxi; Haile 1998: 492.

62. Beverley 1947 [1705]: 230; 2013 [1705]: 182.

63. Lawson 1967 [1709]: 176.

64. Hariot 1955 [1590]: 341–42; 1972 [1590]: 14–15; 2007 [1590]: 40; Spelman 1910 [1613?]: xci; Haile 1998: 492.

65. North Carolina: Hariot 1955 [1590]: 342; 1972 [1590]: 15; 2007 [1590]: 40. Powhatan: Smith 1986b [1612]: 157; Strachey 1953 [1612]: 118; Spelman 1910 [1613?]: cxi; Haile 1998: 676 (Strachey), 492 (Spelman). It was Robert Beverley who specifically mentioned beans climbing the cornstalks (Beverley 1947 [1705]: 144; 2013 [1705]: 109).

66. North Carolina: Lane 1955 [1586]: 279; Barlowe 1955 [1585]: 105. Virginia: Strachey 1953 [1612]: 79; Haile 1998: 636; Hariot 1955 [1590]: 343; 1972 [1590]: 15; 2007 [1590]: 41.

67. Hariot 1955 [1590]: 422; 1972 [1590]: 68; 2007 [1590]: 70. Hulton (1984: 126) says the scaffold was manned by "a watchman"; it is my own suspicion (Rountree 1989: 49) about boys getting target practice, given how much pressure was put on young males to become sharpshooters.

68. Hariot 1955 [1590]: 337–41; 1972 [1590]: 13–14; 2007 [1590]: 39–40. No North Carolina source mentions harvesting and drying; the most complete description comes from Henry Spelman in Virginia: Spelman 1910 [1613?]: xcii; Haile 1998: 492. Editor D. B. Quinn identified one grain-producing wild plant as an *Atriplex* species.

69. Mush: Hariot 1955 [1590]: 339; 1972 [1590]: 14; 2007 [1590]: 39. Ashcakes: Smith 1986b [1612]: 157; Strachey 1953 [1612]: 80–81; Haile 1998: 638. Rockahominy: Hariot 1955 [1590]: 339; 1972 [1590]: 14; 2007 [1590]: 39; Banister 1970: 376.

70. Hariot 1955 [1590]: 339; 1972 [1590]: 14; 2007 [1590]: 39.

71. Hariot 1955 [1590]: 340; 1972 [1590]: 14; 2007 [1590]: 39.

72. Radford, Ahles, and Bell 1968: 1117 shows it growing wild only in counties bordering the Chowan River, and being more common in the piedmont and mountains. It was probably encouraged rather than domesticated.

73. Both native species of *Atriplex* grow wild in counties closest to the sounds (Radford, Ahles and Bell 1968: 419).

74. Lane 1955 [1586]: 283.

75. For a description of Eastern Woodland Indians as travelers, see Rountree 1993b.

76. One such cairn was explained to Edward Bland in 1649; it marked a vicious skirmish between some Chowanokes and some Powhatans earlier in the century: Bland et al. 1911 [1651]: 12–14.

Chapter Three

1. Nancy Shoemaker (1997) points out that the term "redskin" came two centuries later, originating in the Deep South for political reasons: differentiating Native Americans from both Europeans and Africans.

2. Stallybrass 2007: 22ff.

3. Skin and hair coloring: Barlowe 1955 [1585]: 102. Facial hair: Hariot 1955 [1590]: 419; 1972 [1590]: 52; 2007 [1590]: 64; Hulton 1984: 115. Eyes: Hariot 1955 [1590]:

439–40; 1972 [1590]: 49; 2007 [1590]: 62; Hulton 1984: 112. Never bald: Lawson 1967 [1709]: 174.

4. Ubelaker 1993: 72.

5. Men: Hariot 1972 [1590]: 74; 2007 de Bry engravings of various people, some of whose captions change in the different editions. Text: Hariot 1955 [1590]: 420, 424, 441, 443–44; Hariot 1972 [1590]: 53, 47, 46, 129; 2007 [1590]: 63, 64, 61, 72.

6. See the White painting and de Bry engraving of a man in body paint. Hariot 1972 [1590]: 46, 2007 [1590]: 127 (de Bry engraving); Hulton 1984:78 (White painting).

7. Pictures' order: *Great Lord of Virginia* [man with bow and arrows], *Chief Man of Roanoke* [man with copper pendant], *Aged Man of Pomeioke, Their Sitting at Meat* [man showing tribal markings on his back—de Bry only]. Text of caption only: Hariot 1955 [1590]: 441–42, 438–39, 419, 430, 443–44; Hariot 1972 [1590]: 46, 50, 52, 61, 74; Hariot 2007 [1590]: 61, 63, 64, 68, 72 (English text) and 127, 135, 139, 153, 167 (colorized illustrations). White paintings [in same order]: Hulton 1984: 78, 76, 64, 71.

8. Pictures' order: *Chief Lady of Secota, Young Gentlewoman Daughter of Secota* [John White's caption: "One of the Wives of Wingina"], *Chief Lady of Pomeioke* [with her daughter], *Their Manner of Carrying Their Children, Their Sitting at Meat.* Text of caption only: Hariot 1955 [1590]: 424, 440, 418, 420, 430. De Bry engravings with their captions: Hariot 1972 [1590]: 47, 49, 51, 53, 61; Hariot 2007 [1590]: 63–64, 63, 62, 68, and 62–63 (English text), and 137, 141, 129, 153, and 133 (colorized illustrations). John White paintings [in same order]: Hulton 1984: 67, 77, 63, 65, 71.

9. Pictures' order: *An Aged Man in His Winter Garment, Their Sitting at Meat.* Engravings and their captions: Hariot 1972 [1590]: 52, 61; Hariot 2007 [1590]: 64 and 68 (text), 139 and 153 (illustrations); Hulton 1984: 115, 122. White paintings: Hulton 1984: 64, 71.

10. Lawson 1967 [1709]: 200. The mantles he saw may or may not have belonged to Algonquian speakers, although William Strachey described a similarly made cloak among the Powhatans (1953 [1612]:65; Haile 1998: 625).

11. Lawson 1967 [1709]: 223.

12. Loin coverings: see notes 5 and 6 for illustrations. Prepubertal girls: Quinn 1955: 446. Menstruating women: Lawson 1967 [1709]: 200.

13. Lawson 1967 [1709]: 200. Leggings: Archer 1969 [1607]: 102; Haile 1998: 122; Strachey 1953 [1612]: 73; Haile 1998: 631.

14. Hariot 1955 [1590]: 418, 424, 438–39, 441; 1972 [1590]: 51, 47, 50, 49, 46; 2007 [1590]: 63–64, 62, 63, 61. Mixed-size beads: Hariot 1955 [1590]: 425, 440; 1972 [1590]: 71, 49; 2007: 71, 62.

15. Barlowe 1955 [1585]: 102.

16. Lane 1955b [1586]: 281, 284.

17. Hariot 1955 [1590]: 437; 1972 [1590]: 60; 2007 [1590]: 67; Hulton 1984: 121.

18. Lawson 1967 [1709]: 194 (refusal), 193 (men's vigor).

19. Lawson 1967 [1709]: 194.

20. Lawson 1967 [1709]: 194.

21. Lawson 1967 [1709]: 193.

22. Lawson 1967 [1709]: 192–93.

23. Lawson 1967 [1709]: 193 (divorce), 192 (children), 189 (remarriage), 194–95 (husband's debts).

24. Human skeletal data from Virginia: Donna Boyd, personal communication, 1992.

25. Long rushes: Hariot 1955 [1590]: 370; 1972 [1590]: 24; 2007 [1590]: 48. Dyeing: Hariot 1955 [1590]: 335; 1972 [1590]: 11; 2007 [1590]: 38. Size: Lawson 1967 [1709]: 195. Uses: Barlowe 1955 [1585]: 99, 109. Bedding: Smith 1986b [1612]: 162; Strachey 1953 [1612]: 79; Haile 1998: 636. Burials: Smith 1986b [1612]: 169; Strachey 1953 [1612]: 95; Haile 1998: 651. Drying: Spelman 1910 [1613?]: cxii; Haile 1998: 492.

26. Strachey 1964 [1610]: 81; Haile 1998: 430.

27. I.e., Jamestown Rediscovery in the early 2000s. At this writing, it has not been included in any of that organization's publications.

28. I have tried working with them myself. Indian hemp grows readily on my family's nonworking farm.

29. Banister 1970: 40.

30. Illustrated in Beverley 1947 [1705]: 167; 2013 [1705]: 131.

31. Lawson 1967 [1709]: 217; he noted that a solution of water and beaten-up green corn could be used as well.

32. White painting: Hulton 1984: 79. Engraving "the Conjurer": Hariot 1972 [1590]: 54; 2007 [1590]: 143; Hulton 1984: 117. Virginia (text and illustration): Beverley 1947 [1705]: 184 (text), 183 (illustration); Beverley 2013 [1705]: 145 (text), 144 (illustration). Ashmolean purse (which I have seen twice): Feest 1983.

33. White painting: Hulton 1984: 74. Engraving *Their Seething of Their Meat*: Hariot 1972 [1590]: 60; 2007 [1590]: 151; Hulton 1984: 121.

34. Jamestown Settlement Indian Village interpreters, personal communications.

35. For a detailed list, econiche by econiche, see appendix C of Rountree and Davidson 1997.

36. Lawson 1967 [1709]: 196.

37. Hariot 1955 [1590]: 351; 1972 [1590]: 18; 2007 [1590]: 43. Powcohicora: Powhatan term: Smith 1986b [1612]: 152; Strachey 1953 [1612]: 129; Haile 1998: 685. The term has been adopted into English as "hickory" for certain kinds of nut-bearing trees.

38. Hanson 1977 [1728]: 24–25. Hanson had been captured by Abenakis and dragged a long way to the Indians' town, during which her milk dried up and her baby began to starve. A woman traveling with the warriors' party took pity on her and the child. The text reads: ". . . she advised me to take the Kernels of Walnuts, and clean them, and beat them with a little Water, which I did, and when I had so done, the Water look'd like Milk; then she advised me to add to this Water, a little of the finest of the *Indian* Corn Meal, and boyl it a little together. I did so, and it became palatable, and was very nourishing to the Babe, so that it began to thrive and look well." Nutrition: Mary C. Rountree, Ph.D., nutritionist: personal communication, 2017.

39. Smith 1986b [1612]: 162; Spelman 1910 [1613?]: cix; Haile 1998: 490. Secret name: Purchas 1617: 943 (marginal note). Earning names: Strachey 1953 [1612]: 56, 113–14; Haile 1998: 613, 671. Name-changing: Lane 1955 [1586]: 265 (Wingina); Kingsbury 1906–35: III: 584 (Opechancanough); Smith 1986c [1624]: 294 (Opitchapam).

40. Shown in Beverley 1947 [1705]: 172; 2013 [1705]: 135.

41. Lawson 1967 [1709]: 196–97.

42. Personal observation, Shoshone fieldwork (in Nevada), 1967. Restless infants, like those of today when fastened into car seats, quieted down in the familiar security of the cradleboard and fell asleep.

43. Hulton 1984: 65; Hariot 1955 [1590]: 420; 1972 [1590]: 53; 2007 [1590]: 64–65.

44. Lawson 1967 [1709]: 210.

45. Wax and Thomas 1961: 306–8, 312–13.

46. Nonhunting men: Lawson 1967 [1709]: 216–17. Wooden platters: Barlowe 1955 [1585]: 109. Illustration: White painting: Hulton 1984: 71. Engraving *Their Sitting at Meat*: Hariot 1972 [1590]: 61; 2007 [1590]: 153; Hulton 1984: 122.

47. Evidence that it was men's work: Lane 1955 [1586]: 279.

48. Lawson 1967 [1709]: 241–42. The best description of the process comes from Virginia: Beverley 1947 [1705]: 207–9; 2012 [1705]: 163–65. Illustration of a wicker-work huskanawing cage: Beverley 1947 [1705]: 165; 2012 [1705]: 129.

49. Smith 1986b [1612]: 171; Strachey 1953 [1612]: 98; Haile 1998: 211.

50. Banister 1970: 376: "They make excellent broath of the head & humbles [entrails] of a deer which they put in the pot all bloody, this seems to resemble the jus nigrum of the Spartans made with the blood & bowels of a hare. They eat not the brains with the head."

51. White 1955 [1587]: 525; Hariot 1955 [1590]: 431–32; 1972 [1590]: 48; 2007 [1590]: 62 (text); Hulton 1984: 111.

52. Lawson 1967 [1709]: 215–16.

53. Lawson 1967 [1709]: 206.

54. Hariot 1955 [1590]: 361–62; 1972 [1590]: 21; 2007 [1590]: 45. Hariot wrote only of seasonal reliance on shellfish, but he made his observations before the drought of 1587–89 really got underway; see Stahle et al. 1998.

55. Depths: common sense plus Gabriel Archer's mentioning that one of the Powhatan chiefs sent boys "to dive for mussels" (1969 [1607]: 31; Haile 1998: 113). Indian populations were much gentler on shellfish populations not only because their own population was much smaller, but also because they lacked dredges, oyster tongs, thousands of crab pots, etc.

56. White painting: Hulton 1984: 73. Engraving *Their Manner of Fishing*: Hariot 1972 [1590]: 56–57; 2007 [1590]: 67 (test), 147 (illustration); Hulton 1984: 119. White text: 1955 [1587]: 525. The 1590 edition of Hariot called the animal "a fish"; "sea crab" is the new translation from the Latin published in 2007.

57. White painting: Hulton 1984: 73. De Bry engraving: Hariot 1972 [1590]: 56–57; 2007 [1590]: 146–47.

58. Glover 1904 [1676]: 23–24 (bow of cane); Beverley 1947 [1705]: 149; 2013 [1705]: 113 (at gunwale).

59. Beverley 1947 [1705]: 149; 2013 [1705]: 113.

60. Rountree 1993b: 27–28, 38, 213, 222.

61. Text on rattles and illustrations of singing and dancing: Hariot 1955 [1590]: 429; 1972 [1590]: 62–65; 2007 [1590]: 68–69; Hulton 1984: 123–124; Lawson 1967 [1709]: 178, 180. Varying size of rattles: Strachey 1953 [1612]: 85; Haile 1998: 642.

62. Flutes: Percy 1969 [1608?]: 137; Haile 1998: 93; Smith 1986b [1612]; 167; Strachey 1953 [1612]: 85; Haile 1998: 642; Spelman 1910 [1613?]: cxiv; Haile 1998: 495. Drums: Smith 1986b [1612]: 167; Strachey 1953 [1612]: 85; Haile 1998: 642.

63. Lawson 1967 [1709]: 178, 180. Analogous to the Powhatan game (Strachey 1953 [1612]: 84; Haile 1998: 641; Clayton 1965 [1687]: 38–39; Pargellis 1959 [1688]: 232; Beverley 1947 [1705]: 221; 2013 [1705]: 174).

64. Strachey 1953 [1612]: 84; Haile 1998: 641.

65. Lawson 1967 [1709]: 184.

66. Lawson 1967 [1709]: 175.

67. Wax and Thomas 1961: 310.

68. Lawson 1967 [1709]: 184. Fighting was unforgivable, unless the combatants were drunk (early eighteenth century).

69. Lawson 1967 [1709]: 206.

Chapter Four

1. Lawson 1967 [1709]: 206; Beverley 1947 [1705]: 200; 2013 [1705]: 158.

2. Lawson 1967 [1709]: 219–20.

3. Mantoac: Hariot 1955: 372; 1972 [1590]: 25; 2007 [1590]: 48; translation, Geary 1955: 892. Ahone: Strachey 1953 [1612]: 89; Haile 1998: 646. Human form: Hariot 1955 [1590]: 373; 1972 [1590]: 26; 2007 [1590]: 49. The sun: Percy 1969 [1608?]: 148; Haile 1998: 98–99. Dangerous forces, things, and animals: Smith 1986b [1612]: 169; Strachey 1953 [1612]: 88; Haile 1998: 645. *Mantóac:* Wes Taukchiray (personal communication, 2017) suggests that the word was more probably *montàoc*, in keeping with the common Algonquian plural form *oc*.

4. Hariot 1955 [1590]: 373; 1972 [1590]: 26; 2007 [1590]: 49; Rountree 1989: 135–36.

5. Smith 1986b [1612]: 169; Strachey 1953 [1612]: 88–89; Haile 1998: 645–46.

6. Unfamiliar things: Hariot 1955 [1590]: 375–76; 1972 [1590]: 27; 2007 [1590]: 49. Reactions to Bible: Hariot 1955 [1590]: 376–77; 1972 [1590]: 28; 2007 [1590]: 50.

7. Hariot 1955 [1590]: 372–73; 1972 [1590]: 25–26; 2007 [1590]: 48–49.

8. Rountree 1989: 137–38.

9. Sixteenth-century Carolina: Hariot 1955 [1590]: 373; 1972 [1590]: 26; 2007 [1590]: 49. Seventeenth-century Carolina: Lawson 1967 [1709]: 187. Seventeenth-century Virginia: Smith 1986b [1612]: 172; Strachey 1953 [1612]: 100; Haile 1998: 657.

10. Lawson 1967 [1709]: 219.

11. Hariot 1955 [1590]: 378; 1972 [1590]: 28; 2007 [1590]: 50.

12. Percy 1969 [1608?]: 147; William White, quoted in Purchas 1617: 952; Haile 1998: 141.

13. Strachey 1953 [1612]: 98; Haile 1998: 655.

14. Hariot 1955 [1590]: 345; 1972 [1590]: 16; 2007 [1590]: 41.

15. Banister 1970: 378; Beverley 1947 [1705]: 191; 2013 [1705]: 150.

16. Hariot 1955 [1590]: 429; 1972 [1590]: 62; 2007 [1590]: 68; Hulton 1985: 123.

17. Purchas 1617: 943.

18. Spelman 1910 [1613?]: cix; Haile 1998: 490.

19. Strachey 1953 [1612]: 113–14; Haile 1998: 671.

20. Smith 1986a [1608]: 59; Haile 1998: 164; Smith 1986b [1612]: 169; Strachey 1953 [1612]: 95; Haile 1998: 651–52.

21. Hariot 1955 [1590]: 374; 1972 [1590]: 26; 2007 [1590]: 49 (no details of burial); Lawson 1967 [1709]: 185, 187–88.

22. Lane 1955 [1586]: 281.

23. The words are Hariot's: 1955 [1590]: 428; 1972 [1590]: 64; 2007 [1590]: 69.

24. White painting: Hulton 1984: 69. De Bry engraving: Hariot 1972 [1590]: 64–65; 2007 [1590]: 156–57.

25. Smith 1986b [1612]: 168; Strachey 1953 [1612]: 111; Haile 1998: 669. Taste: personal experience, thanks to the late Charles Hudson, who brewed some of the stuff for our class (National Endowment for the Humanities Summer Institute for College Teachers) in 1989. Archaeologist George Szabo refined the description of the taste for us: old sweat socks left in old rubber boots. Well, medicine isn't *supposed* to taste good.

26. Hariot 195 [1590]: 373; 1972 [1590]: 26; 2007 [1590]: 49. We have to question this term. The Powhatan word *machacomico* meant "meeting" or "meeting place," while the only term used for temples in the Virginia records is "*quiocasin* house." The latter term, plainly derived from the word for "gods," is more likely for the Carolina Sounds region.

27. Barlowe 1955 [1585]: 105; Hariot 1955 [1590]: 414, 422–23, 428; Hariot 1972 [1590]: 66, 68, 64; Hariot 2007 [1590]: 69, 70; Hulton 1984: 125, 126.

28. Pictures' order: *The Town of Pomeioke*, *The Town of Secota*, *The Tomb of Their Werowans*. Text only: Hariot 1955 [1590]: 416, 421–22, and 426–27. Engravings and their captions: Hariot 1972 [1590]: 66–67, 68–69, 72–73; Hariot 2007 [1590]: 69, 70, 71 (text), and 159, 161, 165 (illustrations); Hulton 1984: 125, 126, 128.

29. Hariot 1955 [1590]: 373; 1972 [1590]: 26; 2007 [1590]: 49.

30. White painting: Hulton 1983: 68. De Bry engraving: Hariot 1972 [1590]: 71; 2007 [1590]: 163.

31. Barlowe 1955 [1585]: 112. John Smith, remembering (accurately?) an actively hostile encounter at Kecoughtan in October 1607 (his earlier writings omit the hostility), wrote in 1624 that those townsmen had attacked him, bearing their "idol" in front of them: Smith 1986b [1612]: 144; Haile 1998: 232.

32. Beverley 1947 [1705]: 197; 2013 [1705]: 155.

33. Hariot 1955 [1590]: 426–27; 1972 [1590]: 72; 2007 [1590]: 71 (text) and 165 (illustration); Hulton 1984: 128. Also caption on John White's painting: Hulton 1984: 68. This method does not correspond exactly with the Powhatan one (Smith 1986b [1612]: 169; Strachey 1953 [1612]: 94; Haile 1998: 651; Beverley 1947 [1705]: 214, 216; 2013 [1705]: 168, 170), nor with the mat-wrapped bone bundle found in a (probably Chickahominy) temple by Robert Beverley in 1694 (Beverley 1947 [1705]: 196; 2013 [1705]: 155). The method also does not fully correspond with John Lawson's description (1967 [1709]: 188), which has the chief's corpse decaying naturally in an underground coffinlike structure, then dug up as a skeleton, cleaned, the bones articulated and wrapped in deerskins, and then placed as a bundle in the temple. Lawson's mention of commoners being allowed to pay for such a burial also seems not to have been an Algonquian speakers' practice. His term for the temple, however, is Algonquian: *quiogozon* (*quiocasin* in Powhatan). Valuables buried with chief: Smith 1986b [1612]: 173; Strachey 1953 [1612]: 62; Haile 1998: 620.

34. White painting: Hulton 1984: 72. De Bry engraving: Hariot 1972 [1590]: 48; 2007 [1590]: 131.

35. White painting: Hulton 1984: 79. De Bry engraving; Hariot 1972 [1590]: 54; 2007 [1590]: 143.

36. No definite reference backs this up, but it was true for the people's Powhatan relatives. John Smith had the luck to be "conjured" by diviners who wanted to know if his people were well-intentioned or not. See his earlier (therefore more reliable) and more detailed description in Smith 1986a [1608]: 59; Haile 1998: 163–64.

37. Lawson 1967 [1709]: 226.

38. Banister 1970: 379.

39. Smith 1986b [1612]: 168; Strachey 1953 [1612]: 111; Haile 1998: 669.

40. Banister 1970: 379.

41. Lawson 1967 [1709]: 229–30.

42. Term used for "Asclepias or swallow wort": Quinn 1955: 444–45. General term: conclusion reached by Merrill and Feest 1975.

43. *Wapeih*: Hariot 1955 [1590]: 328; 1972 [1590]: 8; 2007 [1590]: 36. Bloodletting: text accompanying the engraving *A Great Lord of Virginia*: Hariot 1955 [1590]: 441; 1972 [1590]: 46; 2007 [1590]: 61 (text), 127 (illustration); Hulton 1984: 109.

44. Quinn 1955: 444–45.

45. Lawson 1967 [1709]: 175.

46. Hariot 1955 [1590]: 380; 1972 [1590]: 29; 2007 [1590]: 51.

47. For further details, see Park 2006 [1938]. In the mid-1960s, after reading Park in an earlier edition, I worked with an elderly Shoshone Indian lady in Nevada who had had experiences with all three kinds of illness. One of her sons, sick with double pneumonia, had been diagnosed with "object intrusion," and when the (female) Indian doctor sucked out the object during an all-night ritual, the boy recovered. I met him, now in his sixties, during that summer. One of her daughters, sick with whooping cough, had been diagnosed with "soul loss"; another (male) Indian doctor retrieved her soul, and she had a period of remission, though she subsequently died. Her mother, my friend, had then gone into a deep depression from grief, diagnosed as "ghost possession," and the doctor had brought her out of it by driving away the ghost. Do some patients cure themselves? Yes, with help they believe in.

Chapter Five

1. It lacked glass, and the only metal the people knew was soft native copper.

2. Rountree 1993b: 27–28. Much more about Indian travel was recorded elsewhere in the Eastern Woodlands; for a summary, see Rountree 1993b.

3. Lane 1955b [1586]: 268, 270.

4. Radford, Ahles, and Bell 1968: 883; in Jasper, Hampton, Allendale, Barnwell, Aiken, Edgefield, Lexington, Orangeburg, Calhoun and Colleton Counties. Also Sussex County, Virginia: Weakley et al. 2012: 427.

5. Lawson 1967 [1709]: 174–75. Lawson says this was not the same as "pecoon," but his account of the limited location of the plant's growth corresponds with true puccoon. Lawson's "pecoon" was probably bloodroot (*Sanguinaria canadensis*), which

grows mainly in North Carolina's inner coastal plain, piedmont, and mountains (Radford, Ahles, and Bell 1968: 882, 479).

6. Abbott 1974; Barlowe 1955 [1585]: 110; Lane 1955b [1586]: 260.

7. Lawson 1967 [1709]: 98.

8. Lawson 1967 [1709]: 203–4; Banister 1970: 373; Beverley 1947 [1705]: 227–28; 2013 [1705]: 279–80.

9. Archer 1969 [1607]: 83; Haile 1998: 103 (oysters). Deer suet "made up handsomely in cakes" was "sold" to the Jamestown English and possibly to other Powhatan Indians: Strachey 1953 [1612]: 115; Haile 1998: 673.

10. See the map in Rountree 1993b: 34, which is based on the work of Myer 1927, Wallace 1965, and Tanner 1989.

11. Barlowe 1955 [1585]: 100, 103.

12. Rountree 1993a: 13–18; Obert (2020) has reached the same conclusion.

13. Lane 1955 [1586]: 279 (inviting to join, 284 [chief's town declined while other towns accepted the invitation]).

14. North Carolina: Lawson 1967 [1709]: 204. Virginia: Smith 1986a [1608]: 59, 61; Haile 1998: 164; Smith 1986b [1612]: 174; Strachey 1953 [1612]; 44, 77; Haile 1998: 604, 634. Since the limited historical record in both Virginia and North Carolina indicates that commoners were not matrilineal, it is possible that the practice for chiefs was borrowed from other, more elaborate (and matrilineal) Indian nations to the southwest.

15. Rountree 1989: 93, 118.

16. North Carolina: Hariot 1955 [1590]: 374–75; 1972 [1590]: 26–27; 2007 [1590]: 49. Virginia: Smith 1986b [1612]: 160; Strachey 1953 [1612]: 76; Haile 1998: 634.

17. Paint: Hariot 1955 [1590]: 334–35; 1972 [1590]: 11; 2007 [1590]: 38. Jewelry: Barlowe 1955 [1585]: 101–102, 103. Cloaks: analogy from Virginia: Smith 1986b [1612]: 160–61; Strachey 1953 [1612]: 71; Haile 1998: 630.

18. Barlowe 1955 [1585]: 103.

19. Detailed account: Barlowe 1955 [1585]: 98–100. Also analogy with Powhatans in Virginia: Percy 1969 [1608?]: 135–36, 137; Archer 1969 [1607]: 84, 92, 103; Haile 1998: 91–92, 93, 104, 112, 123.

20. Lawson 1967 [1709]: 175.

21. Analogy from a 1615 feast in Virginia: Hamor 1957 [1615]: 43–44; Haile 1998: 835–36.

22. Rountree 1989: 108.

23. Smith 1986a [1608]: 60; Haile 1998: 163–64.

24. A newly captured John Smith was interviewed by Opechancanough in December 1607 only after Smith had had a night's rest (Smith 1986a [1608]: 47, 49; Haile 1998: 157–58). A couple of months later, he and Christopher Newport met Powhatan for the first time, gave him presents, and were feasted before "he [Powhatan] began his discourse" (Smith 1986a [1608]: 65; Haile 1998: 166–67).

25. Documented only for Virginia in the early years (Smith 1986b [1612]: 167–68; Strachey 1953 [1612]: 84–85; Haile 1998: 641–42) but well attested later for Eastern Woodland peoples when entertaining foreigners.

26. Barlowe 1955 [1585]: 107–10.

27. White 1955 [1587]: 526 (Manteo); Lane 1955b [1586]: 280 (Wanchese); Quinn 1955: 119 (both went to England and back).

28. Lane 1955b [1586]: 258 (Menatonon); Barlowe 1955 [1585]: 110; a note to that page gives Quinn's opinion that Pooneno may have governed a Tuscarora, rather than a Chowanoke, town.

29. Barlowe 1955 [1585]: 113.

30. Lane 1955 [1586]: 265, 279, 280.

31. Lane 1955b [1586]: 258, 279.

32. Barlowe 1955 [1585]: 111, if Barlowe got it right while lacking an interpreter.

33. Barlowe 1955 [1585]: 113.

34. Barlowe 1955 [1585]: 113–14.

35. Barlowe 1955 [1585]: 113.

36. Strachey 1953 [1612]: 64; Haile 1998: 622.

37. Ethnographic analogy from Virginia: Rountree 1989: chapter 6, especially p. 101.

38. Barlowe 1955 [1585]: 114; what happened after arrival at the captors' village is deduced by analogy with Powhatan examples.

39. Lawson 1967 [1709]: 207–8.

40. White 1955 [1587]: 528–29.

41. Barlowe 1955 [1585]: 113–14.

42. Lane 1955 [1586]: 281–83.

43. Lane 1955b [1586]: 270; this is a mention of a Chowanoke chief's son who had been captured and then released by Mangoags (Meherrins?) to the west.

44. The English of the Roanoke colonies recorded nothing about this, apparently having seen nothing of it in their short stays. Such treatment for captured men is, however, copiously documented for other Eastern Woodlands peoples, including the Virginia Algonquian speakers: White 1969 [1608?]: 150; Percy 1921–22 [1625?]: 263, 266; Smith 1986b [1612]: 175; Strachey 1953 [1612]: 60; Haile 1998: 141 501, 504, 617. Strachey (1953 [1612]: 109; Haile 1998: 667) recorded a derisive song sung about it and noted that "they never bemoan themselves, nor cry out, giving up so much as a groan for any death how cruel soever and full of torment."

45. Swanton 1946: 717.

46. That was true for all of the Atlantic Coast colonies. See Kupperman 2000.

Chapter Six

1. Worked out in some detail for the Powhatans: Rountree 1993b.

2. Barlowe 1955 [1585]: 111, 111n.

3. Lewis and Loomie 1953: 58; Scisco 1945: 278.

4. Barlowe 1955 [1585]: 97; Quinn 1955: 78: Quinn adds, "We know nothing, directly, of the preparation of the 1584 expedition." That includes the number of people and their roles to play, as well as what supplies they took along.

5. Barlowe 1955 [1585]: 100.

6. Barlowe 1955 [1585]: 98.

7. There is no record of which inlet they used, Roanoke or Gunt. But with the kind of watercraft they had, they probably played it safe as long as possible and took the inside route down to Gunt.

8. Barlowe 1955 [1585]: 99–101.

9. Barlowe 1955 [1585]: 104 (swords), 105 (fires). Quinn (1955: 15–16) posits that Barlowe's account sounds so sunny because he knew his writings would be used as procolonizing propaganda in London. So he left out any negative incidents that would almost certainly have occurred.

10. This is not uncommon when very different-looking people see each other for the first time. It happened to my own father in the 1930s in rural Haiti.

11. Barlowe 1955 [1585]: 106–10.

12. Barlowe 1955 [1585]: 111–14.

13. White 1955 [1587]: 526.

14. The largest ship's journal (printed in Quinn 1955: 189) says arrival at Croatoan (near Cape Hatteras) on June 26.

15. Quinn 1955: 173n.

16. Quinn 1955: 176 (livestock); this is the account in *Holinshed's Chronicles*, not an eyewitness one. Quinn 1955: 503 (mules); those visitors were fleeting precursors of White's 1587 colony. Mastiffs: missionary George Thorpe, trying in 1621 to allay the fears of Indians afraid of the dogs, had several of them killed in sight of his would-be converts: Kingsbury 1906–35: 3:552–53; Smith 1986c [1624]: 294–95. The only mention of dogs, confusingly, is in Ralph Lane's writing about his starving men, on an expedition up the Chowan River the next spring, having had to eat "dogs porridge, which they had bespoken [prepared] for themselves": Lane 1955b [1586]: 272.

17. Journal of the *Tiger*, printed in Quinn 1955: 189–91.

18. White 1955 [1587]: 531.

19. Lane 1955b [1586]: 280; White 1955 [1587]: 527–28.

20. Rountree 1990: 62–63; 2005: 178–79.

21. Quinn 1955: 192 and 192n. The names of the 107 colonists besides Ralph Lane: Quinn 1955: 194–97. Some animals may have been killed or drowned in the violent grounding of the *Tiger*. In addition, a maritime anthropologist told me decades ago that horses were the chanciest animals to survive the long, southerly looped Atlantic crossing, because they require more fresh water than the other kinds of livestock.

22. Lane 1955b [1586]: 257–59.

23. Opechancanough took the name Mangopeesomon after his brother Powhatan died, at which time he became the real power in the region and could speed up his preparations for the Great Assault of 1622: Strachey 1953 [1612]: 113–14; Haile 1998: 671 (naming customs); Kingsbury 1906–35: 3:584 (Opechancanough's change); Rountree 2005: 211 (my deduction about change).

24. Rountree 1990: 75, 84.

25. Lane 1955b [1586]: 264–66.

26. Lane 1955b [1586]: 270–72.

27. Lane 1955b [1586]: 259.

28. Records lost: Quinn 1955: 245. Little is known in detail about either that wintering expedition or what plans the English laid for shifting their efforts northward.

Quinn suggests (1955: 246) that the fact that all of the Mid-Atlantic coast was then claimed—and sometimes defended militarily—by the Spanish was threat enough to the "encroaching" English to make them keep any documents relative to their Chesapeake explorations a secret.

29. Lane 1955b [1586]: 276–77.

30. Lane 1955b [1586]: 279.

31. Lane 1955b [1586]: 275–76. The phrase is "The king was advised and of himself disposed."

32. Lane 1955b [1586]: 280–83. "China," or china-root, a species of greenbrier, is mentioned.

33. Lane 1955b [1586]: 285.

34. Lane 1955b [1586]: 286–88.

35. Lane 1955b [1586]: 289–92.

36. Quinn (1955: 469), writing from the English perspective, merely calls it "rash." The ships were the tardy relief fleet, expected long before by Lane. His report to the Roanoke chief about seeing them arrive the previous month had been a ruse.

37. White 1955 [1587]: 528–59; Quinn 1955: 504. Most of the small English contingent were not killed outright. Instead, they escaped in their boat to a nearby island, where they presumably starved to death. Nothing more is known of them.

38. Names of 91 men, 17 women, and 9 boys: White 1955 [1587]: 539–43.

39. White 1955 [1587]: 523.

40. Smith 1986a [1608]: 90; Haile 1998: 179.

41. White 1955 [1587]: 225–26.

42. White 1955 [1587]: 226–29.

43. White 1955 [1587]: 229–30.

44. White 1955 [1587]: 530–31.

45. White 1955 [1587]: 531–35.

Chapter Seven

1. Lawson 1967 [1709]: 69.

2. Percy 1969 (1608?): 140; Haile 1998: 96.

3. Mortimer 2012: 12.

4. Smith 1986b [1612]: 155; Strachey 1953 [1612]: 125; Haile 1998: 682.

5. Goodman 2015: 2.

6. Goodman 2015: 126; Mortimer 2012: 5–6. The most famous such house, for American tourists at least, remains the oldest section of Penshurst Place, with its fourteenth-century central hearth intact.

7. Beds: Goodman 2015: 6–8. Fleas: English: Goodman 2015: 37–38. Indian: analogy with Virginia: Hamor 1957 [1615]: 43; Haile 1998: 835; Beverley 1947 [1705]: 220; 2012 [1705]: 173.

8. Smith 1986b [1612]: 245; Haile 1998: 297. Lice: English: Goodman 2015: 6–8. Indian: the fact that all Algonquian languages had a word for "louse" (Siebert 1975: 354–55).

9. Goodman 2015: 72.

10. Mortimer 2012: 28ff., 133ff.

11. Goodman 2015: 42–44.

12. The English did have standards of behavioral modesty, especially for women and children, but it was largely concerned with showing deference to one's social superiors.

13. Mortimer 2012: 242.

14. Goodman 2015: 17–25. Goodman, a "living historian," lived for months in the Tudor English way, and she found the linen route to cleanliness just as effective as bathing.

15. Mortimer 2012: 26–27.

16. Goodman 2015: 1.

17. A few such clocks still survive in English cathedrals, whose bells still toll the hours, except during normal sleeping hours (personal observation during multiple trips to the UK).

18. Indian: analogy with Virginia: Percy 1969 [1608?]: 145–46; Haile 1998: 141; Purchas 1613: 640; 1614: 766; 1617: 952; 1904–6 [1625]: 841; Haile 1998: 141. English: Goodman 2015: 12.

19. Hariot 1955 [1590]: 376–77; 1972 [1590]: 27; 2007 [1590]: 50.

20. Goodman 2015: 142, 231–32.

21. Goodman 2015: 149.

22. Goodman 2015: 124–41.

23. *Zizania aquatica* and *Hordeum pusillum*.

24. Suet: Strachey 1953 [1612]: 120; Haile 1998: 677.

25. Goodman 2015: 121ff.

26. Spencer 2011: 251–52: "From the first quarter of the nineteenth century the fate of British cooking was essentially in the hands of a burgeoning [and gentility-seeking yet profit-oriented] bourgeoisie and its kitchen staff. . . . Two factors . . . would generate a decline in [British] cooking; a willingness to connive and abet the master's economy drives in the kitchen could easily succeed in [producing] too many mediocre dishes and in addition it would encourage a tendency towards blandness through a fear of pungent herbs, especially garlic, upon the breath; this was a cardinal social sin which would have been sufficient cause to be ousted from society forever."

27. I regret that I can no longer find the reference; it was in *Natural History* magazine several decades ago. A wife and husband, both cultural anthropologists, went to live with a very traditional ethnic group whose members expected them to do the work appropriate to their sex. The wife fitted in easily, having learned basic housework as a child, while the husband had a foul time of it learning jobs he had never even seen done before.

28. That would have been true even of urban Englishwomen. Many families kept chickens, cows, and perhaps even a pig in their backyards in the city. Unsanitary? Often. Cheaper food? Definitely.

29. Mortimer 2012: 95.

30. Bridenbaugh 1967: 17. See also Stone 1984, especially pp. 14ff.

31. Mortimer 2012: 81.

32. Stone 1977: 77, 78, 80. Stone wrote his book before the explosion of drugs such as cocaine on the American scene in the 1980s.

33. Mortimer 2012: 78, 81.

34. Goodman 2015: 119.

35. Cited in Mortimer 2012: 129.

36. Wax and Thomas 1961: 308; also personal observations when I met conservative Winnebago and Shoshone Indian people in Wisconsin and Nevada, respectively.

37. Stone 1977: 81ff.

38. Mortimer 2012: 51. See also Hogrefe 1977: xv–xxiv.

39. Goodman 2015: 262ff.

40. Stone 1977: 126. In this paragraph I rely heavily on Stone's reconstruction of Tudor English child-rearing, on pp. 113–27.

41. Stone 1977: 125.

42. Mortimer 2012: 81.

43. Stone 1977: 117–18.

44. Griffiths 1996.

45. Pollock 1983: 97–99, 144–49, 188, 199.

46. Stone 1977: 83–84; Kussmaul 1981: 24–27; Griffiths 1996: chapter 1; Fletcher 2008: chapter 2; Shepard 2002: 23–38, 93–126. (I am indebted to Karen O. Kupperman for leading me to the latter four sources.) For an Italian observer's view ca. 1500, see Sneyd 1847.

47. My evidence for this is Uttamatommakin (a priest) telling English priest Samuel Purchas in London in 1617 to evangelize the young people in Pocahontas's entourage, for he himself was "too old" to change (Purchas 1617: 955; Haile 1998: 882). In spite of his arguments with Purchas, he still did not see any threat in the younger people joining a rabidly evangelistic religion. It was their business, not his.

48. Thomas 1971: 115–18. I am indebted to Karen O. Kupperman for pointing out this source.

49. A major source for this statement is the many published accounts of those captivities, notably in the seventy-volume collection published by the Garland Publishing Company.

Chapter Eight

1. Nugent 1934: passim.

2. McIlvenna 2009; Barth 2010.

3. Lawson 1967 [1709]: 232.

4. Lawson 1967 [1709]: 233.

5. Lawson 1967 [1709]: 233; Rountree 1990: 71n. In 1621 Opechancanough tried to stockpile the plant to use on the English.

6. CSR 3:153.

7. CSR 22:734–35. Like many Europeans of his time, he assumed that American Indian tribes were the Lost Tribes of Israel, in which case they would have preserved some biblical traditions. He hoped to find evidence of that among the Indian people he met, so his statement may be wishful thinking.

8. Dunbar 1960; Taukchiray n.d.

9. Brooks 2014.

10. Lawson 1967 [1709]: xxxviii.

11. Lawson 1967 [1709]: 69.

12. The Arab name "Wahab," as either surname or first name (and pronounced "WAY-hab"), survived on Ocracoke Island at least as recently as the 1950s (Rountree, personal observation by her parents, who had friends there).

13. Brooks 2014: 183, 186.

14. CSR 2:129. For more detailed background, see La Vere 2013: 176.

15. CSR 2:171; CCR; Taukchiray n.d.: 60.

16. Cumming 1958: 202–4.

17. CSR 5:321.

18. CGP (Dobbs), No. 5, folder for 1756, letter of August 10, 1756; North Carolina, Secretary of State, Land Grant Office: Patent Book 15: 268; CSR 6:563.

19. Currituck County, Deeds 5:326.

20. Brooks 2014: 195.

21. Brooks 2014: 201.

22. Quinn 1955: 870.

23. Taukchiray n.d.: 43.

24. CCR.

25. For details, see La Vere 2013: 69–73.

26. CSR 2:310.

27. CSR 2:310; Taukchiray n.d.: 28.

28. Lawson 1967 [1709]: 209.

29. CCR; published in Hathaway 1900: 598–99.

30. Lawson 1967 [1709]: 242.

31. Lawson 1967 [1709]: 211.

32. CCR. Governor Walker's May 14 order to militiamen to take the five Indians into custody and John Lawson's June 23 letter to Walker about what he'd learned at Bay River during a visit the previous week are both published in Hathaway 1900: 597–98. Walker's June 2 order remains unpublished.

33. Albemarle County, Papers 1 (1678–1714): folio 56.

34. La Vere 2013: 69–73.

35. CSR 1:875.

36. Microfilm of extracts from *A Book of Orders, Judgements and Decrees from the Honorable Edward Hyde, Esquire, President; and His Council*, reel P56.1P [the Francis Lister Hawkews Papers, 1695–1836], items 14ff.; cited in Taukchiray n.d.: 54a, CCR. Slave traders from South Carolina had also been active in taking Mattamuskeet prisoners during the war. The place the people were sold to is not named, but the Virginia colony had already established a precedent by sending Nanzatico Indian prisoners to Antigua in the Caribbean (Rountree 1990: 121).

37. CSR 2:141; identified as Mattamuskeets by Taukchiray (n.d.: 33).

38. CSR 2:168. North Carolina, Secretary of State, Land Grant Office: Patent Book 2:367 (Coree).

39. For what happened to the Nanzaticos, see Rountree 1990: 121.

40. Frank J. Klingberg, ed., *The Carolina Chronicle of Dr. Francis Lejau* (Berkeley: University of California Press, 1956), 65; cited in Taukchiray n.d.: 55.

41. Lawson 1967 [1709]: 219.

42. CCR.

43. Secretary of State: Land Grant Library, File 76; printed in full in Garrow 1975: appendix 4.

44. Garrow 1975: 20–21.

45. CSR 3:153 (1731), 5:321 (1755). 1761 deed: Hyde County, Deeds, Vol. A, part 2, pp. 793–96.

46. Garrow 1975: 22–23.

47. Garrow 1975: 24–26. For a discussion of what that transition was like among the Virginia Algonquians, see Rountree 1990: chapter 7.

48. The relevant deeds from Hyde County are printed as appendices in Garrow 1975. The 1761 termination deed is appendix 33.

49. CSR 6:563, 995–96.

50. Hyde County Court Minutes 1764–91, March term. Thanks to a two-year break in the minutes at that point, the outcome is unknown. The text, minimal as it is, is printed in Garrow 1975, appendix 35. One of the anonymous readers of this manuscript noted that she was probably held by the Collins Family of Somerset Plantation, which left voluminous papers in the North Carolina State Archives; the family's racial practices may be able to be gleaned from that collection.

51. Taukchiray n.d.: 65a; U.S. Census 1850, Hyde County.

52. Hyde County Deeds 1:51 (text printed in Garrow 1975: appendix 34). Discussion by Garrow 1975: 30–31. Apprentices: Hyde County Apprentice Bonds, 1804 (texts printed in Garrow 1975: appendices 35–37).

53. Garrow 1975: 32–35; Hyde County Apprentice Papers, 1771–1849, 1850–1892 (texts in Garrow 1975: appendices 40–41).

54. Speck 1916.

55. Quinn 1955: 209. Ralph Lane's account has hints about that sojourn and no more, presumably because it was (in twenty-first-century parlance) "classified information." We do know that the third colonizing attempt, in 1587, was originally planned to take place in Chesapeake Indian territory, not on Roanoke Island.

56. Lower Norfolk County, Virginia, Deeds D: 294. We are indebted to Lars Adams for finding and transcribing that document for us.

57. Hening 1809–23: 1:325.

58. 1660: Lower Norfolk County, Virginia, Deeds D: 75; Nathaniel Batts Papers 1655–1660, North Carolina State Archives (cited in Petrey 2014: 96). 1663 deed: CSR 1:19 (1662/3 sale); North Carolina Higher Court Records 1697–1701: 503 (1693 testimony to adjacent land's deed). 1663 patents: Nugent 1934: 426, 427. See also Cumming 1939 and McPherson 1966.

59. Virginia southside counties at that period extended far into what is now North Carolina; the Virginia county that would have claimed the Edenton area in the 1660s was Nansemond County, whose records burned during the American Civil War.

60. Anonymous 1900: 7, 11.

61. Robinson 2001: 11, cited in Petrey 2014: 105. North Carolina's law preceded Virginia's by forty years, but both laws were disastrous for Indian towns.

62. Hawks 1858: 379, quoted in Taukchiray n.d.: 26.

63. North Carolina Higher Court Records 1697–1701: 80, 102.

64. Order: CCR, published in Hathaway 1903: 73. Payment: CSR 2:140. The survey excluded some land—within the Indians' bounds—claimed by an Englishman, who had protested to the governor (Hathaway 1903: 251).

65. Lawson 1967 [1709]: 242. Taukchiray has estimated that in 1703 there had been only two sectors of the Yeopims, with the bulk of them (about three-quarters) living at Poteskeet and the rest (Lawson's Paspatanks) living on the Pasquotank River and calling themselves "Yeopims" (Taukchiray n.d.: 23, 31).

66. CSR 22: 735.

67. Lawson 1967 [1709]: 200.

68. Lawson 1967 [1709]: 192–93. For all of the Native people of the region, the incest taboo extended out through first cousins.

69. CSR 2: 141.

70. CSR 2: 141.

71. Secretary of State: XIX Record-keeping—Probate: Will Books, Box 45, Proceedings of Court of Chancery 1712–54: 23, 54.

72. CSR 2: 204–5.

73. CSR 2: 483.

74. Brickell 1968 [1737]: 282–86.

75. CSR 4: 446.

76. CSR 5: 321.

77. Secretary of State, Land Grant Office, Patent Book 5: 155. Edenton District Superior Court, Civil Action Papers Concerning Land 1766–1779 (DCR.2.022, Boxes 83–84), cited in Taukchiray n.d.

78. Hathaway 1903: 227. Petrey (2014: 164) mistakenly gives the page number as 327.

79. CSR 1: 657.

80. Smith 1986c [1624]: 193, 215; Haile 1998: 296, 323.

81. Smith 1986c [1624]: 291; Kingsbury 1906–35: 3: 641–42.

82. Strachey 1953 [1612}: 64; Haile 1998: 622.

83. Bland et al. 1911 [1651]: 13–14.

84. Nugent 1934: 426, 428.

85. Nugent 1977: 13, 229, 231, 241, 242.

86. Anonymous 1900: 7, 347. Adams (2013) calls that period the "Chowan River War."

87. Bass n.d., third genealogical page.

88. CSR 1: 432.

89. CSR 2: 140. The date of the grant is given as "in the administration of Governor Archdale," which was 1695–96.

90. CCR (published in Hathaway 1903: 242–43).

91. CSR 2:140.

92. Chowan County, Deeds 1:63.

93. CSR 1:852.

94. CSR 2: 141. Chief Hoyter was possibly related to Chief Hiter of the Machapungas/Mattamuskeets of 1699, though evidence is lacking.

95. Lawson 1967 [1709]: 242.

96. For details of one action they were involved in, under an English commander, see La Vere 2013: 129–31.

97. CSR 2:141 (pro-English), 1:891 (delivery).

98. CSR 1:859.

99. North Carolina Colonial Court Records, Box CCR190, Taxes and Accounts 1679–1754: folder "Claims 1713–1720," item "Moneys paid to sundry persons," p. 2, State Archives of North Carolina, Raleigh.

100. CSR 2:297, 308.

101. CSR 2:380.

102. CSR 2:485. The same surveyor had laid out 53,000 acres for the Tuscaroras and the Chowanokes together in 1723.

103. CSR 4:35.

104. General Assembly Records (formerly Legislative Papers) Box 101: petition (dated October 23, 1790) of William Lewis and Samuel Harrell, concerning land formerly belonging to the Chowanokes by patent. The petition appears in full in Taukchiray n.d.: 90p.

105. Diligent searching for the patent itself in modern times has failed to turn it up. Chowanoke tribe's response: CCR, published in Hathaway 1903: 75. A personal letter, undated, from John Hiter, asking for a resurvey of the land, was published in Hathaway 1903: 77.

106. Houn 1983: 6; CCR; CSR 4:33–35, 74–75.

107. CSR 3:153 (census), 282, and 319 (militia captain).

108. CSR 3:537–38; Taukchiray n.d.: 75.

109. Caption to map of Tuscarora land: MC.183.T964.1803b. Population: Taukchiray n.d.: 93–94.

110. Brickell 1968 [1737]: 282–86.

111. Sales: CSR 4:802, 1254; Gates County, Deeds 5:380; Chowan County, Deeds G: 137–39. Encroaching: CSR 4:630–32.

112. CSR 5:162 (quote), 321. Wes Taukchiray (n.d.: 90h) identifies the two men as John Robbins, who had been an adult for at least twenty-four years, and James Bennett, about four years his junior; the sole woman was probably Nan Robbins. The parentage of the four children is unknown.

113. CSR 22:329.

114. Grimes 2000 [1910]: 128; Chowan County, Wills; Chowan County, Deeds M: 216–18.

115. CSR 15:730, 17:243.

116. Robbins: Gates County, Court of Pleas and Quarter Sessions, 1:16. Others: Gates County, Court of Pleas and Quarter Sessions, 1:55, 135; 2:12.

117. Gates County, Court of Pleas and Quarter Sessions, 3:57; Gates County, County Court Minutes 1796–1803, p. 172.

118. Chowan County, Minute Docket Superior Court, 1810–1813 [unpaginated], pp. 39 and 41 from title page.

119. Chowanokes of both sexes were listed—siblings James, Benjamin, Patience, Sarah, Nancy, Elizabeth, Dorcas, and Christian Robbins (Gates County Deeds A [pt. 2]: indenture no. 46; Gates County Deeds 5: 20; Taukchiray n.d.: 90–91). 1793 sale of land adjacent to the 30 A. Gates County Deeds 3: 167. Not in 1724 patent: Taukchiray n.d.: 97.

120. Gates County Deeds 2:153. The signatories were James Robbins, Benjamin Robbins, George Bennett, and Joseph Bennett.

121. Hazel 2014: 38.

122. General Assembly Records, Box 101.

123. Gates County, Deeds 3:207.

124. Unwillingly: Milteer 2016: 43–45. Early 1820s: Gates County, Deeds 5:174 and passim (cited in Taukchiray n.d.); for details, see Hazel 2014: 39ff.

125. Hazel 2014: 34, 58.

126. Governmental acknowledgment, whether state or federal, is for tribes, not for individuals, however authentically Indian they may be. Any funded programs administered by these governments (especially the federal one) are intended to assist groups of people, not individuals, and even then, the largesse, such as it may be, is not handed out automatically. Neither, by any means, is the recognition in the first place. We speak from experience: Rountree has been involved in recognition cases in Virginia (seven state, one federal) and Maryland (one state), either as a researcher/presenter or as an evaluator. Taukchiray has been a researcher for several recognition petitions in the Carolinas.

Bibliography

Abbott, R. Tucker. 1974. *American Seashells: The Marine Mollusca of the Atlantic and Pacific Coasts of North America*. 2nd ed. New York: Van Nostrand Reinhold.

Adams, Lars C. 2013. "'Sundry Murders and Depredations': A Closer Look at the Chowan River War, 1676–1677." *North Carolina Historical Review* 90: 149–72.

Albemarle County, North Carolina. 1664–1738. Records.

Anonymous, comp. 1900. "Indians of Southern Virginia, 1650–1711: Depositions in the Virginia and North Carolina Boundary Case." *Virginia Magazine of History and Biography* 7: 337–352, 8: 1–11.

Archer, Gabriel. 1969 [1607]. "Relatyon of the Discovery of Our River." In *The Jamestown Voyages under the First Charter*, series 2, vol. 136, edited by Philip L. Barbour, 80–98. Cambridge: Hakluyt Society. Also printed, with modernized spelling, in Haile, *Jamestown Narratives*, 101–18.

Banister, John. 1970. *John Banister and His Natural History of Virginia, 1678–1692*. Edited by Joseph and Nesta Ewan. Urbana: University of Illinois Press.

Barlowe, Arthur. 1955 [1585]. "The First Voyage Made to the Coastes of America, with Two Barkes . . ." In *The Roanoke Voyages, 1584–1590*, series 2, vol. 104, edited by David B. Quinn, 91–116. Cambridge: Hakluyt Society.

Barth, Jonathan Edward. 2010. "'The Sinke of America': Society in the Albemarle Borderlands of North Carolina, 1663–1729." *North Carolina Historical Review* 87: 1–27.

Bass, John. n.d. *Sermon Book*. Manuscript book (dating to late seventeenth century) in possession of the Bass family of Nansemond Indians, Chesapeake, Virginia.

Beverley, Robert. 1947 [1705]. *The History and Present State of Virginia*. Edited by Louis B. Wright. Chapel Hill: University of North Carolina Press.

———. 2013 [1705]. *The History and Present State of Virginia*. Edited by Susan Scott Parrish. Chapel Hill: University of North Carolina Press.

Bland, Edward, Abraham Wood, Sackford Brewster, and Elias Pennant. 1911 [1651]. "The Discovery of New Brittaine, Began August 27, Anno Dom. 1650 . . ." In *Narratives of Early Carolina, 1650–1708*, edited by Alexander S. Salley, 5–19. New York: Charles Scribner's Sons.

Blick, Jeffrey P. 1987. "The Huskanaw and Ossuary Rituals of the Quiyoughcohannock Indians of Southeastern Virginia." *Quarterly Bulletin of the Archeological Society of Virginia* 42: 193–204.

———. 2000. "The Archaeology and Ethnohistory of the Dog in Virginia Algonquian Culture as Seen from Weyanoke Old Town." In *Papers of the Thirty-first Algonquian Conference*, edited by John D. Nichols, 1–17. Winnipeg: University of Manitoba Press.

————. 2006. "Canis Familiaris Skeletal Remains from Weyanoke Old Town (44PG51), Virginia." *Northeast Anthropology* 69: 59–85.

Brickell, John. 1968 [1737]. *The Natural History of North Carolina*. Murfreesboro, N.C.: Johnson Publishing Co.

Bridenbaugh, Carl. 1967. *Vexed and Troubled Englishmen, 1590–1642*. New York: Oxford University Press.

Brooks, Baylus C. 2014. "John Lawson's Indian Town on Hatteras Island, North Carolina." *North Carolina Historical Review* 91: 171–207.

Bushnell, David Ives. 1937. "Indian Sites Below the Falls of the Rappahannock, Virginia." *Smithsonian Miscellaneous Collections* 96, no. 4.

Ceci, Lynn. 1975a. "Fish Fertilizer: A Native North American Practice?" *Science* 188 (4183): 26–30.

————. 1975b. Reply to letters in 1975a. *Science* 189 (4207): 946–49.

Chowan County, North Carolina. 1739 to present. Records.

Clayton, John. 1965 [1687]. "'The Aborigines of the Country': Letter to Dr. Nehemiah Grew." In *The Reverend John Clayton*, edited by Edmund Berkeley and Dorothy S. Berkeley, 21–39. Charlottesville: University of Virginia Press.

————. 1968 [1687]. "Another Account of Virginia." Edited by Edmund Berkeley and Dorothy S. Berkeley. *Virginia Magazine of History and Biography* 76: 415–36.

Cresson, Hillborn T. 1892. "Report upon Pile Structures in Naaman's Creek, near Claymont, Delaware." In *Archaeological and Ethnological Papers of the Peabody Museum* 1, no. 4. Cambridge, Mass.: Peabody Museum of American Archaeology and Ethnology at Harvard University.

Cumming, William P. 1939. "The Earliest Permanent Settlement in Carolina." *American Historical Review* 45: 82–89.

Currituck County, North Carolina. 1739 to present. Records.

————. 1958. *The Southeast in Early Maps*. Princeton, N.J.: Princeton University Press.

Dixon, Bradley J. 2019. "'His One Netev Ples': The Chowans and the Politics of Native Petitions in the Colonial South." *William and Mary Quarterly* 76: 31–74.

Dunbar, Gary. 1960. "The Hatteras Indians of North Carolina." *Ethnohistory* 7: 410–18.

Fagan, Brian. 2000. *The Little Ice Age*. New York: Basic Books.

Feest, Christian F. 1978a. "Nanticoke and Neighboring Tribes." In *Handbook of North American Indians*, vol. 15, *Northeast*, edited by Bruce G. Trigger, 240–52. Washington, D.C.: Smithsonian Institution.

————. 1978b. "Virginia Algonquians." In *Handbook of North American Indians*, vol. 15, *Northeast*, edited by Bruce G. Trigger, 253–70. Washington, D.C.: Smithsonian Institution.

————. 1978c. "North Carolina Algonquians." In *Handbook of North American Indians*, vol. 15, *Northeast*, edited by Bruce G. Trigger, 253–70. Washington, D.C.: Smithsonian Institution.

————. 1983. "Powhatan's Mantle" and "Skin Pouch" [the "Virginia Purse"]. In *Tradescant's Rarities*, edited by Arthur MacGregor, 130–35, 135–37. Oxford: Clarendon.

Fletcher, Anthony. 2008. *Growing Up in England: The Experience of Childhood, 1600–1914*. New Haven, Conn.: Yale University Press.

Garrow, Patrick H. 1975. *The Mattamuskeet Documents: A Study in Social History*. Raleigh, N.C.: Department of Cultural Resources, Division of Archives and History.

Gates County, North Carolina. 1779 to present. Records.

Geary, James A. 1955. "The Language of the Carolina Algonkian Tribes." In *The Roanoke Voyages, 1584–1590*, series 2, vol. 104, edited by David B. Quinn, 873–900. Cambridge: Hakluyt Society.

Glover, Thomas. 1904 [1676]. *An Account of Virginia, Its Scituation, Temperature, Inhabitants, and Their Manner of Planting and Ordering Tobacco, etc.* [Originally published in *Philosophical Transactions of the Royal Society*.] Oxford: B. H. Blackwell.

Goodman, Ruth. 2015. *How to Be a Tudor: A Dawn to Dusk Guide to Tudor Life*. New York: Liveright Publishing Corp.

Griffiths, Paul. 1996. *Youth and Authority: Formative Experiences in England, 1560–1640*. Oxford: Oxford University Press.

Grimes, J. Bryan, ed. 2000 [1910]. *Abstracts of North Carolina Wills from about 1663 to 1760*. Baltimore: Clearfield Publishing Co.

Haile, Edward W., comp. 1998. *Jamestown Narratives: Eyewitness Accounts of the Virginia Colony: The First Decade; 1607–1617*. Champlain, Va.: RoundHouse.

Hamor, Ralph. 1957 [1615]. *A True Discourse of the Present State of Virginia*. Richmond: Virginia State Library. Also printed, with modernized spelling, in Haile, *Jamestown Narratives*, 795–856.

Hancock, William H. 2006. *Building an Indian House*. Yorktown, Va.: J & R Graphics.

Hancock, William H., and Helen C. Rountree. n.d. "Building a Powhatan House: A Guide to *Yeehawkawn* Construction for Museums." Manuscript with accompanying digital photos and video, on file with the authors, Jamestown Settlement, and Historic St. Mary's City.

Hanson, Elizabeth. 1977 [1728]. *God's Mercy Surmounting Man's Cruelty*. Garland Library of Narratives of North American Indian Captivities 6, compiled by Wilcomb Washburn. New York: Garland Publishing.

Hariot, Thomas. 1955 [1590]. *A Briefe and True Report of the New Found Land of Virginia*. In *The Roanoke Voyages, 1584–1590*, series 2, vol. 104, edited by David B. Quinn, 317–87. Cambridge: Hakluyt Society.

———. 1972 [1590]. *A Briefe and True Report of the New Found Land of Virginia*. New York: Dover.

———. 2007 [1590] *A Briefe and True Report of the New Found Land of Virginia*. Charlottesville: University of Virginia Press.

Hathaway, J. R. B., ed. 1900. "Governor Walker and the Bay River Indians." In *North Carolina Historical and Genealogical Register* 1(4). Edenton, N.C.

———. 1903. "Miscellaneous items of interest." In *North Carolina Historical and Genealogical Register* 3(2): passim. Edenton, N.C.

Hawks, Francis L. 1858. *History of North Carolina*. Fayetteville, N.C.

Hazel, Forest. 2014. "Looking for Indian Town: The Dispersal of the Chowan Indian Tribe in Eastern North Carolina, 1780–1915." *North Carolina Archaeology* 63: 34–64.

Hening, William Waller, comp. 1809–1823. *The Statutes at Large, Being a Collection of All the Laws of Virginia from the First Session of the Legislature.* 13 vols. New York: R. & W. & G. Bartow.

Hogrefe, Pearl, 1977. *Women of Action in Tudor England.* Ames: University of Iowa Press.

Houn, Weynette Parks. 1983. *Chowan County North Carolina County Court Minutes, Pleas, and Quarter Sessions, 1730–1743.* Durham, N.C.: W. P. Houn.

Hulton, Paul. 1984. *America 1585: The Complete Drawings of John White.* Chapel Hill: University of North Carolina Press.

Hyde County, North Carolina. 1739 to present. Records.

Johnson, Frederick. 1942. "The Boylston Street Fishweir." Andover, Mass.: Phillips Academy, Robert S. Peabody Foundation for Archaeology, *Papers* 2.

————. 1949. "The Boylston Street Fishweir, Part II." Andover, Mass.: Phillips Academy, Robert S. Peabody Foundation for Archaeology, *Papers* 4.

Kingsbury, Susan Myra, comp. 1906–1935. *Records of the Virginia Company of London.* 4 vols. Washington, D.C.: Library of Congress.

Kupperman, Karen Ordahl. 2000. *Indians and English: Facing Off in Early America.* Ithaca, N.Y.: Cornell University Press.

Kussmaul, Ann. 1981. *Servants in Husbandry in Early Modern England.* Cambridge: Cambridge University Press.

Lamb, H. H. 1995. *Climate, History, and the Modern World.* 2nd ed. New York: Routledge.

Lane, Ralph. 1955a [1585]. Letter to Sir Francis Walsingham (8 September 1585). In *The Roanoke Voyages, 1584–1590*, series 2, vol. 104, edited by David B. Quinn, 210–14. Cambridge: Hakluyt Society.

————. 1955b [1586]. "Discourse on the First Colony." In *The Roanoke Voyages, 1584–1590*, series 2, vol. 104, edited by David B. Quinn, 255–94. Cambridge: Hakluyt Society.

La Vere, David. 2013. *The Tuscarora War: Indians, Settlers, and the Fight for the Carolina Colonies.* Chapel Hill: University of North Carolina Press.

Lawson, John. 1967 [1709]. *A New Voyage to Carolina.* Edited by Hugh T. Lefler. Chapel Hill: University of North Carolina Press.

LeMaster, Michelle. 2006. "In the 'Scolding Houses': Indians and the Law in Eastern North Carolina, 1684–1760." *North Carolina Historical Review* 83: 193–232.

Lewis, Clifford M., and Albert J. Loomie. 1953. *The Spanish Jesuit Mission in Virginia, 1570–1572.* Chapel Hill: University of North Carolina Press.

Lippson, Robert L., and Alice Jane Lippson. 2009. *Life along the Inner Coast: A Naturalist's Guide to the Sounds, Inlets, Rivers, and Intracoastal Waterway from Norfolk to Key West.* Chapel Hill: University of North Carolina Press.

Lower Norfolk County, Virginia. 1637 to present (as City of Chesapeake). Records.

Mallinson, David F., Stephen T. Culver, Stanley R. Riggs, J. P. Walsh, Dorothea Ames, and Curtis W. Smith. 2007. *Past, Present and Future Inlets of the Outer Banks Barrier Islands, North Carolina.* Published online at www.ecu.edu/icsp/ICSP /Reports_files/Past-Present-and-Future-Inlets2008.pdf.

McIlvenna, Noeleen. 2009. *A Very Mutinous People: The Struggle for North Carolina, 1660–1713*. Chapel Hill: University of North Carolina Press.

McIlwaine, H. R., comp. 1915. *Journal of the House of Burgesses*. 13 vols. Richmond: Virginia State Library.

McPherson, Elizabeth Gregory, ed. 1966. "Nathaniel Batts, Landholder on Pasquotank River, 1660." *North Carolina Historical Review* 43: 66–81.

Merrell, James H. 2012. "Second Thoughts on Colonial Historians and American Indians." *William and Mary Quarterly* 69: 451–512.

Merrill, William L., and Christian F. Feest. 1975. "An Exchange of Botanical Information in the Early Contact Situation: Wisakon of the Southeastern Algonquians." *Economic Botany* 29: 171–84.

Milteer, Warren E., Jr. 2016. "From Indians to Colored People: The Problem of Racial Categories and the Persistence of the Chowans in North Carolina." *North Carolina Historical Review* 93: 28–57.

Mires, Peter B. 1994. "Contact and Contagion: The Roanoke Colony and Influenza." *Historical Archaeology* 28: 30–38.

Mook, Maurice A. 1944. "Algonkian Ethnohistory of the Carolina Sounds." *Journal of the Washington Academy of Sciences* 34(6): 181–97.

Mortimer, Ian. 2012. *The Time Traveler's Guide to Elizabethan England*. New York: Viking.

Myer, William E. 1927. "Indian Trails of the Southeast." *Annual Report of Bureau of American Ethnology* 42: 727–857. Washington, D.C.

North Carolina, Secretary of State, Land Grant Office. Warrants, Surveys, and Related Documents. Microfiche. Raleigh, North Carolina State Archives.

Nugent, Nell Marion, comp. 1934. *Cavaliers and Pioneers: Abstracts of Virginia Land Patents and Grants, 1623–1800*. Vol. 1. Richmond: Dietz Press.

———, comp. 1977. *Cavaliers and Pioneers: Abstracts of Virginia Land Patents and Grants, 1623–1800*. Vol. 2. Richmond: Virginia State Library.

Oberg, Michael Leroy. 2008. *The Head in Edward Nugent's Hand: Roanoke's Forgotten Indians*. Philadelphia: University of Pennsylvania Press.

———. 2020. "Tribes and Towns: What Historians Still Get Wrong about the Roanoke Ventures." *Ethnohistory* 67(4): 579–602.

Pargellis, Stanley, ed. 1959 [1688]. "The Indians of Virginia" [author possibly John Clayton]. *William and Mary Quarterly*, 3rd series, 16: 228–53.

Park, Willard Z. 2006 [1938]. *Shamanism in Western North America*. Mansfield Center, Conn.: Martino Publishers.

Pentland, David. 2000. "Lawson's Pamlico Vocabulary." *Southern Journal of Linguistics* 24: 218–27.

Percy, George. 1921–1922 [1625?]. "A Trewe Relacyon." *Tyler's Quarterly* 3: 259–282. Also printed, with modernized spelling, in Haile, *Jamestown Narratives*, 499–519.

———. 1969 [1608?]. "Observations Gathered out of a Discourse of the Plantation of the Southern Colonie in Virginia by the English 1606." In *The Jamestown Voyages under the First Charter*, series 2, vol. 136, edited by Philip L. Barbour, 129–46. Cambridge: Hakluyt Society. Also printed, with modernized spelling, in Haile, *Jamestown Narratives*, 85–100.

Petrey, Whitney R. 2014. "Weapemeoc Shores: The Loss of Traditional Maritime Culture among the Weapemeoc Indians." M.A. thesis, Department of Maritime Studies, East Carolina University.

Pilkey, Orrin H. 1998. *The North Carolina Shore and Its Barrier Islands: Restless Ribbons of Sand.* Durham, N.C.: Duke University Press.

Pollock, Linda A. 1983. *Forgotten Children: Parent-Child Relations from 1500 to 1900.* Cambridge: Cambridge University Press.

Purchas, Samuel, comp. 1613. *Purchas His Pilgrimes.* London.

———. 1614. *Purchas His Pilgrimes.* 2nd ed. London.

———. 1617. *Purchas His Pilgrimes.* 3rd ed. London.

———. 1904–1906 [1625]. *Hakluytus Posthumus or Purchas His Pilgrimes.* 20 vols. Glasgow: James MacLehose and Sons.

Quinn, David Beers, ed. 1955. *The Roanoke Voyages, 1584–1590.* Series 2, Vol. 104. Cambridge: Hakluyt Society.

Radford, Albert E., Harry E. Ahles, and C. Ritchie Bell. 1968. *Manual of the Vascular Flora of the Carolinas.* Chapel Hill: University of North Carolina Press.

Riggs, Stanley R., Dorothea V. Ames, Stephen J. Culver, and David J. Mallinson. 2011. *The Battle for North Carolina's Coast.* Chapel Hill: University of North Carolina Press.

Robinson, W. Stitt, ed. 2001. *North and South Carolina Treaties, 1654–1756.* Vol. 13 of *Early American Indian Documents: Treaties and Laws, 1607–1789,* Alden T. Vaughan, general ed. Bethesda, Md.: University Publications of America.

Rountree, Helen C. 1989. *The Powhatan Indians of Virginia: Their Traditional Culture.* Norman: University of Oklahoma Press.

———. 1990. *Pocahontas's People: The Powhatan Indians of Virginia through Four Centuries.* Norman: University of Oklahoma Press.

———. 1993a. "Who Were the Powhatans and Did They Have a Unified 'Foreign Policy'?" In *Powhatan Foreign Relations, 1500–1722,* edited by Helen C. Rountree, 1–19. Charlottesville: University Press of Virginia.

———. 1993b. "The Powhatans and Other Woodland Indians as Travelers." In *Powhatan Foreign Relations, 1500–1722,* edited by Helen C. Rountree, 21–52. Charlottesville: University Press of Virginia.

———. 2005. *Pocahontas, Powhatan, Opechancanough: Three Indian Lives Changed by Jamestown.* Charlottesville: University of Virginia Press.

Rountree, Helen C., Wayne E. Clark, and Kent Mountford. 2007. *John Smith's Chesapeake Voyages, 1607–1609.* Charlottesville: University of Virginia Press.

Rountree, Helen C., and Thomas E. Davidson. 1997. *Eastern Shore Indians of Virginia and Maryland.* Charlottesville: University Press of Virginia.

Sawyer, Roy T. 2010. *America's Wetland: An Environmental and Cultural History of Tidewater Virginia and North Carolina.* Charlottesville: University of Virginia Press.

Scisco, Louis. 1945. "Discovery of the Chesapeake Bay." *Maryland Historical Magazine* 40: 277–86.

Seib, Rebecca, and Helen C. Rountree. 2014. *Indians of Southern Maryland.* Baltimore: Maryland Historical Society.

Senter, Jim. 2003. "Live Dunes and Ghost Forests: Stability and Change in the History of North Carolina's Maritime Forests." *North Carolina Historical Review* 80: 334–71.

Shepard, Alexandra. 2002. *Meanings of Manhood in Early Modern England*. Oxford: Oxford University Press.

Shoemaker, Nancy. 1997. "How Indians Got to Be Red." *American Historical Review* 102(3): 624–44.

Siebert, Frank T., Jr. 1975. "Resurrecting Virginia Algonquian from the Dead: The Reconstituted and Historical Phonology of Powhatan." In *Studies in Southeastern Indian Languages*, edited by James M. Crawford, 285–453. Athens: University of Georgia Press.

Sloan, Kim, Joyce E. Chaplin, Christian F. Feest, Ute Kuhlemann. 2007. *A New World: England's First View of America*. London: British Museum.

Smith, John. 1986a [1608]. "A True Relation." In *The Complete Works of Captain John Smith (1580–1631)*, vol. 1, edited by Philip L. Barbour, 3–118. Chapel Hill: University of North Carolina Press. Also printed, with modernized spelling, in Haile, *Jamestown Narratives*, 143–82.

———. 1986b [1612]. "A Map of Virginia." [Historical section compiled from various texts by William Simmond.] In *The Complete Works of Captain John Smith (1580–1631)*, vol. 1, edited by Philip L. Barbour, 119–90. Chapel Hill: University of North Carolina Press. Also printed in part, with modernized spelling, in Haile, *Jamestown Narratives*, 205ff., 569ff.

———. 1986c [1624]. "The Generall History of Virginia, New England, and the Summer Isles." In *The Complete Works of Captain John Smith (1580–1631)*, vol. 2, edited by Philip L. Barbour, 25–488. Chapel Hill: University of North Carolina Press. Also printed, with modernized spelling, in Haile, *Jamestown Narratives*, 215–347, 857–64.

Sneyd, Charlotte Augusta, transl. 1847. *A Relation, or Rather a True Account, of the Island of England, with Sundry Particulars of the Customs of These People, and of the Royal Revenues under King Henry the Seventh, about the Year 1500*. London: Printed for the Camden Society by John Bowyer Nichols & Son.

Speck, Frank G. 1916. "Remnants of the Machapunga Indians of North Carolina." *American Anthropologist* (n.s.) 18: 271–76.

Spelman, Henry. 2019 [1613?]. "Relation of Virginea." In *The Travels and Works of Captain John Smith*, edited by Edward Arber and A. G. Bradley, ci–cxiv. New York: Burt Franklin. Also published, verbatim but with modernized spelling, in Haile, *Jamestown Narratives*, 481–95.

———. 2019 [1613?]. *Relation of Virginia*. Transcribed and edited by Karen O. Kupperman. New York: New York University Press.

Spencer, Colin. 2011. *British Food: An Extraordinary Thousand Years of History*. London: Grub Street.

Stahle, David W., Malcolm K. Cleaveland, Dennis B. Blanton, Matthew D. Therrell, and David A. Gay. 1998. "The Lost Colony and Jamestown Droughts." *Science* 280: 564–67.

Stallybrass, Peter. 2007. "*Admiranda narratio*: A European Best Seller." In *A Briefe and True Report of the New Found Land of Virginia: The 1590 Theodor de Bry Latin Edition*, 9–20. Charlottesville: University of Virginia Press.

Stone, Lawrence. 1977. *The Family, Sex, and Marriage in England, 1500–1800*. New York: Harper and Row.

———. 1984. *An Open Elite? England 1540–1880*. Oxford: Clarendon Press.

Strachey, William. 1953 [1612]. *The Historie of Travell into Virginia Britania*. Series 2, Vol. 103. Edited by Louis B. Wright and Virginia Freund. Cambridge: Hakluyt Society. First book also published, verbatim but with modernized spelling, in Haile, *Jamestown Narratives*, 569–689.

———. 1964 [1610]. *A True Reportory of the Wreck and Redemption of Sir Thomas Gates. . . .* In *A Voyage to Virginia in 1609, Two Narratives*, edited by Louis B. Wright. Charlottesville: University of Virginia Press. Also printed, with modernized spelling, in Haile, *Jamestown Narratives*, 382–443.

Swanton, John. 1946. *Indians of the Southeastern United States*. Smithsonian Institution Bureau of American Ethnology no. 137. Washington, D.C.: U.S. Government Printing Press.

Tanner, Helen Hornbeck. 1989. "The Land and Water Communication Systems of the Southeastern Indians." In *Powhatan's Mantle: Indians in the Colonial Southeast*, edited by Peter Wood, Gregory Waselkov, and Thomas Hatley, 6–20. Lincoln: University of Nebraska Press.

Taukchiray, Wesley. n.d. "North Carolina in the Fall of 1754, with Emphasis on the American Indian Population." [Copy in North Carolina Archives is mistitled "Indians of the North Carolina Coastal Plain."] Copy in possession of both Rountree and Taukchiray, also in the Wesley D. White Papers, South Carolina Historical Society. [1977, revised in 1984].

Thomas, Keith. 1971. *Religion and the Decline of Magic: Studies in Popular Beliefs in Sixteenth- and Seventeenth-Century England*. New York: Oxford University Press.

Ubelaker, Douglas H. 1993. "Human Biology of Virginia Indians." In *Powhatan Foreign Relations, 1500–1722*, edited by Helen C. Rountree, 53–75. Charlottesville: University Press of Virginia.

Wallace, Paul F. W. 1965. *Indian Paths of Pennsylvania*. Harrisburg: Pennsylvania Historical and Museum Commission.

Wax, Rosalie, and Robert K. Thomas. 1961. "American Indians and White People." *Phylon* 22: 305–17.

Weakley, Alan S., J. Christopher Ludwig, John F. Townsend, comps., and Bland Crowder, ed. 2012. *Flora of Virginia*. Fort Worth: Botanical Research Institute of Texas Press.

White, John. 1955 [1587]. "The Fourth Voyages Made to Virginia, with Three Shippes, in the Yeere, 1587. Wherein Was Transported the Second Colonie." In *The Roanoke Voyages, 1584–1590*, series 2, vol. 104, edited by David B. Quinn, 515–39. Cambridge: Hakluyt Society.

White, William. 1969 [1608?]. "Fragments published before 1614." In *The Jamestown Voyages under the First Charter*, series 2, vol. 136, edited by Philip L. Barbour,

147–50. Cambridge: Hakluyt Society. Reprinted, with modernized spelling, in Haile, *Jamestown Narratives*, 138–41.

Winne, Peter. 1969 [1608]. Letter [of November 16, 1608] to Sir John Egerton. In *The Jamestown Voyages under the First Charter*, series 1, vol. 136, edited by Philip L. Barbour, 245–46. Cambridge: Hakluyt Society. Also printed, with modernized spelling, in Haile, *Jamestown Narratives*, 203–4.

Index

Page numbers in *italics* refer to figures, maps, and tables.

www.ingramcontent.com/pod-product-compliance
Lightning Source LLC
Chambersburg PA
CBHW020057311224
19730CB00002B/129